Tommy Robinson

Enemy of the State

The Press News Ltd

This edition published March 2017
by The Press News Ltd

ISBN: 987-0-9570964-9-3

Body text set in 11pt Century Schoolbook

Printed in Great Britain

CONTENTS

Remembering Les Gearty, one of the
best and maddest men I've known,
who was always by my side
no matter what situations we faced.
A loyal and faithful friend.
We all miss him.

INTRODUCTION

I WAS HOPING to shout out loud 'three cheers for Tommy Robinson' on the morning of Thursday July 23rd, 2015. I say Tommy Robinson. It's sometimes Stephen Lennon in the media, or occasionally a long-ago name, Stephen Yaxley. Whatever. It was going to be three cheers for me, the founder and former leader, now officially retired, of the English Defence League.

It had been a dramatic, often wild six years, of street battles and police stitch-ups, of fearing for my family's lives and resisting attempts by Scotland Yard to recruit me as some kind of undercover snitch. Six years of mad laughs with the lads, but also of long weeks and months in solitary confinement. Six years of having my life turned upside down and inside out by the state – all for being a British patriot. For trying to wake my fellow countrymen and women up to the dangers of radical Islam.

And as of Thursday July 23rd I would be a free man. I would be able to take my family on holiday, to speak on a public platform without having my collar felt, to go about my business like any other citizen of the United Kingdom.

The licence period of an 18-month prison sentence for lending my brother-in-law the deposit on his first house – yes, really – was due to end on Wednesday July 22nd. Finally I could say without fear of being handcuffed again, 'Luton and Bedfordshire Probation Service, Scotland Yard and the entire British constabulary – kiss my arse'.

I could have shouted as loud as I liked, but no one would have heard. Not while I was locked in yet another concrete box of a solitary confinement cell in the bowels of HMP Peterborough, waiting for someone to tell me what the hell I'd been jailed for this time. Just days before being a free man at last, and thrown in a cell once again on the whim of

1

some sadistic so-and-so just trying to squeeze one more ounce of misery out of me, while they still could.

Even the screws in Peterborough nick could hardly believe it – that someone would get recalled to prison just a week or so before their licence was up. I was in solitary confinement, yet again, because despite all of my warnings to the screws, including a note to the prison governor not to do it, they put me on an open wing, two cells away from a Muslim murderer doing 28 years.

He promptly put a massive bounty on my head and after I gave a Somali prisoner a slapping – I was told he'd taken the contract to attack me with boiling water – I finally got my wish, the safety and sanctuary of being in solitary. It was only a few days until I was free of the system. I could handle that.

But the day and night of July 22nd came and went, with no explanation. They kept me locked up another 48 hours. It was probably because 'they' (whoever is watching, and believe me 'they' are) knew that I was due to be making a public appearance at the House of Lords on the 23rd. 'They' were desperate to keep disrupting my life for as long as they possibly could.

So for all of you history buffs who celebrated 800 years of the signing of Magna Carta this summer – be my guest and shove your Habeas Corpus up your deluded liberal backsides. There isn't much 'justice' in the British justice system that I've come to know and hate.

Indeed, for someone who has bent over backwards to avoid trouble in recent months and years, I've spent more time in English prisons than some of the Great Train Robbers. If this book-writing gig catches on, my next effort might be a guided tour to the many and varied institutions of HM's prison service.

Still, better late than never. I'm out. No more weekly sermons from the Marxist matron at the probation office, no more messing with mine and my family's lives just for the hell of it. I'm done with bowing and scraping to busybody do-gooders, to looking over my shoulder for the police every time I tweet something mildly offensive to a Home Counties communist.

I'm free of the English Defence League and, mostly, I'm finally free to make my own choices. With my track record, I suspect that will include making plenty more mistakes. I just hope that whatever they are, they don't involve hearing the clanging door of a jail cell behind me. I've had enough of them – fairly or unfairly – for a lifetime.

Don't worry, you're not going to need a box of Kleenex at your side as you read this. It really isn't Tommy-does-tearjerking. It's not a sob story. The trouble I've found myself in has been at times clearly self-inflicted. But only at times. You might just learn something about the workings of a British police state that I doubt you believe exists.

My over-arching crime, at least in the eyes of the British establishment, has been to be a patriot. I love my country. I think that St George's Day, April 23rd, should be a public holiday. I resent the fact that people who hate the country they call 'home' are pampered and protected by a state that places their so-called rights above those of young men who risk and sacrifice their lives for British democracy.

Oh, and just to make things clear from the outset, I really, really don't care about the colour of those people's skin or the nature of their religion. I never have and I still don't. I'm sorry if that disappoints a few of you.

But here's something else I believe – that if you publicly declare war on me, my family and my country, it's only to be expected that some of us will offer resistance. Clearly I'm in the minority – or at least so it's seemed, since this 'life' of Tommy Robinson began in 2009.

My name will forever be connected with the English Defence League, I know that. But this isn't a book about the

EDL, although it obviously plays a major part in it. Theirs is a different story, perhaps for another day. For now this is my story, my attempt to make sense of a life, and especially a recent past, that even I find barely believable.

None of it was planned. But despite everything that I've been through, I have no regrets, other than what my family has been put through – and that wasn't always of my doing. You'll notice that I don't name my wife and children in the book. That's deliberate. They still occasionally pay too heavy a price for having me as a father and husband.

Coming home from Peterborough nick, albeit a couple of days late, marked the end of an 18-month prison sentence, all because I lent my brother-in-law £20,000 for a deposit on a house and he overstated his earnings on a self certification mortgage, which made it 'criminal'. No one lost a single penny, but having tried and failed on numerous counts to put me away, to silence me, the state finally did.

I would argue that they also tried to have me killed in the process, but that's for you to decide.

It had taken the police and the state long enough. It had taken them pretty much every day since a group of angry Luton residents shouted 'enough', having watched extremist Muslims being encouraged by the police to scream their hatred at the returning soldiers of the Royal Anglian Regiment in March 2009.

But they'd done their worst, I was still standing, and I was free to speak my mind. Finally.

1: TIME ON MY HANDS

WHEN YOU are sent home from prison part-way through a custodial sentence, it's with many and varied limitations on where you can go, what you can do – even who you can talk to or communicate with via social media. You might have an ankle tag on, a curfew ... whatever the state decides.

In my case, and although I'd quit the English Defence League more than a year before, when I came home to my wife and kids, one of the stipulations that might see me recalled to prison was not communicating with members of the EDL, either directly or indirectly – which meant by Twitter or social media. I'd been sent down for doing a family member a favour and now here I was back home, still getting 'we hate Tommy Robinson' death threats, but among my many other restrictions, I couldn't respond to them. I couldn't even join in the debate about whether I deserved to have my head chopped off.

It meant that I had a lot of time on my hands and I'm the type of bloke who gets bored easily anyway. It's why I probably spend too much time on Twitter, letting off steam about this and that, or watching Youtube videos on my mobile phone. You can only go to the gym and run the kids backwards and forwards so much.

Let's face it, if your main area of interest is the Islamic war that's being waged against the west, then there's no shortage of news, either from home or abroad. As I finish this book, the November 13 Paris massacre has shaken the world to its boots. However the world has tried to handle radical Islam so far, it hasn't worked.

I use my phone to check out the web and do all of my emails and social media stuff because I don't have my own computer – not since the police decided the best way to tackle the creation of the EDL was to hit me and my family, by sometimes fair means but mostly foul. No trumped up or imagined crime was off limits if it meant putting me behind bars. They shut down my businesses, bank accounts, took our computers, lied in statements, lied to judges ... it was anything goes, if it meant nailing Tommy Robinson.

As such I don't doubt for a minute that the authorities could find a way to put any manner of incriminating stuff on a computer that I owned if they really wanted, by way of another excuse to knock me down again, possibly finish me off. If you think I'm being paranoid, then read on. What's that old saying? Just because you're paranoid doesn't mean the bastards aren't out to get you.

I spent a lot of that time making plans for what I was looking at as basically a new life, a fresh start, once my licence period ended that 18-month sentence.

But it was a period, it still is a period, when there was and is no shortage of explosive – literally explosive – issues of the sort that spawned the birth of the English Defence League. I don't mind saying that I feel massively vindicated by events that have simply confirmed the fears and warnings we were expressing, albeit pretty crudely, as far back as 2009. But still it seems that no one is listening. What will it take? The assassination of the Queen perhaps? The Prime Minister?

We are still seeing British Muslim men and women acting like persecuted Jews in Nazi Germany, with their efforts to 'escape' the UK and reach the supposed safe haven of Islamic State in Iraq and Syria – ISIS. To my mind that should be a cause for celebration. Good. Sod off and don't come back.

And yet we have a government, politicians and liberal do-gooders bending over backwards to prevent them going in the first place, and even then, trying to facilitate their safe return. Why? Good riddance. If they hate the British way of life that much, if they don't want a tolerant democracy, our benefits and tax credits, if they don't want the privileges that our state and legal system bestow upon them at the expense of non-Muslim Britons, then who are we to try to convince them otherwise?

They've been allowed to set up sharia courts outside our legal system, to create Muslim enclaves that are literally no-go areas for non-Muslim people, and no government grant is too big or small to try buying their favour – to encourage them to 'love' their so-called country.

Stop them joining ISIS? We should put on special planes for them – with one-way tickets only. Why would you want your sworn enemy breeding his or her poison in your own back yard? Clearly in this country, we do.

The Charlie Hebdo massacre in Paris took Islam's war into the very heart of a French nation that was already tougher on Muslim citizens who oppose a secular state than Britain is. And now even that atrocity has been dwarfed.

At least the French had the courage to ban the face veil, the niqab, one of the first laws I believe our government should consider if it's ever serious about breaking down barriers between communities. The niqab isn't a religious necessity under Islam and our politicians know that full well. What it is, is two fingers in the face of every living, breathing Englishman and woman, on a daily basis. It's an up-yours that shows exactly how the hardline, majority Muslim community regards the rest of us. The problem is, we can't deal with the truth of it.

If recent history has taught us one thing, it's that there will be other outrages like Charlie Hebdo, like the Bataclan atrocity. Inevitably. Those kinds of attacks, which we then saw again with the massacre of mostly British tourists in Tunisia, could have happened on the streets of Dewsbury in 2012. I failed to turn up at an EDL rally there, which as a result of finishing early averted a planned attack by five Muslim terrorists who, some time later, I would have an amusing encounter with during a stay at one of Her Majesty's Prisons. I think I got the last laugh on that one.

Among the Muslims fleeing Britain to join ISIS, there were two Dewsbury teenagers, Hassan Munshi and Talha Asmal, the 17-year-old who blew himself and a bunch of innocent fellow Muslims up with a suicide bomb. Don't doubt for one minute that a great many of those young men and women will be returning amongst the flood of refugees, fully trained killers, hell bent on reaching the Paradise their death cult promises.

Unfortunately, the British establishment's only plan to combat Islamic extremism seems to be to throw more and more money at the Muslim community and hope one day it might respect us, or at least hopefully respect our laws. And if Muslims don't? If it's sharia or nothing? No one seems comfortable even asking that question, probably because they are scared stiff of the answer.

And it's not just the terrorists in our midst and abroad. In the last couple of years, a period when I've been effectively under house arrest and gagged by the state, we've seen the continued scandals of Muslim grooming gangs across the country.

Rochdale was bad enough. Rotherham, not even a town you would identify as being a typical hotbed of widescale Muslim criminality, rocked the country to its boots. More than a thousand children, systematically abused and raped over years and years, with the tacit approval, a nod and a wink, of Social Services, councillors and the police. It is a disgrace and still, apart from a token resignation or two, it looks like the real guilty parties will plod on without having their collars felt. Not the rapists, but the people who silently allowed it to happen for fear of offending a few medieval sensitivities.

But because me and my mates shouted and complained up and down the land about these instances of criminal appeasement, we were boxed into a convenient 'far right' cage and I was declared an enemy of the state.

I was locked up once for trying to exercise my simple right to walk through the London Borough of Tower Hamlets. No one wanted to acknowledge what was going on there and they certainly didn't want the inconvenience of me making the point. It's taken long enough, but the corrupt empire of Tower Hamlets' Muslim mayor Lutfur Rahman has eventually been brought tumbling down. Will he ever see the inside of a prison cell though? Don't hold your breath. He's still part of the system.

I ought to feel vindicated at all of these EDL bogeymen-issues coming home to roost and our warnings proving to be not scaremongering, but well-founded fears. The fact is that I'm not, because it's blindingly obvious that still, no one is learning any lessons.

The latest Muslim grooming gang to get banged up for the systematic rape of our children (September 2015) was in Aylesbury. They've gone down for 82 years. Outside the Old Bailey the council's jobsworth spokesman for children's services admitted, 'There were probably indications that may have been there which our staff didn't pick up on.' No shit, Sherlock! The EDL demonstrated in Aylesbury to highlight exactly that. I guess bureaucrats can't hear when they've got their fingers in their ears and their heads up each other's arses.

Yet it goes on. Ministers announce commissions and inquiries, reports everywhere, which will not make one blind bit of difference – because no one has got the guts to talk about the real problem, let alone do something about it. They still have their heads in the sand and their arses pointed skywards. No wonder we all keep getting shafted.

All of the points we made, the reasons for our protests, keep being proven right, week after week. No one seems to be any learning lessons though.

ALL OF MY LIFE I've been a worker, a grafter, though not necessarily in the classroom at Putteridge High School, in what passed for a nice part of Luton when we were kids. I always managed to get in the top set without ever really knuckling down, and did enough to win a highly prized apprenticeship as an aeronautical engineer with Britannia Airways in Luton, where I was born and bred. My mum and her second husband Tommy Lennon worked really hard so that we could afford to live in that part of town.

They were never given a leg up by the state and they never asked for one. Me neither – although the state has tried to give me a few things, most of which I wouldn't wish on my worst enemy. Well, on second thoughts, maybe I would ... because I have quite a few of them. Enemies that is. A big fat proportion of the civilised world, and just about the entire uncivilised world. And counting.

Living there was certainly a big step up from Farley Hill where I lived as a kid, a sprawling hillside estate to the south of Luton town centre, which used to be the biggest working class community in the district and a happy enough hunting ground for young kids like us to play out together. Farley Hill is very different today. It changes by the week, by the month, by the year. It's not a happy place for a lot of the people who live there.

I look at the elderly non-Muslim people being forced out of their homes as one community takes the district over, a street at a time, an estate at a time, and I can't think of a better phrase than 'ethnic cleansing' to describe what's going on there.

Sure, you don't see dead bodies on the scale of global war zones maybe – although in truth there have been plenty of casualties – but the outcome is the same. A settled community, even a mixed community because black and white people have long mixed well in Luton, slowly but surely being forced out, by fair means or foul.

My older brother was the clever one of the Yaxley family, but I was street smart enough and I could pass an exam. I got my 11 GCSEs including an A in maths and won that apprenticeship – only six available for 600 applicants, which I hope says something.

That ended in tears though. As you might have guessed, my day job this past few years hasn't been fixing or building aircraft. It was my own fault, as so many things have been, but even during my five years with Britannia I would spend my Friday nights moonlighting on contracting jobs in London. I always knew the value of a pound and I always wanted nice things.

That's how come me and my Afghan mates Kamran, Imran and a black lad called Andre managed to club together and buy a Porsche when we were still teenagers. Real flash geezers. That ended in tears too.

I've cut a few corners, trying to do well for myself and my family. Not enough that I deserved to go to jail for lending my brother-in-law the deposit for a house and putting him in touch with my mortgage adviser though.

I was basically blackmailed into pleading guilty to that in order to keep my wife from being dragged into a courtroom and having her photo splashed all over the press. That brought my life, the one that I was hoping to build beyond the EDL, to an abrupt and painful halt.

Meanwhile Britain, the world, continues daydreaming, in a state of complete denial over the dangers presented by an ideology that has effectively declared war on us. I find it impossible to just sit and watch it happening.

From the moment we started the English Defence League and began aggravating the authorities, the British state decided that it would do the same back to us. Or specifically to me, as the public face of the EDL.

They – the police, Special Branch, MI5 and James Bond too for all I know – descended on me and my family like a ton of bricks. They scrutinised every penny I had ever earned, every bill, invoice and receipt I'd ever issued or collected.

They swarmed all over my family. They even got a warrant to go through my mum and dad's bank account – they did it to anyone I had ever done business with. And after years of trying, on that at least, they got absolutely nowhere, found nothing wrong.

It took them long enough, but they eventually found something they could hang on me, the mortgage case. That's why I ended up with the time to tell this story. It's why I've spent probably too much time tweeting about the evils and dangers of radical Islam.

Even that isn't without its dangers. I was convicted of a minor white collar offence, but I was hit with licence conditions that all related to the EDL, for some inexplicable reason. People could tweet death threats to me, say they were going to rape my mum and behead my children, but simply by responding to them my liberty was physically taken from me. I was locked back up.

And did the police go after those haters, the people making those vile threats? Don't be silly. There's only room for one pantomime villain in this story.

Until July 23rd 2015, I had to keep my nose clean, and if I knew what was best for me, my mouth shut. I had to report regularly to a pain-in-the-arse probation officer in Bedford who saw her main goal in life as turning me into one of her Politically Corrected puppets, and I now have to somehow plan a life beyond the EDL and, most probably, beyond Luton.

It isn't as if I can go down Bury Park – the town's hotbed of extreme Islam – and fix Mrs Khan's broken boiler, is it? I used to have a plumbing business among other things, until the state closed me down, froze my bank accounts, declared me a financial non-person.

If I tried plying my trade down Bury Park tomorrow it's a toss up whether they'd find my head in a different part of town from my body, or whether they'd find either of them at all. Tommy Robinson is very well known in that neck of the woods, by the violent Muslim gangsters and the extremist Muslim preachers.

Even the ordinary locals going about their daily business feel justified to take a swing if they see me passing, as has happened more than once, even while working with film crews. But the law doesn't apply in those instances. So I have to be careful where I go, needless to say.

An everyday job in Luton isn't on the cards then, yet my family has taken a massive financial hit of £125,000 over the mortgage case under Proceeds of Crime legislation. I'll go into more detail later, but when I pleaded guilty in that deal with the Crown Prosecution Service, it limited what they would pursue me for financially, along with leaving my wife out of it. That was the axe they hung over my head. Plead guilty Tommy, and we'll leave your wife alone. What would you do? What would any man do?

My agreement with the CPS was that they wouldn't pursue me for getting what they call 'particular benefit' from the offence. I'd lent my brother-in-law £20,000, he overstated his earnings on his mortgage and made £30,000 when he sold the house on and paid me back. That was all.

Then after I pleaded guilty for what my lawyer thought would be a non-custodial sentence, and still got jailed, the police went back on their word anyway, going after me for £315,000, the total value of all the equity in the property my wife and I owned. The lying bastards.

I don't know if that's because I told officers from the Metropolitan Intelligence Bureau, people who claimed to be a division of Scotland Yard, to go fuck themselves. Those people promised to make all of my problems go away, if only I went back to lead the EDL, to be their man on the inside.

What were they after? I'm still not sure. A way of controlling the EDL perhaps, to suit whatever their own political agendas were.

I also think they were worrying about this Paul Golding character, who has started another protest movement, Britain First. He's the man you might have seen in the news but mostly on social media networks, storming into mosques and taking his followers into the fray quite a bit more forcefully than I ever did at the EDL.

Anyway, whoever the MIB really are, they wanted me back on the inside, as their informer, running the EDL. They came to see me in prison, at home, they kept phoning me – every time I was at a low ebb, and thought things couldn't get worse, along came this crew dangling an offer to 'help'. I told them where to shove it. I'd rather do the jail time than be an informer.

IT'S NOT JUST the police and security services who think anyone and everyone is either up for sale, or ripe to be blackmailed. My experience of recent years is that almost everyone has an agenda, especially in public life.

I was in the national news for a few days just before the 2015 general election, which surprised a lot of people when it delivered a Conservative majority. Well I'm sure the Tories wouldn't be particularly thankful to me, but their majority was one MP less thanks to Tommy Robinson. The nation ought to be grateful though.

Unusually for once, it wasn't a case of the world slagging me off in the news. In fact there was almost an uncomfortable silence from all of the usual media suspects, because for once I was portrayed as the bloke doing the right thing – exposing corruption. I don't think some people knew how to handle that. It contradicted all their cosy preconceptions about who and what the supposedly 'far right' Tommy Robinson is.

If there are themes that emerge from writing this book, I expect one to be that you can trust hardly anyone. I certainly can't. When I quit the EDL I got a lot of support from the Quilliam Foundation, the anti-extremist think tank. As part of the process of leaving the EDL and trying to find a constructive way of being involved with the national debate, I met a lot of people who were presented as being progressive Muslims. One such man was Afzal Amin, the Conservative candidate for Dudley North in the general election. I liked Afzal. He talked sense.

He'd been a captain in the British Army who had served in Iraq and Afghanistan and even been a counter-insurgency education officer to Prince William and Prince Harry. We met a few times and he was the kind of straight talking British Muslim you'd like to think we need a few more of in public life. A few more? A few thousand more.

That's what I thought – at first. He talked to me about arranging a dinner with a group of serving Muslim soldiers but it never happened. Afzal kept in touch though. He texted me at Christmas and then in January 2015 he called to say he was coming back from London, and could he drop by and say hello. I wasn't exactly busy, so I said yes.

The EDL were planning yet another protest in Dudley, in his seat, over the building of another of these mega mosques. It had started as a £20 million monstrosity that the local council and residents had been battling over for the past seven years and had been finally given the green light. The EDL had protested there several times.

Afzal told me at first that he wanted to talk to the EDL leadership in the area before their protest at the beginning of February, and could I introduce them to him. Since I left the group, the new chairman and some of the leading figures were from the Midlands anyway, so I said yes.

Afzal was pretty scathing about the mosque plans. He said he'd told the Dudley Muslim Association that if they had £5million in the bank (the plans had been scaled down a lot) they shouldn't be spending it on a lavish mosque, but on their youth, tackling crime and drugs and all the other issues on the streets. He said the mosque plan was little more than a big dick contest for the architects. As I'd thought ever since first meeting him, he seemed to be talking sense.

Since leaving the EDL and being sent down I hadn't spoken to anyone associated with the group, but I called the chairman Steve Eddowes. I also rang my contact Dev, who runs an anti-extremism organisation. Dev has become something of a mentor to me and although we don't always see eye to eye, he always said his two aims were to try to keep me safe, and to keep the public safe. The fact that I'm still here and have spoken at places like the Oxford Union and Harrow, shows he's been at least partially successful.

Dev was from that area, so I told him that I was coming up and asked if he wouldn't mind sitting in. Given what Afzal said later, when he claimed that the story which blew up nationally was all an EDL plot, I'm glad that I did.

When I left the EDL, Steve Eddowes was one of the blokes I was closest to. He understood the need to keep the right-wing nutters away. We'd always been clear about that, not that anyone in the mainstream media or politics wanted to listen. I still have a lot of time for 'Edders'.

I picked Dev up and we went to meet at a Toby Carvery, which was funny in itself, as an entire corner of the restaurant was like a shrine to Winston Churchill. I thought that was great ... Churchill watching over these lads. I was taking photos of it all on my mobile phone.

In fact I'd only been there about 10 minutes, when my wife rang saying there were two cars parked outside the house, men with hoods on, in the dark – it was after 9 o'clock at night, and one had just got something out of the boot and passed it through the window to another man. We

16

don't live on the kind of street where you would expect strangers in cars just to randomly pull up outside.

I screamed at her to hit the panic button and I told the others that I had to go. I was out of there and on the phone to the police before the others got down to discussing anything about whatever Afzal's plans were. You probably can't imagine what it's like to live like that, knowing there are a lot of people walking the streets who would be happy to stick a knife in you, to blow up your wife and kids.

She was peeking out of an upstairs window, telling me she could see one of these men on the phone, that our house phone was ringing downstairs and she was freaking out, with three young children in the house and me miles away.

She hit the panic button, exactly as I'd said. Most people obviously wouldn't have a panic button in their house, but neither would most people have had six different Osman warnings – specific and credible death threats uncovered by the police or security services.

Luckily this was just an unfortunate choice of location by two blokes to hand over a van that one was buying from the other. I say lucky because panic button or not, it took the police 27 minutes to respond to that alarm. There have been major military battles that have been over and done with in less time.

Later I rang Dev, Edders and Afzal. It seemed things had gone well at their meeting. Afzal said: 'They're fine English men, just like the men I met in the military.'

Dev reported that Afzal spoke about himself a lot and Edders was pretty much wondering the same as me – is Afzal just being a politician, or is he really on the case? Is this actually someone on the inside who sees the light, who wants to do the right thing? We were hopeful.

What was strange was that they then had another meeting with the EDL and Afzal turned up with some blokes who were recognised as former members of the

Birmingham City football hooligan gang, the Zulus – except these blokes were all Muslim converts. I had no idea at the time what that was all about.

Afzal rang me the day before the EDL's Dudley demo in February and asked if I could go up there, but I couldn't. He went along to it and when he phoned me he said, 'I was treated very well'. He seemed surprised. I told him that he would be, that it wasn't quite what he thought, or what the media portray it as.

Some 1,000 or so EDL supporters demonstrated and it went off peacefully – not that that's what you would have read in the papers. The headlines were all about 30 people being arrested, but what the police didn't say is that they were all Muslims or Unite Against Fascism members, the left-wing rabble-rousers who followed us everywhere. There were no EDL arrests, but by the time the police came out and confirmed that, it was too late – they'd already run the headlines. As usual.

After that Afzal contacted me in the first week in March, with the general election getting closer and asked if I was looking for work. I told him, 'I'm unemployable pal'. He didn't elaborate, didn't suggest anything dodgy, he just said that he had a way for me to earn some money.

He was chasing after the Dudley North seat held by Labour MP Ian Austin, in an area with a big mixed Muslim/ non-Muslim electorate and the Tories thought it was ripe for Afzal to win.

I left it at that however. I didn't ring him back. Then he phoned on my daughter's 4th birthday, and my dad's 68th birthday – the same day, Sunday March 9th. We were having a family meal at TGI Friday's in Milton Keynes but he asked if he could come to see me. He seemed pretty desperate to talk so I agreed.

The first time I'd seen him he'd turned up in a black Mercedes. This time he was driving a big cream Jeep, about

60 or 70-grand's worth of motor. Except he also had this big fat Pakistani bloke with him, and I thought, 'Bugger me – he's his chauffeur!' Not the fat bloke, but Afzal. He was driving his money man around, it appeared.

We went into the Harvester in Milton Keynes and this character with Afzal, called Naeem, was talking about all of his businesses, all the staff he has, all of his money.

They asked if I minded going to a different restaurant in Luton. I told them I'm not exactly Mr Popular in that part of town, but Naeem said, 'When you're with me, no one will say a word'.

I'm not being funny but this tub of lard couldn't protect himself, let alone me – if he could ensure my safety that would be down to who he was, and how well known. I got that message loud and clear, as was clearly intended.

So off we went to the Irmak Grill, a Turkish restaurant in the town centre. It's the type of place that has curtained cubicles so that Muslim women can take their veils off to eat. Once we got settled Naeem asked me what my household outgoings were. I said a couple of grand a month and he said, 'Easy, not a problem'. He said they were trying to get Afzal into Parliament and that they wanted me to help their cause. I remember his exact words being, 'So long as we're eating, you won't go hungry'.

I asked if they were offering me a job and the pair of them said they 'knew' I still controlled the EDL – I didn't by the way – and how much the members and leadership respected me. It was complete bollocks, at least the leadership bit, but not in their minds.

Afzal reckoned that if he could get some credibility in the white working class community, then he could swing it, win the seat. Labour had a small majority and obviously he thought he had the Muslim vote sewn up, but he wasn't leaving anything to chance. He mentioned me coming along and appearing at some public meetings that would be called

'An Evening with Tommy Robinson' where I'd just turn up, talk about whatever, but basically give my support to him.

The line was, 'This man has fought for our country in Iraq and Afghanistan, now he'll fight for us'. He said I'd be paid for my time which sounded fair enough at that point. I still thought he was pretty much on-message, even if this mug Naeem was a bit suspect.

Things changed though when Afzal said he wanted to talk to the EDL leadership about setting up another demo, a repeat of the anti-mosque protest, but with a twist. This time he wanted to stage manage it. He wanted me to have the EDL call the follow up demo the weekend before the election on May 7th, then announce a meeting with him and the police chief and finally agree to call it off, with Afzal being able to take the credit.

I couldn't believe what I was hearing. He'd always been nice enough with me, and seemed to be in tune with a lot of the concerns I've raised both inside and outside the EDL, but this was outrageous. He said he was all for tackling the grooming problems, restricting the growth of sharia courts, the building of mosques and all those issues. Like I said, he really seemed to 'get' people's concerns about how Muslim communities and organisations were getting out of control and Islamifying whole areas, whole towns and cities.

But now here he was basically trying to use a legitimate street protest group, which I've always insisted the EDL is, as a device just to get him elected. When the story broke in the Mail on Sunday soon afterwards, people demanded to know if I was still in the EDL, through the back door or whatever, but really, I wasn't.

During that call Afzal and his man Naeem said they wanted the meeting with the EDL leadership to happen in two days, but I explained that Steve Eddowes wasn't around and it would have to be the following Monday. That bought me a week to sort something out, to work out what to do. And as I said earlier – I had plenty of time on my hands, waiting for my licence period to wind down.

I had to go into London anyway so I trotted along to the Spy Shop, off Oxford Street, to see about getting some surveillance equipment, but that was going to cost £900. So then I rang a contact from a television production company, who was working on a documentary about me, and explained it all to him. I wasn't sure exactly what they were going to offer but I wanted it all recording either way.

The tv documentary bloke Mike was worried about us being involved in some kind of covert entrapment, but I said, 'I've done sod all – this is entirely these guys!' And it was. Here was a completely corrupt would-be Member of Parliament intent on buying his way into government, and with his eyes on 10 Downing Street.

Somehow I'm not expecting a knighthood for the public service I did the country though.

2: THE STING

IF ALL OF THIS sounds a bit James Bond, then it's probably because it was – although it turned out being more like Mr Bean when we were getting ready to go see Afzal and his people.

Was I scared? Not really. My life would undoubtedly have been a lot calmer if I did get scared more easily. I'm only 5ft 6ins tall. I hardly scare people to death with my intimidating physique. I'm not sure if that leads to people thinking they can push me around, but those situations usually end up in blood and tears for someone.

I've also been around the houses enough times to know that this bloke Naeem fancied himself as something of a gangster. He was making sure he sent me that message loud and clear. Just how close that was to the truth I discovered when we sat down at the restaurant he owns in Broad Street in the centre of Birmingham.

Mike went out and bought £3,500 of surveillance gear and on the Monday of the meeting we set off, calling to pick up Steve Eddowes in Wolverhampton. When we got to Edders' place the room was full of the EDL leadership, blokes I hadn't seen in a long time.

I think some of them thought – hoped even – that I was coming back to the organisation, but I put them right about that. It wasn't even up for debate. However I had to explain everything that was going on with Afzal to them, and insist the information didn't leave those four walls. This wasn't something that could be made public, otherwise I was in serious trouble. One of the lads said, 'I thought you'd given up the fight'. I replied, 'No, I'm just looking for a different way to fight.'

Those blokes are all good men. They know when to keep their mouths shut. Mike had booked a hotel room near

Birmingham airport to get me wired up, but it was miles from the meeting and we were already late. I called Afzal and bought some time saying Edders had been held up.

We had one device on my watch and Mike had bought a camera that was built into a pair of glasses. Great, eh? Except I don't wear glasses. I'd look a right tit showing up in a pair of specs. There was one recording gizmo on my key ring, a white USB stick that was a listening device, then one that was a camera and a microphone in a phone case. Talk about overkill.

All of that was straightforward enough, but the main camera was going to be in my jumper, which I'd left with Mike that morning to get it ready. That's where the trouble started, because the power pack for this thing was about twice as big as a cigarette pack and needed to be strapped round my pudgy belly. I thought, 'wonderful, absolutely effing wonderful.' I looked like I was wearing a colostomy bag.

It's customary with Asians to greet one another with a hug, but these guys would put their arms around me and grab a handful of listening equipment between my shoulder blades. And that wasn't all. We were in a rush, Mike was trying to get this thing sorted, and I ended up with gaffer tape wrapped round me like a corset, which had the effect of shoving all my fat belly down and out. I looked like a boozy darts player, with a tub of lard poking over my belt.

If you can get something good out of bad, it was that I'd been in a car accident a few days before, so when we got to the restaurant I explained that I had whiplash and just shook hands. It's a wonder I was there at all – I'd pulled out of a road and got hit sideways on by a lorry. The car was written off, but I climbed out without a mark on me.

The policewoman who came to attend the accident said hello and told me she'd once sat outside my house for a week. Small world.

Apparently that was after one of the death threats we got which resulted in a Muslim bloke chasing my cousin Kevin Carroll down his road, trying to get in range to use his shotgun. Kev broke his toe hurdling the fences making his escape. We laughed our arses off at that, although it might not have been so funny if the bloke had caught him.

Anyway, back to the restaurant and having avoided the hugs I then had to try to sit down. Bugger me. I almost went pop. We'd put this thing on with me standing up. When I sat down in the restaurant that pot belly suddenly looked like I was going to give birth.

Naeem took one look at my gut, laughed and said, 'Fucking hell Tommy!' It's a wonder I didn't lose my bottle and just scarper. That seemed an even better idea given what happened when Naeem's brother Bibi came in.

There are four brothers in the family firm but this character Bibi clearly fancied himself as the hard man. Gold tooth, the whole gangster approach. When he walked in and got introduced, Naeem said to me, 'Know what my bruv said Tommy? He said "get him shot, he's a wanker".'

They told us they had the building surrounded by their boys. It was straight out of Goodfellas or The Godfather. Edders told them, 'And you don't think we haven't got lads all round this place looking out for us?'

Naeem said he'd spoken to Luton's Muslim gangsters, blokes like Nigel Khan who's notorious around the place. He said that they'd got the inside track on me, that I was the bloke they thought I was, whatever that was supposed to mean. The loud and clear message was that they were hard cases and it wouldn't be a good idea to cross them.

'None of us are stupid, right Tommy?' said this Bibi bloke. I chuckled, which you could hear on the tape. 'Yes you are pal,' I was thinking.

So there I was, wrong 'uns to the left and right of me, a wanker to the front – Afzal – and the whole place was surrounded by blokes who wouldn't think twice about killing us. Shit, these were people whose spiritual leaders had put out an order to execute me at any cost, the first chance they got.

There was also a Sikh man present who was a captain in the army. It seemed to me as though Afzal was using him to get the Sikh vote, but I don't think he was involved in anything underhand, he was just there for show. I didn't particularly want him there if I'm honest, because as far as I was aware he'd done nothing wrong. I've always got along well with Sikhs. I have a lot of respect for them.

It all got a bit embarrassing when Bibi started on him. I'd sort of guessed the bloke was probably gay, but Bibi started busting his chops, asking him if he was married, if he had kids, all that stuff. Bibi kicked my leg under the table and winked. I just thought, 'so what?' Arsehole.

We got down to business and Afzal and Naeem came out with all of it – what they wanted from the EDL with Edders and the boys, calling a follow-up demo which they'd cancel and credit Afzal for. He talked about these 'Evening with Tommy Robinson' events, although it would have to go under the name of some made up community group, not the Tories. I could say what I normally would, but finish with, 'Vote for the army guy, he's fought for us in Iraq and Afghan, he'll fight for us now.'

I was careful not to lead anyone into saying anything, by the way, but I needn't have worried, these blokes were so full of themselves. Naeem was talking about Afzal when he was the MP being able to intervene with the chief of police when they had any 'business' problems, going on about him being their bloke in Parliament.

Afzal even bragged about him and Naeem being at a meeting the week before with David Cameron. He said that people were milling round the Prime Minister, but that he told Naeem, 'We're not going over there, just wait. He'll come to us.' And sure enough, David Cameron pushed past these people and made a beeline to Afzal, shaking his hand and asking how the campaign was going.

Afzal talked about Conservative HQ asking him which committees he wanted to be on when he got elected. He even said he wanted to be Prime Minister. 'I'm not going into politics just to be another MP Tommy,' he said. 'I'm ambitious, I want to go places. I want the top job.'

It was unbelievable. Honestly, it was. He said that after a year or so in Parliament he'd tell Cameron the EDL were right all along, that one bloke was speaking the truth about the Muslim problem – Tommy Robinson.

Did I believe it? What do you think? I can tell the difference between a drop of sweat and someone pissing down the back of my leg. He would use me, use the EDL, and when he got where he wanted, by hook or by crook, he'd dump on us from the top of Big Ben. There was nothing more certain.

And what if me or Edders spoke up? Who would the media believe, do you think? And even if we did blow the stunt later, how would that reflect on us – that we'd been happy to get involved in such shenanigans? There'd be a queue of people from all quarters wanting to string me and Edders up.

And of course there were also the big bad brothers, Naeem, Bibi and company. They'd made a song and dance about their close friend 'Tony' who'd been shot coming out of a gym ... the geezer was a notorious gangster who had survived one shooting because he was wearing a bulletproof vest, but not the next one.

It was all for show, to impress us with how bad they were. We finished the meeting about 11pm and dropped Mike back at the hotel. I took Steve Eddowes home, briefed the EDL boys who had waited around, about what was going on, and pressed home the point that it all had to stay absolutely under wraps. Then it was back to the hotel and the drive home. The motorway was shut and it was 4.30am when we got back to Luton.

AT THAT POINT I didn't even know what I was going to do, if anything, with whatever was on the tape. As much as anything it was for my own protection, because I've been stitched up by more than enough people that I've trusted over the years. I try to record as much as I can.

This could have been a stunt to get my licence revoked – again – and the last thing I wanted or needed was to find myself back on a prison wing for another four months, full of Muslim extremists all out to kill me. That couldn't happen, you say? It already had. More than once.

At least with the recording I knew that no one would be able to twist my words or make out that this scheme had been my idea all along. That's why I wasn't worried when the story broke in the Mail on Sunday and Afzal tried to claim that it was all my idea, or that I'd never actually left the EDL and this was us trying to stitch him up.

Everything was there on the tapes. A two-and-a-half-hour meeting with him leading the way, all the way. He was bang to rights, his career finished before it started.

When we'd left the meeting about 11pm, Steve Eddowes was absolutely raging. Think about it. Whatever people say and think about the EDL, blokes like me and Kevin Carroll, men like Steve Eddowes, have risked an awful lot putting our heads above the parapets to speak our minds.

It's not fun living under a death threat. Under a bunch of death threats. Al-Shabaab have said it's every Muslim's duty to kill me in the name of Allah. You don't think there aren't a few who would take that as a direct order?

Most people have probably read in their newspapers about Twitter trolls being arrested and prosecuted for abusing celebrities or politicians. I remember one man being jailed for 18 weeks for making threats against the Labour MP Stella Creasy after she supported putting Jane Austen on the new £10 note. Would he ever have carried out his threat, or tried? Who knows, but probably not.

However I've given police print outs of more than 300 identifiable tweets from people threatening to kill and chop up my kids, rape my wife and my mother. I've even looked them up, found out who they are and done the job for the police. And guess how much action has been taken?

That's right, sweet FA. Not once.

Yet when a Nazi fanatic tweeted that he was going to rape my mum, find my address and kill me, and I told him I'd be outside the probation office the next morning if he was that desperate, I was found in breach of my licence conditions – apparently I was openly inciting violence – and thrown back in jail for a month. Again, I'll explain that in more detail later, but it's still very fresh in the memory, and I had sworn to my family that the law would not have reason to put handcuffs on me ever again.

I don't generally hold out much hope of getting a fair crack of the whip from anyone in authority, so, sitting on this outrageous plot by a Conservative high flyer like Afzal Amin, what I could mostly think of was the variety of ways the whole scenario could blow up in my face. What's more, I could picture Afzal's musclemen backers sending their boys to look for me, in addition to everyone else out there.

The next morning, after the meeting in Birmingham, I was talking to a journalist who's been helping me with this book, not sure what to do. I think at that point Mike and I intended keeping the recordings for the eventual documentary, but the journalist said the story was absolutely dynamite and to let him make a few calls. That's how the Mail on Sunday got involved and the story broke.

We were never going to go ahead with the fake EDL demo anyway – can you imagine what the reaction from the

EDL rank and file would be if that came out? That it was a Muslim plot they'd been duped into, by the former and current leaders of the EDL? It didn't matter because what counted was doing the right thing in the circumstances.

During those next few days Afzal kept pressing me for news of when the EDL would announce the demo, which meant there was a bit of a problem. This was going off on Tuesday and Wednesday, while the Mail couldn't break cover until Saturday, in order to keep their story exclusive.

Afzal and I spoke on the phone – which I also recorded – but he was very careful not to mention the money he'd pay me and the EDL, saying he'd rather talk about those things face to face. I went down to meet him at a Pizza Express on Abbey Road near the Oval cricket ground in London, on the Thursday afternoon, all wired up again, and he came right out with it. I didn't look like Nellie the Elephant with the recording gear this time, I just put the bloody camera battery pack in my pocket. I don't know why we didn't think of that the first time – probably all too caught up in the James Bond stuff.

At that meeting Afzal explained that the Tories couldn't be seen to be paying EDL members but he wanted a couple of them working on the patch with him, canvassing on his behalf. He said he'd pay me £2,000 for my help, and that the EDL boys would get £250 a week each. He said that he knew that it was in breach of election law, but his backer would give me the money to pass onto them. It was as plain and as blatant as that.

I was told I'd never have to worry about things financially again, that any legal problems I had would be made to disappear, because he'd intervene on my behalf. He obviously believed his own bullshit because Naeem was already talking about him like he was a lifelong get out of jail free card. By this time I think I was more disappointed than anything. Here was a supposedly intelligent man, someone who was on first name terms with the Prime Minister, who could even imagine himself in the most powerful position in the land, and he was talking complete and utter rubbish.

A senior Tory Muslim championing the EDL in Westminster? He wouldn't last five minutes, either with the establishment or with British Muslims. He'd get more death threats than me. But of course it would never work out like that. It was never going to work out like that, but this man was so stupid as to believe that everyone was as readily for sale, as corrupt, as he obviously was.

Except we weren't – neither for sale nor corrupt – and his dream was going to turn into a nightmare very shortly. Because I had Afzal Amin bang to rights.

For once, for probably the first time in the public eye, Tommy Robinson was the good guy. It's a nice feeling, but I'm not taking it for granted just yet.

The Mail on Sunday got their teeth into the story and the two reporters on it, Nick Craven and Ben Ellery, went to work digging into Afzal's background for a follow up story. It turned out that when he was younger he was credited with authoring a radical Islamic pamphlet under the name Raja Afzal Raza Amin al-Quraishy.

Among a slew of extremist views, he appeared to call for Indian restaurants to be burned – and this was someone who insulted the staff in a curry restaurant by saying, 'I'm not a Paki am I?' as he had that night in Birmingham. The pamphlet called for the Muhajideen to form enclaves across the country, from which they could wage jihad against the kuffar. Does the state do any homework on these people?

When the Mail on Sunday ran that follow-up story Afzal claimed that his work had been tampered with and the extreme views had been inserted into the pamphlet without his knowledge. I'm not sure I'd believe him anyway, but he didn't dispute membership of the group.

Clearly Afzal Amin reinvented himself after that and he seems to have been given plenty of legs up the greasy pole of the good old British establishment. And until me and Steve Eddowes went into that restaurant and called his bluff, the entire British political establishment was only too happy to swallow, hook line and sinker, this completely fabricated front. They always do. Mugs.

In a matter of days lots of Afzal's old pals were turning on him, revealing he'd been kicked out by a group of Muslim friends for his radical views. Meanwhile the chairwoman of the Dudley North Conservative party, Anne Millward, was quick to criticise him for spending more time abroad in Dubai and Somalia than canvassing in Dudley.

I still wonder what Afzal was doing in those places – and how he managed to pay for it. Both of his children went to Eton, he swanned about in big motors, but I couldn't fathom where all of the money came from. I can guess though.

Mrs Millward came out and blasted Tory Central Office for not vetting him sufficiently, as if it was none of their fault in the Dudley North constituency. Not that you'd expect anyone to take responsibility for it, because these people never do.

Just think, this bloke could have been sitting round the Cabinet table as you read this. Would he have been representing dodgy Muslim businessmen, middle east terrorists or just chancing it for his own ends and means?

Or was his agenda to bring the English Defence League to the high table of mainstream British politics? I know what I think, and I reckon you do too.

Still, who could have imagined this ordinary Luton lad in a situation where he could bring down a corrupt Muslim politician who had mighty ambitions to hold the highest office in the United Kingdom?

Lord Lennon of Luton – it has a ring to it, don't you think?

3: BACK IN THE DAY

I WAS BORN in the L&D – the Luton and Dunstable Hospital – in November 1982. I have an older brother. There's just 18 months between us.

My first memories revolve around mum. She was with my birth dad, Malcolm Yaxley, but they soon split up. Mum told me she was in a battered wives hostel with both of us kids in those early days. I remember him later on, but we didn't call him dad, we called him Malcolm. It must have been awkward for him. He only used to come to see us on birthdays and Christmas and suchlike.

The man who is my dad, Tommy Lennon, got together with mum when I was two. So from my earliest memories Tommy was dad, and Malcolm Yaxley was just the bloke who came along once or twice a year to bring us a present.

He always had a quality car, Malcolm, I remember that much. I used to like him coming along on Sports Day when I was in junior school, in his nice sports car. I was too young to remember much, but by all accounts he sounded like a cruel, vindictive bastard. He stopped coming to see us when I was about 11 and died two or three years ago, I heard.

In the early days of the EDL, The Times was doing a story 'exposing' my identity. I'd always tried to avoid it but there came the time I was going to be revealed to the world and a journalist called Stephen Bird found me. I met him in a pub in Farley Hill, The Parrot. He said he had tracked down my dad and told me that he was in Bulgaria, which was news to me.

So I told him, 'Stick his name in the article – Malcolm Yaxley'. I thought someone would ring him up and ask what the hell his son was up to. That would be a laugh.

When I had kids I dropped the name, Yaxley, because I didn't want to carry on with it. Mum told me Malcolm had died, but I don't know how she found out. There were a couple of times that I looked him up through Google, like you do, but to be honest he was nothing to me. I think if I ever had bumped into him, he'd have got a smack in the teeth and a reminder that DNA doesn't make you a dad.

My dad was and is Tommy Lennon, Scottish and Glaswegian, a great man and a real hard-working bloke too.

My mum, Rita Carroll as was, is Irish. Her family came over here when she was a youngster. She's one of eight, a proper Irish Catholic family. She's a tiny thing, my mum, which is probably why I stopped growing when I was about 14. I got to 5ft 6ins in good time, but that was that. Just a little chubby kid with a big attitude.

But mum and Tommy worked really hard for us. He was a specialist pipe fitter who was always working away, here, there and everywhere, so mum brought us up mostly and she did a lot of childminding and fostering too.

Lots of times there was another kid in the house being looked after by mum. She and Tommy never had kids together and I sometimes think mum was mindful of what having two families under one roof might do, but it matters not, because Tommy's my dad. We've worked together for a lot of years.

My first memories were of growing up in Layham Drive, in Stopsley and going to Wigmore Junior School although my first vivid memory is of a really bad asthma attack when I nearly died. The next door neighbour jumped over the fence and gave me mouth to mouth and resuscitated me. I can remember having a bloody nose from my brother as part of the whole incident but mum says that I got it wrong, that my brother wasn't even there.

It's certainly in my memory banks, even though I was only aged about two and I still get occasional flashbacks from it, of being in the ambulance, even though the family can't believe it. I had bad asthma when I was younger.

Mum and Tommy owned the house we lived in. As a family we were very close to my auntie June and uncle Bill, who lived across town in Farley Hill and we moved back there to live with them at one point, while mum and dad were waiting for a new house to be built.

We all mucked in with auntie June and Bill and some other cousins, as families did back then. It was a very family-oriented part of town with a healthy mix of people from different backgrounds and certainly in my younger days none of that was an issue. It still wouldn't be, if one community didn't like to make it a problem.

One of my friends from primary school was a Sikh lad called Jatin. It was quite funny, years later, because when the police were turning my life upside down, they went to London where Jatin owns a business, investigating a financial transaction we'd had.

I'd bought something from him, nothing more than that. The police thought that because he was Asian, and I couldn't possible have friends from that community, that I must have been up to something dodgy, which just about sums them up. Jatin rang me saying not to worry – that they were just trying to find something, anything, to stitch me up on. He said the copper told him that his boss was pulling his hair out because they couldn't pin anything on me. Funny.

During that period living back in Farley Hill, it was my first memory of being let loose, of being able to go out with mates, just kids being kids, being mischievous and having fun. I was about nine or 10 then.

We'd build dens and all kinds of stuff from whatever we could scavenge and collect. Healthy stuff. We still had to be back in the house earlier than the other kids though. Mum was pretty strict like that. And it was the same when we moved back to the Stopsley area, to Wigmore, for the next few years. There were woods nearby and we'd hunt out planks and all kinds of rubbish and carry it for miles to build tree houses. Just normal growing up.

I got into motor bikes a little bit in my early teens. A neighbour moved in next door and he owned a Lotus and a Ferrari; very flash. He raced bikes professionally and had a Ducati, and then he bought these little rev-and-go track bikes that he used to let us have a go on. After that my dad got us trials bikes, but mum and dad were quite strict about when we could take them out. So as you'd expect, we'd wait until they were out, then go burning round the estate, creating havoc, being a nuisance.

I remember when Princess Diana died, my mum went to watch the funeral and all we could think of was 'great, mum's out' – and we were out bombing around on the motorbikes. The flash bloke with the sports cars and bikes ended up on the run for a massive fraud, apparently. There's always been a lot of crime around Luton, as you'll discover soon enough.

AT THAT TIME, going into my teens, I wasn't really aware of race or religion being any kind of an issue. Sure, their colour identified people, but it never registered as being a barrier to anything. Not at first, at least.

Bury Park is an overwhelmingly Muslim enclave now, but we used to go because there was a McDonalds and some shops which mum used.

Kenilworth Road, the home of Luton Town FC, is smack bang in the heart of Bury Park, which contributed to some of the later trials and tribulations when Luton's Muslim radicals were the trailblazing poster boys for al Qaeda and Osama bin Laden, and me and my football pals were starting to stand up for the other side. It can't have been easy but the police, as usual, managed to turn a difficulty into a disaster. Give coppers a 50-50 choice and they seem to have close to a 100 per cent record of right royally messing things up. The truth is that by the time the conflict became focussed on religion and nationalism, there had been trouble brewing in Luton for many years. That was more about gang territory and activity than any disputes over faith and religion.

When we were kids, Wigmore was a new school and a big estate was built at Cutlers Green, right in the middle of the area – probably one of the last large estates to be built.

A lot of Muslim families moved in and when I was about eight I was probably one of the first kids to become friends with some of them. There were also brothers Daniel and Dean Grozetti, whose dad came from Trinidad originally.

People talk about the current asylum crisis but a proper, early refugee family moved in a few doors from us, as a result of the Bosnian conflict. Amir's dad was killed over there and he arrived amongst us with his mum. A good lad and a success story of a man too. The last time I saw him he told me he was embarrassed at how other British Muslims were acting.

My pal Briso and I – Paul Brisland – were glued at the hip for years. With my mum being quite strict and his mum letting him stay out until all hours, I'd often stay at Briso's and we'd be out on the street. One of my cousins, Declan Carroll, used to spend most weekends with us, and he knew the Grozetti boys. We were all good mates growing up and I wasn't aware of other kids being Muslim. I didn't know anything about their religion, it was just a simple fact that a lot of them were either Pakistani or Bangladeshi.

My brother's best friend at the time, Dobbsy – Stephen Dobbs – has remained a close family friend all these years on. Lads like 'Big Mike' and Abella, pals through thick and thin. We were all just a big melting pot of kids and if there was any name calling or racial bullying going on, then I wasn't aware of it. I do think though, in hindsight, that there's probably a lesson to be learned in terms of cultures mixing. At that time you had quite a slow influx of pupils from other nationalities and communities coming into the school at Wigmore and I think that's when you're far more likely to see integration.

Things changed quickly though, and the problems started once we got into high school. That's when I became aware not so much of the religious issues yet, but certainly the prejudices and the physical differences between cultures and communities.

My first school girlfriend, Becky Ling, had a terribly sad story. She was at our house when news came that her dad had dropped dead at the gym from a heart attack. Becky's mum got terminal cancer not long after and she moved away to Norwich to live with her older sister.

When I was about 14 I had a girlfriend from an Irish family, Charlotte McCormack. Charlotte's best friend, Lisa Day, was going out with my pal Kamran – as in Kamran and Imran, the twins whose family came here from Afghanistan. One day Kamran's family went to see Lisa's mum to say that the relationship was killing their dad, he was dying from the shame of his son being with a white girl, a Christian girl. He did die eventually, but I doubt it was anything to do with that.

But I remember seeing Lisa crying over it. They were forced to stop seeing each other and that didn't seem right. It was particularly strange because with a big black community in Luton, mixed relationships were everywhere – black girls with white boys, white girls with black boys. It was normal. There were lots of mixed race young people.

The changes kept on coming and I remember suddenly that we weren't supposed to say 'Pakistanis' any more, because some of the new pupils coming to our school were from Afghanistan. They would all be bussed in to our high school, Putteridge, as they didn't live on the estate or in the area, which I suppose reflected the growing numbers within the Muslim community, meaning that they were having to be shipped out to schools three or four miles away.

The first time I was aware of racial trouble would probably have been in year nine, when I was about 13.

There was a growing gang mentality among the Muslim kids, mainly in that they hung out tightly and pretty exclusively together. We had a boy from Nigeria start school, who had moved to Luton from Leicester. He said the Muslims there didn't act like this, although I didn't know quite what he meant.

Anyway, my high school mate Dean Gilheaney had a fight with a Pakistani pupil, a boy from the year above us called Majid. You have to understand that this was normal knockabout school stuff. Boys had playground scraps and all that. Always have and always will.

Except this was different. This time it was very different. All the Muslim lads rushed Dean, younger ones, older ones – Dean was in year nine with me and even boys from year 11 attacked him, which never happened. They jumped him down on the school service road and they put him in hospital. There were about 20 of them. Police came to the school and the teachers had to put all the Muslim kids in one classroom because by then all of Dean's pals were suddenly looking for payback.

From thereon I was aware of the tensions more and more, but it was still generally about a gang mentality rather than having any religious overtones. When we got to year 11 I remember a young lad called Bowler, two years below me but a game kid, and he got in a scrap with one of the Muslims who was supposed to be a real hard nut, and whose brothers were in the Gambino gang. We'll get to Luton's criminal gangs shortly.

All the Muslims in our year were going to rush young Bowler and it ended with a big group of the black and white lads getting together to say that no one was touching the kid. I had massive respect for this lad, Bowler – I can still picture him walking through the school with a can of coke amongst 20 Pakistani lads, all older than him. He threw the coke all over them, called them a bunch of wankers, and ran off laughing. He was game, for sure.

That wasn't the end of it though. It never was, because it quickly became clear there was no such thing as a one-on-one fight where these lads were concerned. By the end of the school day there was a big crowd of Pakistani men waiting outside school. It's a wonder no one got killed.

When I was about 15 my brother, who went to the Catholic high school, Cardinal Newman, not Putteridge like me, got jumped on, robbed and beaten up. He knew who had done it and I went round to the ringleader's house – he was quite a bit older than us, about 19 or 20. A big group of us all used to congregate on Friday nights and hang out and Kamran came along, which was unusual for the Muslim lads who were our friends.

This lad who'd jumped my brother had an Irish mum, but his dad was a Pakistani taxi driver which I didn't know at the time. I've always been a bit more fiery than my brother and despite him being the older one, I wasn't taking it lying down.

We went round to his house, I knocked on the door and his mum answered at which point I saw him look out of the window. His mum slammed the door shut just as Kamran pushed at it and his hand went straight through the glass. He ended up with stitches.

I also used to hang about with some of the gypsy kids from the travellers' site at Stopsley and we found out there was a party at the Catholic church hall which ironically was in Bury Park. Some of the other lads who'd jumped my brother were there, so a group us went looking for them. We couldn't get in and later, when they all started leaving and found just four of us still hanging about, I got a few slaps for my trouble. The whole thing was no big deal – or at least it wasn't a big deal until we went to school on Monday.

As I said, I didn't know the race of the main lad's dad, but when I came out of school there were about 30 Pakistani men waiting for me. All of our teachers came out to try to defuse things and the police turned up too, so nothing happened, but these conflicts seemed to be building. It was strange. You could laugh and joke with the Muslim lads during class but once school was over they were back in their community, amongst their own, again.

There was a barrier that just came down and there was no moving it. I've not seen anything before or since to suggest the situation is going to improve, either. Whatever rivalries and tribal allegiances they had in their own communities, between different mosques and sects, there was one common enemy that united them every time – non-Muslims. I don't see anything, not in our country, not across the world even, that contradicts that.

I had Muslim mates I thought I could trust and rely on, but I've seen the look in their eyes, seen them shrug their shoulders, when the line's been drawn in the sand, when it's been backs to the wall. Islam trumps everything.

Every year just brought more instances of conflict between the Muslim community and everyone else. Every year you just became more aware of the widening differences and the fact there wasn't much common ground between us. Not much at all.

AT ONE POINT some bright spark within the education system thought it was a clever idea to promote integration by sending us on a visit to a Muslim school, Denbigh, which is right in the middle of Bury Park. This wasn't a mixed school by any means. It was 100% Muslim and here we were, rolling up on a bus to come look at them like it was a trip to the local zoo.

Is that how it was intended? Of course not. But is that how they took it? I don't know, because there was absolutely zero conversation going on. We got off the bus, walked into the school and the next thing anyone knew the teachers were locking us in a classroom. There was panic on their faces because all of the Muslim kids were trying to get to us. A great idea that turned out to be.

And as for sport bringing communities together – think again. We were scheduled to play a school rugby match one time against Challney. We were beating them and it all kicked off. The next thing you knew, people were pouring over the horizon, screaming and howling for blood. The teacher called the game off and tried to pack us all back on the mini bus in a hurry, as they came charging after us, with reinforcements arriving from every direction.

Did that make us angels? Not really. There were three high schools in Stopsley so when we then heard Challney were playing rugby against Ashcroft, another one of our local schools, all of we Putteridge lads went there looking for trouble. The Ashcroft teachers called the game off.

My mate Sappy, who by this time had moved in next door to us, went to South Luton which was a 50/50 mixed school. They played Challney at football and that turned into a riot by all accounts.

Even their teacher got involved in the fighting and it made front page headlines in the local press. After that the police had to basically set up camp outside South Luton school because the Muslim gangs kept heading that way after school looking for revenge.

It probably wasn't any different than the school and gang rivalries that you find in a lot of basically working class towns. Teenage lads have always had scraps, established the school pecking order, all of that stuff. This wasn't unique to us I don't think, but there was definitely a different mindset where the Muslim lads were concerned.

The first real fight I ever had was with a black lad called Moses, from Ashcroft, supposedly the toughest kid in their school. It was my fault because I started an argument with him at a firework display. There were loads of us and not many of them, so I was probably a bit too cocky for my own good. I turned up the next day for football training, and Moses showed up with about six lads. We had a one-on-one scrap, and that was that. End of the argument. I even became friends with Moses afterwards and me and my first girlfriend Becky – who went to his school – used to hang out with Ashcroft kids, Tyler, Garvey, Baxter and Ian Thompson. You had a scrap, you settled it, you moved on.

But there was no such thing as a one-on-one fight with the Muslim lads. You had an argument with one, and you might as well have declared war on everyone in his extended community. The older you got, the more aware of the segregation you became.

My friendship with Kamran and Imran endured until well after we'd left school and our adventure with the Porsche we bought. I didn't get invited to their weddings though, non-Muslim people just didn't. I invited Muslim friends to my wedding. What's more, they came.

IT WASN'T ALL conflict, and life growing up in Luton wasn't just about the division between the communities. Football has always been big to me and these days I love nothing more than taking my kids along to watch the Hatters – Luton Town's nickname – just a dad and his family going to the game on a Saturday.

My son's playing football and enjoying it, although there's a lot more for kids at a younger age now than when I was growing up. I joined a local junior team, the Dragons, when I was around 11-years-old, based about three miles from where we lived. Most of my fondest teenage memories would revolve around my time at the Dragons, where basically the same group of boys played together from 11 right up to the age of 17. By the age of 15 or 16 we were probably the best team in Luton. We'd go to training on a Saturday morning with games on a Sunday. I used to walk there mostly, as my dad was working away a lot at the time in Mexico, Germany, all over the world in fact.

The Dragons eventually changed their name and became Crawley and that's where I first met Imran Asmat. Our football club was nowhere near where Imran grew up, but his dad had met Alan Derbyshire, who was a sort of father figure-type who ran our club, and Alan used to pick Imran up. Imran and I became good mates – he once pushed me off the pier on an outing to the coast. Well, pals do that sort of stuff as kids, don't they? No big deal.

Imran used to talk about his older brothers a lot. I hadn't met them at that stage but even as a 12-year-old he always had £100 Stone Island jackets and expensive clothes, which were hand-me-downs from his brothers. I understood they were involved in something lucrative if not strictly legal, but having said that, everywhere you looked it seemed somebody was up to no good.

On one occasion when we were about 13 we went to a football tournament in Newcastle and all stayed at Whitley Bay on a caravan site, Imran was there, plus my good mates Ayling, Bradders and Cheeky. But even that wasn't without its dramas. A few months previously Luton had beaten Newcastle at football, and we ended up getting in a tear-up with a load of Geordie kids who apparently bore a grudge. As we were being chased they were shouting, 'Get the Paki, get the Paki!' and I remember being relieved, thinking, 'I'm alright because they're going after poor old Imran!'

Not funny, I know. But Imran was still my pal.

It was a scrape but the trip was a highlight for all of us. I got a photo of the Newcastle manager Kevin Keegan with me and Imran when we went to meet the team at Newcastle's training ground. It ended up being a bit of a football education in more ways than one, because we played the old junior team of Gazza, David Platt and Alan Shearer, Wallsend Boys. We thought we were the bollocks down in Luton, but we played these lads who were a year younger than us – and they spanked us, a lot to nil.

Still, it was a great memory for a kid. I played up front as a striker when I was younger and I suppose I was okay. I scored a lot of goals, won a lot of trophies, although as the years passed I went to play in defence and then as a sweeper.

I was never good enough to go anywhere with it, professionally or anything, but just loved playing the game. Weekends with the Dragons were great, and after school it was out on the estate kicking a ball about. Kids being kids.

And then one day Imran simply disappeared, just like that. His dad had died, which we didn't know about, and his family took him back to Pakistan. That was the last I heard – one day he was there, one day he wasn't – for a long time. I saw him some years later at a disco and he was with all these bad lads. Word eventually got out that he was heavily involved with the gangs.

Imran died suddenly from a heart attack, very prematurely, during the EDL years. I didn't feel able to go to the funeral – there might have been another one required if I'd shown up – but I dug out a picture and sent it to his brother. It was from our football trip, of me and Imran and our pals with Kevin Keegan.

4: GANGLAND

BY THE TIME I was in my mid-teens I was fully aware of the very real presence and activities of the gangs that effectively ran Bury Park and in turn Luton, certainly in respect of the criminal enterprises which involved mostly drugs and prostitution.

There's not much about the name Gambino that induces nostalgic thoughts of Pakistani Kashmir. Machine guns in New York and the old family home in Sicily maybe. Gambino relates to most people as pure Mafia. But the self-styled Gambinos of Luton were at the forefront of the Pakistani gangs that took over the town through the 1990s.

The 'Reds' of the Raja tribe and 'Yellows' of the Choudary and Jats, the Khwajas, Khans and Ghaffours, they all fought for control of their patch and whatever was going on in and around it. Drugs, prostitution, robbing, fraud, money-laundering, you name it.

I've read that these Muslim gangs formed originally to defend Bury Park from football gangs, Luton Town's Kenilworth Road ground being right in the middle of the patch. For sure the club had its own groups like the Bolts and the MIGs – Men in Gear. Members of my family were influential figures in the MIGs and when I gravitated towards the footy as I got older I was right in that world.

Which came first and which initiated the violence however, the football gangs or the Muslim ones, I'm not so sure. The reality was probably that for both there was relative safety in numbers.

Exactly how that translates into the Muslim gangs running industrial levels of drug trafficking, prostitution, protection rackets and lots, lots more, as close to a scaled down model of the New York mafia as you can get, someone a bit cleverer than me will have to tell you.

You might have noticed by now that I steer clear of calling these communities and gangs and groups 'Asian'. I see that as one of modern Britain's biggest, most Politically Correct cop-outs. I'm not talking about Asian people as in Chinese or Japanese, Vietnamese or Korean.

Whether from Pakistan or Bangladesh, these communities and groups were defined by their ideology, which was and is Islam. They were all Muslim which to my mind makes it the most accurate way to describe them collectively. It's what broadly defines their own identity, so I really don't understand why we get so uptight, so sensitive about using the word 'Muslim' to describe a community.

Most of Luton's Muslim community came originally from Pakistan and within that specifically from Kashmir, and as I understand it, for them the tribe is everything. That would obviously have a lot to do with how the factions and gangs in and around Bury Park and Luton at large developed.

Some years later two gangs of lads who had all gone to Challney Boys' School got into a massive brawl that left one young man, Wajid Khan, battered to death. They were from two gangs called the Runley Road Boys and the Saints Boys and had been rivals when they were at school, but who continued the feud on for years afterwards. One night they went at it with everything from cricket and baseball bats to a machete and a Samurai sword.

Apparently Khan was the leader of the Saints and he and some pals were cruising round Luton in a car, tooled up with weapons, when they ran into the Runley Road Boys and it all kicked off. When Khan's pals legged it he was smashed about 30 or 40 times and died from his brain injuries.

The Runley Road gang members admitted the attack, although they only pleaded to manslaughter saying that they were provoked. How long do you think they got for smashing a young man to death with bats in the middle of the street? Life? Ten years maybe?

You're kidding, aren't you? The longest sentence handed down was five years. One of the thugs got just three years for his part in killing that young man. I got nearly that long for lending my wife's brother a deposit on a house.

THERE WAS another killing in Luton in not too dissimilar circumstances which absolutely outraged most local people – the cold-blooded murder of Mark Sharp.

Mark was 37 and was on his way to get a takeaway in 1995 when he had a bit of an altercation with some blokes in a car who'd cut him up. He flipped a vee-sign at them. There were four of them, and he was alone with his young son, but they still rang for reinforcements before they set about him right there on High Town Road.

All of them were armed, metal bars, part of a snooker cue, and they battered and battered Mark to his knees before one of them finished him off with a knife in his head. Even when he was down they kept on kicking and stamping on him. He hung on for three days before he died.

Two of his attackers got life for murder, but three of the others were acquitted of murder and were given just four years for manslaughter. The judge told the jury they could downgrade it to manslaughter if they felt Mark had done or said anything, 'enough to make a reasonable young Asian male act'.

Can I ask you something? What has 'Asian' got to do with anything, even though it wasn't 'Asian' but 'Muslim'?

It was a something and nothing moment in a car. It happens in every town, every day. But these characters still had to call more of their mates and murder a bloke in cold blood – and the judge felt he had to find a way to let them off easy, by inviting a jury to find an excuse for their behaviour.

That was a turning point for a lot of local people. A few years ago I was in Hemel Hempstead and got talking to a man. It turned out he was a close friend of Mark Sharp and after the case he and his family moved away from Luton. He said a lot of people did. They still are if the truth's told. Non-Muslims are fleeing, at a rate of knots.

It was interesting. That man made the point that no one commemorated the murder as a moment in time, as a social landmark, like they did with the Stephen Lawrence race murder. They were both totally random racial killings, but one was clearly of far lesser importance than the other.

Everyone in Luton remembers the Mark Sharp murder – but violence from the Muslim gangs was an everyday occurrence that everyone was having to learn to live with.

Not long after Mark was killed there was an incident that brought it really close to home. One of my cousins nearly lost his hand because he was stabbed in a confrontation with some Muslim blokes in the town centre. He was rushed to a London hospital, and I can remember all of my aunties and uncles coming up to the house.

News was filtering through what had happened, and when they heard that it involved Pakistanis, everyone in the house was like, 'Oh no – they're going to have done him bad. Because if it's them, they're going to have gone to town on him'. His hand was literally stabbed through, but you could say he was one of the lucky ones.

I suppose these things were bound to have shaped me in some way, growing up. Hearing the stories and experiencing the reality of life on streets that simply didn't belong to us any more. You couldn't help but have it touch your life in some way or another.

It was around then, when I was about 12, that me and some pals were going to the main Luton swimming pool, which was over near Bury Park. My mum used to say, 'No eye contact with the Muslims'. Really. 'Put your head down when you go past the Muslims, when you go out of our area'. It was one of the first times that I was allowed out with my brother and his friends, Roy Frater, a big black lad, who was older, 16, and his younger cousin Wesley. The Fraters were a big family with a big reputation in the area – one of the older brothers had recently been shot dead.

Wesley moved into Cutlers Green near us and we had been allowed to go to the swimming pool so we walked there – probably a two-hour walk, about five miles from home. It was on Bath Road, the other side of Wardown Park, at the back of Bury Park. There were about six or seven of us and we came across a group of around 15 to 20 Pakistanis just hanging about near Wardown Park.

They asked who we were and where we were from and the main one, the gang leader, said to 'leave them two' – indicating Roy and Wesley. Well, everyone knew who the Fraters were and the reputation they had. You messed with the black lads and you could expect repercussions. The rest of us were fair game though. They mugged us, spitting in our faces, calling us white boys, white pigs, knocking us about and then searching us, taking our money.

I was probably the youngest and my brother and his mates were that bit older, so they were the ones being physically beaten up. They took my brother's hat for some reason. They searched us all and took our money. That was the first time I had come into contact with a big group of Pakistani lads. The first time but not the last. If you wanted to go out and about in Luton you ran the gauntlet of those kinds of confrontation, simple as.

Later, when we started going to the under 18s disco, we used to walk through High Town, through the train station up to the town centre, and you were taking a chance every time you made the trip. I got mugged twice one night, but then almost every white kid got stopped and robbed at some time or another. When my mum used to give us money for the youth group, we had to hide it in our shoe under our sock, because we knew that we would be stopped and patted down by these lads, these men.

Some time later when I was on the fringes of the Luton Town football scene, I went to a game against Rochdale and saw a bunch of the older blokes stopping a gang of Pakistani lads. They made them take their shoes off and gave them a few slaps, saying, 'This is what you lot are doing to our youths ... doesn't feel nice, does it?'

Looking back, and although I never thought about it at the time, belonging to the Luton Town football supporters – football hooligans even – was the way a lot of young black and white lads found their own gang. There was only ever safety in numbers if you were out and about around Luton and unless you were part of some gang or other, you were vulnerable.

For me, not just with my interest in football, but with members of my family being part of that Luton Town scene, I suppose it was only natural that I gravitated towards that gang. I'm not going to pretend that it wasn't exciting, being in a big crowd of mates, having a ruck with lads from another club. I suppose I was a bit starry-eyed with listening to the stories, all the rivalries and fights and running battles with different hooligan outfits.

Once when we were staying at my auntie's lots of the blokes came round to watch a video, CCTV coverage of a Luton against QPR game, where trouble broke out. Was it attractive because I was young and impressionable? Possibly. It sounded glamorous and exciting. These men belonged together, had a brotherhood of their own, they had something special, unique to them.

I don't suppose it's any different from any number of gang affiliations or the kind of things young men are drawn to the world over, and always have been. I was about 17 or 18 and on my apprenticeship when I was first allowed to go away on my own to watch a Town game. It was to see them play at Mansfield and I got such a buzz from watching things kicking off, even though I wasn't involved in it.

For my 18th birthday we hired a 52 seater bus to go for a night out in Watford, which might not have been the best idea a group of young blokes ever had, because Luton and Watford have always had a fierce rivalry. We sat down in a pub and a lad strutted in wearing this flash gear and said, 'Who's from Luton then?' And that was it, it was on. Only about half a dozen lads made it home on the bus.

It was tribal, just like when our school would fight another school, or kids from different estates would confront each other. Luton and the football just became another extension of that. I was going to games with lads my own age and they were all willing to stand up for each other. That was a tie that meant something – although it came to an abrupt end for a long period in 2001, after a now notorious Luton battle with Watford.

It was chaos. The game was on a Tuesday night and we all met up at around 10 or 11 in the morning in London, in order to head back up to Watford. There were probably 250 to 300 of us.

The police tried blocking the railway station off and it was then that I heard the chants, 'MIGs, MIGs, MIGs' like a big roar. It sent a shiver down your spine. Everyone ran through Watford, and when we got to the ground it was all kicking off. We went into the ground and there were no police present because they were all outside, dealing with the trouble kicking off there.

The Luton fans ended up on the pitch and went straight over to the Watford end. The match had to be stopped for 15 minutes and it was all over the news, a full scale football riot. Exciting? You got caught up in the frenzy of it, the adrenaline of it, for certain. It was a massive buzz. At least it was in the brief time that it lasted – not later.

Everyone was running backwards and forwards and people got caught up in the madness of the moment – but when everything calmed down it started very quickly to dawn how stupid it all was. I was properly scared, because I had the apprenticeship which, much as I wasn't happy with a lot of things about it, I really didn't want to lose. My mum would have gone through the roof, for starters. As tiny as she was, she was still the gaffer. Still is.

After that Watford game I was talking to one of the older apprentices at work about the buzz from the game. Except this time what had always seemed to us like pretty harmless fun turned into something extremely serious. Suddenly, people's doors started being bust open, with the police piling in behind. I think 18 lads went to jail for their parts in that Watford brawl. And I really, really didn't want anything like that.

It became clear that if people were identified in any way as being part of the Watford riot they were going to prison. One of the lads, an old friend of my brother, got 12 months just for kicking a bottle on the pitch. Twelve months for running on the pitch, chanting, and kicking a bottle?

I remember seeing a picture in the paper and one of the blokes looked a bit like me – I was properly shitting myself. I was a bit pudgy at the time and I even ended up losing a lot of weight. I'm not sure if it was a conscious decision to not look like that bloke, but it was a massive wake up call.

I'd never been much of a drinker at that time and I didn't do drugs, even though I hung about with a couple of groups of lads on Friday nights. One of the gangs would smoke drugs and get pissed and get into plenty of trouble, but although I got along with them in a sociable manner, I would always step away from that stuff. I always kept my head on straight. Back then at least.

After that Watford game, with lots of friends finding themselves in court and worse, I got a full scale reality check. I pretty much stayed away from the football until I finished my apprenticeship. A lot of the lads stayed away from the game altogether until all of the Watford trouble had blown over.

And then the fates conspired against me and I ended up in jail anyway. I'd managed to successfully finish my apprenticeship, but my career was finished before it ever really started.

5: RUNNING WILD

RUNNING A LITTLE bit wild around Luton at times hadn't prevented me from managing a bunch of reasonable GCSE results and getting that Britannia apprenticeship in aeronautical engineering was probably the biggest achievement in my short life. Straight after school I'd landed a full time job in the Asda bakery, which lasted six months or so until the apprenticeship started.

I was working close to home at Luton Airport and attending Bedford College full time for the first year. We were bussed over there by Britannia, but I was a bit of a fish out of water in that company. One of the lads on the course was called Sultan and, not surprisingly, it turned out he was supposed to be a prince – the United Arab Emirates had sent around 50 lads over to study on this course and others like it. None of the people were working class, and they weren't from Luton either. I used to go home and tell my mum that I had nothing in common with them.

I thought I was normal, but I guess it's all about perspective and when you're young you don't see things that clearly. If you were from Luton and you had a punch up, that was quite normal. It wasn't uncommon. Luton was and still is a rough town, and growing up there most people have had a bloody nose at some time or other.

Then all of a sudden I was with these people who'd had a completely different life experience from me. That was the first thing I would ask them, 'Where are you from, where did you grow up?'

They were from villages and places a lot further afield and they just had a different mindset. I'm not saying that I felt exactly inferior, or that they went out of their way to make me feel that way. I was just out of my comfort zone for the first time, that's all.

I had bits of bother while I was at college. A gang of Muslim lads jumped me and stole my phone, a Nokia 8210 – a good phone, that – and I was also jumped by a big lad on another occasion, but I was constantly aware of the danger of losing my job, so I didn't retaliate. That took some doing.

The job was a big deal for me, a huge opportunity. I was still living at Stopsley with my mum and dad but after about two years I told them I didn't want to continue with the apprenticeship. It was for four years and all my mates were employed on building sites and were getting good money. I wasn't and I felt, I don't know, a bit out of my depth, but I stuck with the apprenticeship anyway.

Instead and to make some extra cash I started moonlighting for a local man, an Irish developer, Dave, who was really good to me, not just then but over the years to come. Every Friday night I'd head down to London to work for him labouring. We did a huge job at Merrill Lynch, working when the building was closed, and I could make £160 for that – which was as much as I was making for a full week at Britannia.

I've mentioned my girlfriend Charlotte McCormack, who lived near Putteridge High School and became my high school sweetheart. Her family were lovely to me and even took me on a family holiday to Portugal.

But when I was about 15 or 16 I noticed a really pretty girl walking in the road near our house as I was on my way out with my pals. Just for a bit of a joke, I wrote a note to her on the back of a photograph of me and my mates Tom Stoker and Mark Seymour, and stuck it through the letterbox of the house she'd gone into.

I didn't see that girl again for two or three years because she was from over in Bushmead, a different area of Luton, but then one night I saw her out with friends in town. And that girl is now my wife, the long-suffering mother of our three children.

I tried it on with her that night in town but she wasn't having any of it. The best I could manage was to swop phone numbers with her, which was lucky, given the manner in which we eventually met and got together.

I loved my cars but I reckon she must sometimes shake her head at what happened the next time she saw me and my poxy little Vauxhall Corsa! Well, I say that. As Corsas go this was the business. It had TVs in the headrests and a TV in the front, and the car was two-tone so it even changed colour in the sun. The number plate was C13 RSA. I thought I was the boy, no messing.

I was out in the motor one day with a couple of mates, just cruising around and we had porn playing on the car videos. I know, random! Suddenly I got a text message saying, 'You dirty so-and-sos!' and it was her. She was in a car behind us and could see the porn on the Corsa's tellies.

On that occasion she agreed to go out with me and, as the saying goes, the rest is history. I've already put that poor girl through a lifetime's worth of grief.

I WAS STAYING away from the football at that time, but living in Luton, trouble was never far away. You didn't have to go looking for it – it found you, just going about your business. Even that car got me in trouble.

Because I wasn't a drinker I'd go out in my car and on one occasion I was at the Space nightclub in town. When I came outside there was a big gang of Pakistani lads who started shouting at me, 'Corsa boy, Corsa boy'. Their ringleader was a well-known character called Chopper. That night I was with two black lads Brucie and Nelson and another mate Scott, also known as 'Shit Hair'.

We were standing there minding our own business and the Pakistanis were shouting, 'Corsa Boy, white and black don't go, so fuck off.' I was just standing with my mates, so I said, 'You what?' and they shouted back, 'Go on, fuck off, white boy'. The next thing you know it all kicked off and ended with me and my little mate Scott being chased down the road by this gang.

We jumped in Scott's car and the Pakistanis put all his windows through. More importantly, as a result of that I had this gang looking for me, hunting for blood. I was young I suppose, but I learned a massive lesson out of that episode.

I tried to smooth things over, ringing them up saying I didn't want any trouble, but I wasn't getting anywhere. It went on for months. It was my cousin who told me I couldn't do that with these people, not in this town. I had to stand up to them, not show weakness, or my life wouldn't be worth living. So I rang Chopper and I told him straight. 'It doesn't matter how many of you get me, I know that you live opposite PJ Shoes and if you keep this up, I am going to fucking hurt you. You are getting it mate. So it doesn't matter if there are 20 or 30 of you involved, even if it's your pals who get me, what you need to know is that it's going to be on your head.'

They'd been jumping out of cars up in Stopsley with baseball bats, and going up to my mates' cars demanding to know, 'Where's this Yaxley, where's this Yaxley?'

A decision had to be made, and it's one I've tried to live by ever since – with mixed results it must be said. It's cost me a lot of time in hospital beds and prison cells. Straight after that I had Chopper on the phone saying, 'Aw bruv, let's leave it.'

It worked. And I thought, 'Shit, these geezers have been bullying me for the last six months. I have been looking over my shoulder every time I've stepped outside.'

I suppose it's the same with bullies the world over. Let them get away with it once and your life's a misery, not worth living. Show them one sign of weakness and they will walk all over you.

It was the same when the EDL first started. I thought that if I ran once, I would run every week. People will chase you all the time, but once they know you're not going to run, it's a whole different mindset. That will focus their minds pretty sharpish if they know that when they give it, it's coming straight back at them.

The country could do to learn that lesson, if you ask me. It's an approach that's earned me some beatings, some real hidings. Stitches and broken bones and broken teeth. But my pride's intact, my spirit. They've not broken that yet.

TOWARDS THE END of the apprenticeship, I got a six month contract based at Manchester Airport, working day and night shifts, four on, four off, and staying at a guest house in Wilmslow in Cheshire.

It was another world from the one I'd grown up in. Some of the lads would come up for the weekend at times and we'd have a session, going out in Manchester. Great fun, and my first real time away from home. At other times I'd knock off early, shoot back to Luton and then be back down in London working for Dave, earning some more cash.

The problem was that when we finished, there wasn't much work about in the aerospace industry. Of the six of us that got those apprenticeships, not one got a full-time job. The September 11 attacks on the Twin Towers hadn't been long before and the industry had been rocked on its heels.

It probably mattered more for the other lads than it did for me, because my life was about to take a big left turn anyway. I'd never been in trouble with the law before, but I was about to get sent to jail for my first ever offence. That changed a lot of things.

By this time my girlfriend and I were going strong, even though I was based in Manchester. We'd been together more than three years. She was working at a bank in St Albans and things were going along great. We had been on a night out for her birthday, about a dozen of us, and we rented a limousine which took us over to Milton Keynes. I was staying at her mum's house.

It was a great night out and when I went to prison, I had a photo on my cell wall from that evening. Ironically, it probably saved me from some serious grief.

We came back home to Luton about 2 or 3 o'clock in the morning and we were having a bit of a domestic as we walked home. It was an argument, nothing more.

I was shouting, raising my voice, pissed up. Suddenly this bloke appeared out of nowhere, in his shorts and t-shirt and he got in the middle of things. I have never hit my wife in my life, never would raise my hand, but we were arguing and shouting and I suppose I was being aggressive.

This geezer told me to walk a different way home and said that he'd take her back to her mum's house. I was like, 'Fuck off mate, it's none of your business'. I went to walk after her and he ran at me and tackled me to the floor. He accepted all of this when it came to court, that he ran and knocked me down, that he got physical first.

I bust my head and I ripped my best jeans, so that was it. I got up and fought back and got the better of him. The problem was, when he went on the floor, I kicked him. I was drunk, and it didn't do any physical damage, but I was just reacting to him attacking me. At that point he got up – because I hadn't really hurt him – and he said, 'You're fucked pal, because I'm a police officer'.

Later, when I was in jail, the probation officer came to interview me and asked what I would do different next time. I said nothing, which was probably the wrong answer. But it was 3 o'clock in the morning. If he hadn't assaulted me, I wouldn't have assaulted him and life would have gone on in a completely different fashion. But it didn't.

When it went to court the judge accepted that everything was self-defence, until I kicked him while he was down –

that was beyond self defence. Then the bloke told the court that he'd pulled his warrant card out. He said that he rugby tackled me to the floor and then, as we got up, he pulled his warrant card out. He said I'd known he was a police officer when I went back at him. He also said in court that he was too hastily dressed to bring his mobile phone – but he thought to bring his warrant card? Really? I might have been pissed, but I think that if I'd known he was a policeman it might have sobered me up quickly enough.

We went home and about an hour later the police came through the door mob-handed and dragged me down the stairs. Apparently I had just clobbered an armed response police officer and instead of going down the line of reporting it as a normal incident he just rang his pals and they came to get me in force. This all came out in court, but none of it mattered because of that one kick.

After that I left Britannia and returned to Luton. I got a job at a company called Minor Planet selling car trackers while I waited for the case to come to court, which ended up taking nine months. During that time, my girlfriend and I went to Jamaica and got engaged.

The case went to Luton Crown Court, the charges being resisting arrest and assaulting a police officer. I pleaded not guilty, because he didn't have a warrant card, he never produced a warrant card, and he didn't tell me he was a police officer until after the fight – which he started anyway. There was supposed to be an independent witness, but I discovered that she'd lived two doors away from him for 10 years. That's not an independent witness in my book, that's a friend and neighbour.

All else apart, it was the very first time I'd ever been in any trouble of any sort, so I never thought for a minute that I'd get sent to prison for a first offence. I was thinking that even if I was found guilty I'd get community service, probation, or a big fine maybe.

When the judge said I was going down for 12 months I could have cried. I just wasn't ready for it. My mum was there, my friend Sappy, and suddenly they were taking me down. I was going to jail. That wasn't supposed to happen.

About a year later, when I'd got out, I was getting a jacket potato at a catering van at Luton Airport and there was a police car parked up. One of the geezers in the catering van who I knew, Gary, said that one of the coppers in the patrol car was giving me a funny look.

The bloke got out of the motor, came bowling up and stood right next to me and said, 'You don't recognise me?'

And then I clocked who it was. I laughed. I said, 'Actually mate I didn't recognise you – the last time I saw you, you were on the floor screaming and shitting yourself!'

That wiped the smirk off his face. Arsehole. Liar.

LET ME TELL YOU about Lewsey Farm. It's an estate on the outskirts of Luton, towards Dunstable, and it has had a really raw deal over the years with high levels of neglect, unemployment and deprivation. The residents there do it tough. I know quite a lot of them, good people. Heroin and crack cocaine are sold on a semi-industrial scale, although buying and selling guns might give the drugs a run for its money.

In the first few months of 2013 the place resembled a war zone because of gang rivalries. A lot of the locals must have wondered what they'd done to deserve it. Armed police patrolled the Lewsey Farm and Marsh Farm estates with Heckler and Koch assault rifles after the streets were hit with nine shootings in four months. And that wasn't new, either. Back in 2007 the papers were full of what they called a 'postcode war' between the Lewsey gang – LU4 – and Marsh Farm, which is LU3. At one point a six-year-old girl had a gun put to her head while she was in the back of a car. Madness, complete and utter madness.

When I was sentenced to that 12 months in 2004 I was taken to Bedford prison with a kid from Biggleswade, a small town up the A1. We were told we were being put on D Wing which suddenly took my predicament from being a serious shock to the system, into a serious threat to my health. D Wing was home to a group of Lewsey Farm gangsters who were jailed after a battle in Wardown Park in Luton.

Kamran Shehzad had been stabbed to death in a fight between Muslims and this gang from Lewsey Farm, who were looking to avenge a young black kid who had been beaten up and thrown in the river. None of that was anything to do with me, but I had my own group of mates and we were not what you could call on friendly terms with the Lewsey Farm gang.

So we were stuck on D Wing and as I said to my new pal from Biggleswade, 'We are well and truly fucked here'.

The first day, a big black lad called Foster came into my cell and said, 'Are you Yaxley? I'll see you later.'

The first time I went out on what's called 'association' a couple of them made a grab for me on the landing and tried to drag me into a cell. One of them had some sharpened hair clippers. Luckily the screws rushed in and broke things up and I got back to my cell. That's the kind of place it was.

Another big black lad from Hitchin then came into my cell and asked what was going on. It just happened that I had this picture on the wall from my girlfriend's birthday night out – the night in the limo which ended in the trouble with the off duty copper.

A pal called Les was on the photo and Les is very well known around Luton. He runs a lot of the doors at the pubs and clubs and this bloke saw the picture and asked how come I knew Les.

At that he let the Lewsey Farm boys know that if anyone wanted a piece of the new kid, they'd have to deal with him, which turned out to be a life saver. There's a definite pecking order in the prison system and having someone vouch for you is like a lottery win.

I hadn't been in prison long when I got taken back for my appeal against the severity of the sentence. I was in the prison van with a bunch of boys from A Wing who I knew. And right there in the middle of us was one of the Lewsey Farm geezers who had tried to drag me into the cell. I just asked him, 'How does it feel now? Being stuck on your own?' He was properly shitting himself, but I didn't do anything, because I'm not a scumbag.

I lost the appeal, but after that there was an older bloke, Mark Bates, who also looked after us, who kept an eye on some of the younger kids. He'd been a close associate of the Kray twins in the east end of London back in their day, and I understand he was even a pallbearer at one of their funerals. He had some great stories.

Once things settled down and we got into a routine, I can't say that I minded the time inside. I would far rather not have been there obviously, but I found out that I could handle it.

I've always been comfortable in a bloke-oriented environment, hence a lot of the football stuff – maybe I should have gone in the army. But not being intimidated, knowing you can get through it – that knowledge removes your fear of being sent to jail I think. That's the way it was for me for long enough.

I'm pretty sure that wasn't quite the form of rehabilitation the judicial system looks to achieve. And it probably wasn't entirely helpful to me either, in terms of some of the daft decisions I would make in the future.

THINGS CHANGED AFTER that, once I got out of Bedford. I really hadn't thought I was going to be sent to prison. I might not have been anyone's idea of an angel, but

I wasn't a big boozer, I hadn't touched drugs, and I had never previously been in trouble with the police.

When I came out though, I had a real hatred for the system. It's probably safe to say that that's a common state of mind amongst people who get sent down. Do people learn a lesson? I didn't, because I didn't think I'd done anything wrong to begin with. But my impression was that convicts generally hated the bastards who'd put them away.

I came out with no career, with nothing. I appealed the conviction to the Royal Courts of Justice because they'd asked me in front of the jury if I was currently residing at a particular address, which I was. The prosecution then mentioned that that address had been raided on a drugs charge – but it was absolutely nothing to do with me. It was a different tenant at a different time.

The jury was sent out while the lawyers argued, then when they came back in the judge told them to disregard what had just been said – as if they could possibly erase their own memories!

My appeal was on the grounds that the jury should have been discharged, but I lost that too. If I'd won the appeal I'd have had a chance of getting my old life back on track, going back to my job. Instead I was being thrown on a rubbish heap that I always thought the system was supposed to keep you away from. Upset, angry – yes, totally. Basically, I just thought, 'Fuck you lot'.

A few years later, when I had my tanning shop in Luton town centre, a police car drove past and I shouted out after it, 'Wankers'.

The cop pulled up and asked what I'd said, so I told him – and I told him why I'd said it. I described what his mates had put me through. The bloke, the officer, was really decent actually. He shook my hand and said that he understood, but that the police are not all like that. And as much as I've had more than my share of run-ins with the law, for the most part I've had a decent shake from the individual officers concerned.

Back then though, coming out of jail in 2005 with no prospects, no career, and having been even further ingrained into Luton's criminal fringe, I was seriously pissed off with anything to do with authority.

Also, I wasn't scared any longer. Not of anyone, and certainly not of being thrown in a prison cell. I thought I could cope with anything, although I would discover eventually that I couldn't, I really couldn't.

6: SEPTEMBER 11, 2001

IF THE BLOKE WHO came out of Bedford nick in 2005 had a grudge against the world, I think it's fair to say that it was against a world which was itself changing fast.

A lot of people were increasingly angry – violently and murderously angry, against the western world and specifically the USA and UK. Everything had changed after that terrible Tuesday morning of September 11th, 2001.

I don't think I'm being too melodramatic in saying that. It made some big pretty immediate differences to the airline industry I was working in at the time. Everyone remembers exactly where they were that morning, when they heard the news, saw the images. That massacre woke me up to a great many of the things that had been happening around me in Luton, but which I hadn't really understood or thought too deeply about.

I'm not sure that even now I can get my head around how or why a human being can bring themselves to perform the atrocities that happened in America that day, or what those poor victims went through. Those last moments on those planes, or the dilemma of people in the Twin Towers, having to choose between the flames and jumping to their death. It still chills me to the bone, all these years on.

The first anniversary of 9/11 in 2002 saw Al Muhajiroun stage a Magnificent 19 conference in London. Meanwhile closer to home we suddenly had posters start appearing around Luton, glorifying Islam's so-called 9/11 martyrs.

I was completely pissed off about that. A lot of Luton people were. The Magnificent 19 posters weren't on walls and buildings in Bury Park, on their mosques or meeting places. They were on bus shelters and lampposts all around the predominantly non-Muslim areas. There was only one reason for that – to provoke us, to insult us, to basically say,

'We can do whatever we like and you fools are too weak to do anything about it'.

And they were right. They got away with it time and again. By doing nothing about it – and we didn't – was in my mind physically encouraging it, our authorities telling them to carry on. The insult, the provocation of it was bad enough, but we were effectively giving it the thumbs up. It was race and religious hatred, as clear as daylight, in anyone's right mind. Except that in Luton and in the UK, that's a one-way street. And we're facing the wrong way.

Every Saturday, outside the Arndale Centre in front of Don Miller's bakery shop, groups of bearded extremists would gather to preach hatred and the death and destruction of our country. And what did we do? Luton police? The council? Nothing.

Well that's not quite true – we did something. We let them get on with it, recruiting their own moderate Muslim kids, but also preying on weak non-Muslim people.

You'd be amazed how many people are vulnerable to being radicalised. In the years to come I witnessed first hand how entire swathes of British society are ripe for the Islamic recruiters. I'm not joking and I'm not exaggerating. For every extreme Muslim put into the general population of a prison, we're breeding a dozen or more converts. And what is the state doing about it? Jack shit, that's what.

Every week in Luton those characters were celebrating the murder of thousands of innocent people in America, celebrating right on our doorsteps, displaying their perverted insults to all of those victims, rejoicing in the greatest act of terror the modern world had seen.

Word went around town that Muslim students at Luton 6th Form College were celebrating the killers. Tensions generally were heightened, as I imagine they were in heavily Muslim communities all around the country. As a result of everything that was building, there was talk of a reaction by a group of Luton football hooligans. Apparently there was a meeting at a pub in Dunstable called by the older members of the MIGs and they decided it was time to retaliate against the Muslim extremists. When word of that got out the police leafleted the Bury Park area, telling residents to expect revenge attacks.

After that a young black lad was mugged by a group of Muslims and it cranked things up to another level. Word got out that there would be a confrontation on the day of Town's home game with Rochdale. But on the day it wasn't just the football lads turning out for trouble, because all the bearded mullahs and their supporters came out in force too – as did the police, obviously.

I wasn't involved in any of the aggro, I was just aware of it going on. You couldn't not be aware. I suppose it was fortunate in some ways that soon after that came the riot at Watford with a whole rash of arrests and a lull in the activities of the football lads. To a large extent that element of resisting the Luton Muslim radicals, on a local level at least, died away for a while.

AROUND THAT TIME I first heard of a Muslim dickhead called Sayful Islam – Sword of Islam. That's a nice name to pick for yourself, isn't it? That's love and peace right there. Me and Sayful would cross swords with each other a few times over the coming years.

Just after the Beslan massacre in 2004 a few Luton Muslims, including Sayful Islam, were sitting in a chicken shop in town doing a media interview, and they were welcoming the day when there would be a September 11th type attack on British soil. Were they arrested for it? Don't be stupid.

Al Muhajiroun grew in large part out of Luton's radicals. At this time in 2004 it was still a legal organisation, led by Omar Bakri Mohammed from his mosque in north London, plus Anjem Choudary, and Sayful Islam was the leader of the Luton branch. They regarded Osama bin Laden as their hero, and here they were, in a chicken shop down the road from where I lived, praying for the day that their brothers would bring terror to the streets of England.

Sayful – his actual name is Ishtiaq Alamgir – was taking credit for the Magnificent 19 posters and for drumming up support for Al Muhajiroun, raising local membership from five to 50 potential killers, with the backing of hundreds.

It isn't as though this arsehole swept into town from Saudi Arabia or Somalia. He was born and raised here in Luton, in a middle class family, apparently a bright student who ended up working as an accountant for the Inland Revenue. And then he was radicalised, gave up the job and boasted about living on benefits as he plotted to overthrow the country. If you think I'm overstating this man's evil, listen to these words. They are his:

'When I watched those planes go into the Twin Towers, I felt elated. That magnificent action split the world into two camps: you were either with Islam and al Qaeda, or with the enemy. I decided to quit my job and commit myself full-time to Al Muhajiroun. I am a Muslim living in Britain, and I give my allegiance only to Allah.'

He said the aim of Al Muhajiroun is Khilafah. Again I quote: 'The worldwide domination of Islam achieved by jihad, to include terrorism on UK soil. When a bomb attack happens here, I won't be against it, even if it kills my own children. Islam is clear: Muslims living in lands that are occupied have the right to attack their invaders.'

This man wanted to see our children assassinated, executed, in pursuit of his perverted ideology. And here was the great British public, sitting around listening to it, giving him a public platform and doing nothing about it.

I mean, come on, I ask you – what would you do? I had to do something. I'd seen the Magnificent 19 posters, I'd seen any kind of British advertising billboard they took offence to being covered up and painted out. I'd seen them handing out their leaflets in the town centre.

These men were running an extremist organisation out of a building on Biscot Road, smack bang in the middle of our town and not only were the police and the council not doing anything about any of it, not only was the media pretending everything was hunky-dory, they might all as well have given them written permission to get on with the Islamic revolution.

Things changed a lot for me with the Beslan massacre. Watching television images of parents turning up outside school and hearing them screaming as the gunshots went off inside. Their children were being executed in cold blood. I didn't have children then, but you didn't have to, to imagine what those poor people were going through.

The Muslim terrorists pulled those kids' pants down and if they showed signs of puberty, they were murdered. It's happened more recently in Peshawar where the Taliban killed 120 innocent children. Still, fair play, they're only following their Prophet – it's what Mohammed did to a Jewish tribe according to their own scriptures. Except he was reputed to have killed 600.

It's commonplace today, murdering children, as we've seen with ISIS, but even writing this so many years on, it's as though that happened yesterday. Beslan shook me. And then along came this character Sayful Islam preaching that our kids too are ripe for being rounded up and executed in their classrooms and that he would celebrate it. And we were encouraging him?

I was watching this, listening to this, but it was as if it wasn't really happening – as if no one was seeing what was going on except me. I really struggled with that. I don't know how I kept my hands off him. There's a Youtube video where I'm driving a journalist through Luton for the

70

Channel 4 documentary Proud and Prejudiced, talking about the town, pointing out places of interest. At one point we drove past Sayful Islam in Bury Park. It was a warm, sunny day and I had the car window down. The cameraman was in the back.

Sayful noticed us, noticed me, and started shouting. Traffic is always slow through Bury Park and he walked into the road, demanding to know what was happening. Look it up, see for yourself. Google it on Youtube. You'll see him smack me in the face, completely unprovoked.

I got assaulted by an off-duty copper, retaliated and was given 12 months in prison. This bloke who preaches hatred and murder of British people walked up and belted me in the chops, on camera, and the police were not remotely interested. Not for one second.

So tell me, will you – who's the good guy and who's the bad guy here? Tell me what part of the law I don't understand. I would have a very satisfying moment when I put the shits right up Sayful, one morning in Luton, some time later. The police were all over me yet again for that, as you'd imagine. But Sayful smacks me on film, in the face, unprovoked? Nothing. Zip.

At that point, after the Beslan massacre, I started reading online articles and interviews about this group Al Muhajiroun, who were recruiting and sending people to fight for the Taliban. I hadn't realised that they were basically a Luton product. I don't think I'd even heard of Anjem Choudary at that point. And the thing is, they weren't even hiding the fact about what they were doing. And I thought, who the hell are this lot? And why isn't anyone doing anything at all about them?

I didn't know the first thing about Sunnis or Shias or the differences between them. I might have know that a sharia court was where they decided to cut your hand off for stealing a loaf of bread in Saudi, but my knowledge didn't go much beyond that. The thing is, in terms of the real impact on the people of Luton, the Islamic angle was probably the least of it. People could walk past Sayful Islam and his preachers outside Don Miller's on a Saturday. They might be inconvenienced by calls to prayer, but they didn't have to go into Bury Park if they didn't want to.

If only that was the limit of it all, but nothing could be further from the truth. If everything I've written so far makes it sound like Luton was a town run by gangs and gangsters, then there's a good reason – it mostly was. And most of the drugs and prostitution was either run by the Muslim gangs, or by gangs that got their drugs from them. It was rife, and it was killing people. And if the drugs weren't killing our young people, then the gangs were.

There was a certain helplessness about it all, because everywhere you looked money was being thrown at the Muslim community, and every problem with their young people, their radicals, their piss-and-moan stories about deprivation and prejudice, was met by either the government or Luton Borough Council – or some other do-gooder – throwing more and more money and resources at it. And as time would prove, the people heading up these 'moderate' fronts would turn out being the biggest parts of the problem, not the solution.

I think it's also important to ask the question about the other half of the population, because actually Luton does have a few poor non-Muslim residents too, poor elderly people, trying to get by just on a state pension.

Councillors and execs and managers would be queuing up to get their faces in the local paper, opening a new Muslim community centre here, an outreach project there – and all the time people like Sayful Islam and another character, Abdul Qadeer Baksh, were saying 'thank you very much' and using our money to radicalise both theirs and our kids.

'Our' kids, you say? Don't think that in the brave new British multi-cultural world that the Islamic poison is just spread within their community, amongst supposedly innocent and naïve young Muslims. Far from it.

Abdul Qadeer Baksh is Luton born and bred and the imam for the Salafi mosque in Bury Park. He reportedly has three wives – one white – 14 children and I imagine that by now he must be sick of the sight and sound of me.

At one time he seemed to be everywhere you looked. He had a seat on the council, he had the ear of council leaders, this MP, that organisation ... a poster boy for the 'inclusive' Muslim community. That was then. By now pretty much everyone has shut their doors on him in Luton because he's revealed his true colours.

They were happy courting him for long enough though, a typical example of someone painting himself as a progressive Muslim, yet all the while living a different life within the confines of his community. Apparently he was brought up quite a modern Muslim kid – I heard he was part of a youth dance troupe. And then he went 'home' for a while and came back as this outspoken radical.

I'm going back a while now, way before the EDL, when my cousin Jeanette was just a young teenager. I was about the same age. There wasn't the same awareness then as now about what happens with white girls being groomed, but she was – just the same as all of those young girls up in Rochdale and Rotherham, over in Aylesbury and Oxford. She started going out with a Pakistani bloke and the next thing we knew she was strung out on heroin, addicted.

She woke up on one occasion in a house being gang-raped by half a dozen Muslim men. She was found by some prostitutes, semi-naked, running away from Bury Park back when the working girls used to hang out on the fringes of that district, although they've all been moved on now. The family got her home and the police just remarked that she was a drug addict and basically shrugged their shoulders. Everyone did all they could to help her, but it was useless. They'd lock her in the house and she'd climb out of a window to go back to the Muslims and get her fix.

Jeanette converted to Islam and lives in that community now, apparently with her six children. No one's seen her for 15 years – at least not that we know. We might walk past her in the street every day but we'd never know, because she's clad head to toe in her burkha and niqab.

And it's not an isolated case, it's not just our family. Everyone knows someone in a similar predicament.

Another young girl, Caroline, was a stunning kid, a talented singer. She sang at my brother's wedding actually, but two years later it went down exactly the same path.

Her Pakistani boyfriend took her to her mum and dad's to say that they couldn't see her any longer. What do you think that does to parents? But the kids are brainwashed.

One of her close friends told her that her family were moving and taking her with them, away from all of this. Do you know what she said in reply? 'What, so that men can look at me like meat?'

She was already gone, lost to her family. It was heartbreaking. It still is.

Caroline used to go out with a rough and ready bloke, a bit of a bruiser, Big Mike, who her parents didn't really approve of at the time. But I see her mum now and she asks, quite fondly, 'How's Big Mike?'

And here's the thing – she's had a baby now. The Muslim father doesn't live with her of course, because he already has a Muslim wife. He keeps Caroline in a flat, and goes round to see her three days a week for his bit of fun.

Very holy, don't you think? I talked about the subject once with Abdul Qadeer Baksh. I asked him, 'And we're supposed to keep accepting this kind of behaviour, the way our young women are treated?' He didn't have an answer.

DON'T GET ME wrong, because I was no angel while all of this was going on. When I came out of prison in 2005 I came very close to going off the rails myself. With a lot of the leadership of the MIGs banged up after the Watford trouble I ended up doing a lot of the organising for the lads, arranging transport, pubs where we'd meet before a game, ways in which we'd try to avoid the police.

That's how, when we formed the United People of Luton in 2009 to make a stand against Muslim protests over the homecoming parade of the Royal Anglian Regiment, I was perfectly placed to pull things together. I was hanging out at the 9-Bar pub in the town centre and even ran a football team from there. It was almost like a second home – we had sofas in there and a Nando's across the road. Heaven! We wouldn't even drink much, just hang out mostly.

But there was partying and raving too and there was usually cocaine about and MDMA – ecstasy. I'd never done drugs before I went to jail but when I came out, having to fend for myself, hating the world, I ran with lads who did recreational drugs. It was part of the scene and I was part of it. It's been a long time since I did anything like that.

Does it make me a hypocrite, given where I've already said most of the drugs came from? I'm sure it does, although such as I've ever done joined-up thinking and reasoning, that wasn't the time or place. There was no plan, it was just day-to-day life and gut reaction. Heroin was always completely off limits though.

One night I was walking through town when a female officer in a police van told her colleagues to stop and search me. I wasn't doing anything wrong, but she knew who I was. They found a trace of cocaine – just about enough to make your hamster pedal his wheel a bit faster, but that's all. I got a £300 fine and for the future enemies of Tommy Robinson, my record was elevated onto something close to the level of a Colombian drug baron.

The former Lib Dem leader Nick Clegg wants that stuff making legal, doesn't he? Do you think he fancies going on telly to start a campaign to have my conviction overturned? No, I didn't think so.

I was angry at the time at what was happening in Luton, but I was curious, so I started trying to find out more about these people, and during that process, of looking into what lay behind Beslan, it seemed that the only people talking about it, getting angry, were the BNP. And I didn't know anything much about them either, at the time.

Much is made by the Tommy Robinson-haters of my brief flirtation with the BNP. It was brief. Very brief. And it ended in tears, too. They are a complete set of wankers, that lot.

7: THE BNP – HELLO, GOODBYE

BACK INTO THE football, my social life pretty much revolved around being out with the lads on Friday nights, then the big day out on Saturday and all that involved – from boozing and chanting all the way to a good old ruck with the opposition, as often as not.

A football hooligan? I suppose so. I was working hard, earning some good money finally, and I'd found a group of men who watched my back, who I shared a bond with, even if it was only football. I was making good pals like Little Danny, a ginger kid who never got teased over his hair – he was a bit of a boxer. You didn't mess with him!

It was a part of my life that was running in parallel with what was happening in Luton. I began noticing events like Beslan, becoming aware of Sayful Islam, of the drugs and prostitution gangs, all of it coming together to highlight a massive problem with one specific root cause – the Muslim community. And all the while there was a plentiful supply of people parroting the same old mantra – 'This is a minority, the vast majority of Muslims are peace loving, the vast majority don't agree with this and that....'

Really? I don't see that. I didn't then and I don't now. Ordinary, peace-loving Muslims who just want to get on in life? I'm sure. But they don't care enough about so-called community cohesion to lift a finger. If the vast majority are so offended at what the criminals and the extremists are doing from behind the protective veil of their culture and ideology, then why don't they do something about it?

Why aren't entire Muslim communities, as opposed to a few individuals (who happen to be making a good living out of their token gestures) taking on the extremists and the criminals? Until they do I don't think you can use that 'silent majority' argument. Bullshit then and bullshit now.

But there are other factors too. The Muslim community doesn't look for moderation or progress for two reasons, the first being that their book and prophet are everything. There is no separation of religion from politics from culture from law in Islam. That's its 7th century problem. It's too medieval to progress anywhere.

And then there's the second pragmatic reason – it suits the Muslim community's interests to let the British state pander to a so-called victimised minority. Minority? I don't think so. Not in a Bury Park or even Luton sense. Or a lot of other places in England, either.

As for victimised? Again, not that I see. If there are health and education and social deprivation problems, then it comes mostly from lifestyle choices they make.

I don't remember Parliament passing a law that first cousins have to marry first cousins in forced marriages. In fact most people believe we should be tackling that issue, preventing it. Instead we prefer to sign cheques and quietly ignore massive neo-natal problems, infant mortality rates, and ridiculous numbers of birth deformities in Pakistani communities.

The authorities are too scared to even talk about them for fear of being labelled institutionally racist.

Everything I saw back then told me the government, the council, the police, couldn't bend over backwards far enough to kiss any Muslim arse available. There were grants for this, assistance for that, different rules for the other.

Am I jealous? Not so much jealous as resentful I think. It seemed like there was no shortage of money to buy the friendship and respect of a group of people who just took it and laughed in our faces.

I'm sure there are examples of Sunni Muslim people and groups reaching out to embrace, or at least respect, white Christian ways across the country, but I haven't seen them. I don't think many people in Luton have either.

As for the rise of ISIS in Iraq and Syria? The Muslim states surrounding that region have about 5 million combat troops and some serious air power. They could crush the butchers overnight but they choose not to, while we get our knickers in a twist over whether using a drone the wrong side of a line in the sand is a war crime or not.

And why don't those Arab states act? Probably because the ISIS insurrection suits their longer term agendas.

I THINK IT WAS one of the older blokes at football who started talking about the BNP and mentioned it to a few of us younger lads. I'd been trying to find out more about these issues myself and it seemed like the only people talking about the problems with the Muslim community were the BNP, so I spoke to a bloke who was their organiser for our area, and arranged to attend a meeting they were having at a pub called the King Harry, up in Stopsley.

I went along to the first meeting with my uncle and listened, mostly. They had a guest speaker, gave out loads of literature and they were talking what I thought was plain common sense about the whole range of Muslim/Islamic issues. I suppose I was reasonably impressed with it, so I signed up for a membership and decided to bring the football lads to the next meeting.

These guys had become my best friends, they had become my community. I never gave a minute's thought to their colour or background. We met up and went along to the pub, the King Harry again, which has two bars. As we walked through the door, this organiser said, 'They'll have to wait here', and he was on about the black lads – Isaac, Little Craigy and Webster.

I could not believe it. I simply could not believe it. We stopped the entire meeting, right there and then. In fact Searchlight, the Marxist rag, documented it as the time the Luton MIGs fell out with the BNP. I told them straight out,

'You think you are having a meeting, in our pub, on our estate, in our town, that we have brought you people to, but you're not letting our friends come in?'

They discovered in no uncertain terms that we were about as pissed off as pissed off gets – and that was that with the BNP as far as I was concerned. After that, any time we heard about the BNP, we just told them to go do one. When the United People of Luton started and after that the English Defence League, one thing was clear – the BNP were not welcome. Not as a group, not as individual members, none of them.

Sure, I'd joined the BNP after that first meeting, taken out a family membership on a 12 month deal for only £60. But as people could subsequently see when they hacked the BNP membership list and published it, I didn't renew my membership. It was a very brief relationship.

You probably think that I was naïve for not realising that the BNP was a racist group. I'm sure I was. In those days I didn't even know who Nick Griffin was, let alone that he used to be a senior member of the National Front. I was young and not very well educated in those matters.

After that incident the BNP didn't feature much on the landscape in Luton at all – I don't even think they've stood anyone as a Parliamentary candidate since then.

If there was a non-Muslim or non-criminal gang in Luton of any standing you'd have to say it was the MIGs. They would typically be the people, the recruits that the BNP would appeal to and with that possibility kicked into touch, there wasn't much of a foothold left for them.

I'd grown up with mates of every different colour and background and that was never the issue for me. It was this ideology that was preaching hatred of my country on my doorstep. Why should men and women be discounted from standing up for the nation of either their birth or adoption because they're black, Asian or anything else?

That's racist. And I've never considered myself racist, whatever the world likes to think.

THERE WERE STILL things we could do to make our point on the streets of Luton, although they didn't always turn out quite as planned.

On St George's Day 2004 there were about 200-300 of us in town, hanging out. We'd do this every year and mostly I'd be the one organising things, giving people a nudge to come out. The sun was shining, and we met in the town centre. We had a football, and everyone was having a beer and kicking a football about. It was all quite good natured.

I'd had a black flag made that said Al Muhajiroun on it, and when everyone was there and we'd all had a few beers we pulled the flag out and burned it. Everyone was cheering, we thought it was a complete laugh – except that one of the lads got sent to jail for it, for burning those terrorists' flag. He got done for inciting violence or race hate. Some such bullshit.

We called him Mad Keith – Keith Chambers – he was off his head at times, but a good lad. We couldn't believe it when he got time for that, especially with what happened when Anjem Choudary and his gang started burning poppies on Armistice Day. Talk about double standards, one law for them and one for us.

When I went to jail in 2005, as I was being taken in, Keith was just walking out. I said, 'Bruv, how you doing?'

He wasn't best impressed. He said, 'I'm in for that fucking flag, remember?'

It was the one I made. Poor old Keith.

Later that year, after the flag burning, Luton were playing Peterborough and you might usually have expected a bit of aggro, but on that occasion I got in touch with their lads and said we were all coming out, but not looking for trouble with them.

I said that if they wanted to meet up with us, they were welcome. Whites and blacks were being targeted for random violence by Muslim gangs, our women were being groomed and pimped, shops were pumping out heroin like sweets. I produced a leaflet with all of this on it, basically saying that if we knew what was going on, why didn't the police? And why wasn't anyone doing anything about it?

The leaflet made the point that we wanted this protest to be peaceful. That we were aware the criminality was being carried out by a minority, that Al Muhajiroun was a minority, but that they were minorities that we all needed to do something about.

I didn't know if I was even allowed to hand these leaflets out but the local paper actually helped – they reprinted most of the leaflet, being careful (typically) to remove references to grooming and selling heroin.

On the day the Peterborough fans tried to join us but the police wouldn't let them. Anyone who read the newspaper coverage would have seen that according to the police they stopped the Peterborough fans from starting a ruck. They said it was hooligans trying to fight each other, but it wasn't. It was probably the first time rival football gangs joined together.

So anyway, we handed all of these leaflets out and then I read it out in public, naming the gangs and the gangsters responsible, naming the hate preachers, giving them all a ration. I was wearing a CP Company jacket that pretty much hid my face as I read the leaflet out, which was probably a good thing because the response afterwards was both fast and furious.

My phone didn't stop ringing. Word had got out who was behind it and the Pakistanis were all out to get me.

I just thought 'Let them. I don't run away any more.'

8: THE MISSING YEARS

IF EVER THERE was a bit of a quiet period in my life, and then not much, it was probably after I came out of jail that first time in 2005 and started trying to find my way. I had the comfort blanket of the football lads. In a tribal town like Luton you needed something to belong to and those blokes were my gang. Those were the only places I was safe, or at least where I felt safe, felt at home.

And there was my fiancee. Despite what we'd been through then, like now, we were still the real thing (I don't 'do' romantic much if you hadn't noticed!) She's stuck with me through some serious ups and downs, that girl. Well, perhaps not so many ups as downs.

When I got out of Bedford nick I had three months on a tag and I was at a bit of a loose end. It wouldn't be the last time, but it was probably the first time. I went back to my Irish developer pal Dave, who I call 'Little Legs' (I can get away with calling him that, being about the same size!) and told him I was desperate for some work. The job at Minor Planet had disappeared obviously, while the aeronautical engineering career was a long-gone dream.

I needed to work and Dave was good to me then, as he always has been. He gave me labouring jobs here and there, on all kinds of projects up and down the place. Once I had to shift a thousand sheets of plasterboard from one end of Stevenage town centre to the other. That was hard graft. I did some window fitting for him in London, all kinds of jobs.

I also started doing some buying and selling as well, on the side, getting stuff off one bloke who had some extras for sale, shifting it to other people who were on the look-out for a bargain.

A proper little Del Boy? Too right, in more ways than one. If there was a deal to be done, I was on the phone, ringing around, seeing if I could put Mr A with Mrs B, whatever. I had the big gold chain, thought I was a right geezer. And before you ask, yes – I had the gold medallion too! And a ring with 'Yax' on it. What a wanker.

Some years later when we got married, the lads had a good old laugh at my expense. Listen, at 5ft 6ins I stand out for all the wrong reasons, but given that my mum is only 4ft 8ins and wears size 12 kids' shoes, I'm walking tall by comparison.

My brother was my best man but when it came to doing the speeches, I could hear strange noises coming from behind the curtain at the back of us. Someone was saying, 'You what?' and 'Oy!'

My brother got to the part of his speech where he said, 'Everyone who knows my brother knows him as the small angry man,' – and right on cue, out from behind the curtain walked a midget, wearing an exact replica of my wedding suit, carrying a bottle of blue WKD – which I used to drink. He walked up front, opened his jacket while saying, 'I hate the world, I hate the world,' then he pulled out some perfume and some Ray-Bans – I used to sell perfume and Ray-Bans obviously. The whole place was crying with laughter at my expense. So was I though. It was very funny.

Was all of my wheeling and dealing back in the day legal, above board and straightened away with the tax and VAT man? Absolutely! When the police finally got their teeth into me and turned my business life upside down and inside out, they did everything except send me to the hospital for one of those cameras up your arse, looking for evidence of wrongdoing. They scrutinised every penny I earned from the age of 18. But no one would find anything, because there was nothing to find.

I suppose my big break came when Little Legs's plumber told him that he was leaving the country, emigrating to Australia, and he had to find someone to replace him.

Luckily for me there was a gap of a few months and I asked who was going to take over – and then if Dave would at least let me price his jobs up, to see if we could get involved doing his contract plumbing. Dad was a specialist pipe fitter so he could plumb and I was pretty handy, so we formed a business partnership. Little Legs let us put a price in for his next job and bingo – off we went.

We had a great couple of years, straight into it. We fitted out an entire block of 22 flats in Luton, another 20 flats round the corner, and then another 16 on the back of that.

I bought a couple of them off-plan from one of the jobs and we ended up with all of Dave's plumbing contracts. I got my wife's brother Little Stevie an apprenticeship – he's a great kid – my good mate Sappy, another pal's dad, there was Gollum, another young lad who was a plumber, and there was also my mate Isaac. In the end we had seven or eight blokes working for us. Things were going great.

At one point Dave bought a building and turned part of it into a hairdresser's salon for his daughter. The shop next door to it was available and Dave offered me it at cost, which was too good a deal to turn down, because I'd been looking a lot at property prices with a view to doing some letting of my own.

Payments on it were only £500 a month so all that I needed was something to turn that amount and a bit more over. I found a bloke who was looking to find an earner of his own, he bought some sunbeds and that was that – we were in the tanning salon business!

I even had the foresight to do all of our signs in English and Polish, because the Polish girls like to keep their colour up – they were the bread and butter of the business. I even had all the exterior signage done in the same style as Dave's daughter in the hairdresser's next door, although I don't think she thanked me for that when the EDL stuff started kicking off and people knew where I was based.

It would end up causing me no end of grief, if only because tanning salons are by nature a mostly cash business and when I started the EDL and brought the police crashing down on me, that was the first place they looked.

That shop was doing £2,000 a week, but only about £400 of it was in credit or debit cards. The authorities thought they had me bang to rights for all kinds of tax evasion or money laundering. And then I showed them my garage, with six bin liners packed with till receipts for virtually every single penny that came through the business.

Some poor bastard from the police had to spend two years going through those bin liners, squaring away every boring receipt. We had 60 clients a day, all their account details on their till receipts and there were thousands that this geezer had to synchronise in time and date order. They thought we were taking a grand and putting two through the till, but I knew it was all clean. It didn't stop them finding a different way to ruin my life though.

MEANWHILE, APART from watching Luton Town, my other passion was following the England football team, wherever they were playing.

The highlight of the adventures – and there were a few – was when a group of us went to the World Cup in Germany for a month in 2006. It's a wonder I got home from that in one piece. Fantastic times, even if the memory of climbing on the window ledge of a hospital, about six floors up wearing just a hospital gown with my arse hanging out, is still enough to wake me up in a cold sweat.

We didn't go looking for trouble, but it had a funny way of finding us. We were traveling around in a motorhome, a bunch of mad lads in their early 20s, a couple of great blokes in Kev Mac and Morris, plus one geezer in his 40s, Lee Middleton. Poor Lee. He probably still hasn't gotten over that trip. He seemed to think he could be a calming influence on us, but it didn't quite work out that way.

As far as the football side of things went, we kicked off with the 1-0 win against Paraguay in Frankfurt, then it was onto Nuremberg for the 2-0 win against Trinidad and Tobago and the final group stage match, a 2-2 draw with Sweden in Cologne. There was a 1-0 win against Ecuador in Stuttgart and finally the inevitable quarter final defeat on penalties, against Portugal in Gelsenkirchen.

It was a great time – the German people were very friendly, and there was something about being in such a large group of England fans, men who didn't know you but had your back, come what may. But then there was the trouble too. With football hooligans being football hooligans the world over, there was usually a ruck awaiting not too far away. It probably didn't help that someone in our group had a bunch of counterfeit euros that the German polizei took an understandable interest in.

They raided the motorhome and it ended up with me and one of the lads Kylie being arrested – except that I had some kind of fit when I took a whack over the head from one of the police. I really don't remember much except waking up in a hospital, with a police guard at the door, and realising this was very bad news indeed.

Don't ask me what I was thinking. It was like a cross between The Great Escape and something out of Carry On Nurse, because the first chance I got I unplugged the IV tube in my arm, climbed out onto the window ledge about six floors up, edged along and clambered back in through another window further down the corridor.

I grabbed a bunch of towels which I pretended to be carrying – I could see the copper outside my room – and legged it. I flagged down a bloke in a car and he very kindly took me back to the motorhome. Poor old Kylie was kept banged up for a fortnight.

Lee meanwhile had had enough of it all and moved out. He might have been close to a breakdown, but he certainly was when we dropped him at his hotel, parked outside and all got naked on the motorhome roof as he tried to check in.

He didn't deserve it. And he didn't deserve what happened next, because he flew home to get away from us, then thought he'd sneak back on his own to watch the rest of the footy in peace. Except they nicked him at the airport and gave the poor bloke a football banning order. I'll bet he wished he'd never set eyes on us. Great times.

It wouldn't be my last football-related experience (briefly) in Germany, although there wasn't a ball – or a player – in sight on the next occasion. To flash forward in time briefly, it was one of the craziest stunts we ever pulled while running the EDL. I suppose it shows just how mad things got, and how close to being out of control we were. Or should I say, I was.

I know the leader of world football Sepp Blatter is having his problems these days, but it isn't the first time. I might only be a short arse, but I made Blatter look up to me – quite literally.

This would be in November 2011, when England were playing a friendly against Spain and the match was on the weekend of Remembrance Sunday. A lot of British teams wear poppy emblems on their shirts at this time of year and it seemed a good idea for England to do the same – except that Fifa came out and said they couldn't.

Me and a few of the boys were sitting around, raging about how unjust that was ... and the next thing you know we were on a plane to Zurich, where Sepp Blatter and Fifa have their headquarters. I'd rushed out and had this banner made, but it was all so manic that I actually got on the plane without it.

My cousin and EDL sidekick Kev came over all boy scoutish over that. He said, 'You have one bloody job – one bloody job! – and you balls it up!' He wasn't wrong, but then again I probably hadn't been to bed for the best part of two days. This was when things were altogether too wild. We booked into this plush hotel in Zurich, me and Kev, Nick Read, Davy Cooling and Tim Ablitt. They gave us a plastic room card and while the lads went out on the piss, I got drinking with the other guests – a bunch of Americans were good company I think I remembered through the haze. The trouble was, coming down for breakfast the next morning, they told me the room card was maxed out – €1,000. I'm not surprised all the guests were saying, 'Morning Tommy!' and waving. I'd got the entire hotel pissed on our room bill.

When I told Kev he laughed his arse off. And then I reminded him that we'd booked the rooms on his credit card. He nearly shit himself. In fact I turned round, and he'd already grabbed his stuff and bolted.

We found a Pakistani taxi driver to run us around and organise making a new banner, which cost another £250. There was a slight problem picking it up though – we were in Switzerland and the banner was in Germany, and I hadn't paid the fine I got landed with on the World Cup jolly, so that was a worry. Anyway, long story short, we got the banner, our little Pakistani taxi driver took us back to the Fifa HQ and at that point the other lads had second thoughts. So the driver took me and Kev up to the gate and said he had delegates from the English FA.

That got us into the grounds at least, but they wouldn't let us in the building, so we walked round the back and hung out by a service door until someone opened up – and then we were in.

We worked our way all the way to the top of the building like that and the next thing you know, we were climbing out onto the roof and holding up our banner.

Down on the street this little Pakistani geezer was with the other lads and he couldn't believe his eyes. And there was the one and only Sepp Blatter and all his executives, standing outside, looking up at us and wondering what the hell was going on. They sent up security and the police – but we said we'd jump if they came any closer, and that we weren't coming down until they changed their minds over the poppy on England's shirts. We must have been there six hours and my toes were like little blocks of ice. It was freezing and we really hadn't thought things through.

It had the required effect though. I was phoning back home and we eventually got the word that Fifa had backed down – England could wear black armbands with a poppy insignia. It was a great result, although Prince William and the Prime Minister appealing to Fifa might also have helped a bit. Certainly everyone was eager to give them the credit and avoid saying anything positive about the EDL. Not that that was a surprise, obviously.

As for us? Well, not so good. And certainly not for Kev. When we came down from the roof they nicked us and put us in a Swiss jail for three days. I was in with a Liberian geezer who spoke a bit of English, a decent bloke. I don't know if the locals never break the law, but there didn't seem to be any Swiss people in the cells.

The treatment was good and one police officer told me they understood why we'd done it – to honour our soldiers – and that they respected our protest. Given that I'd been on a bender for the past few days, I welcomed the peace and quiet, the chance to catch up on some kip.

When we got out I was buzzing. Hilarious. Wild. What a piece of PR for the EDL it had been. Or so I thought.

You should have seen Kev's face. 'Funny?' he said. 'You fucking what? I've been banged up with a cell-full of violent Somalians for three days, sleeping with one eye open because they were looking at me like I was an unopened fucking Christmas present!' I said, 'But it wasn't all bad Kev. What about the English radio station?'

'Radio station? What English radio station?'

'That button on the wall by the door. For the radio, mate. You mean you didn't push it to see what happened?'

I thought he was going to have a fit. Again.

When we went to court, this gorgeous female officer was busting a gut trying to keep a straight face over it all. We got a fine and we had just enough money left for a McDonald's when we got out.

I rang my mate Kealey back home. He wasn't one of the EDL or football lads, just one of those great, stand-up friends you make as kids, who's there for you through thick and thin. Later, when I was inside, I got my one phone call and it was the day before my wedding anniversary. I didn't call my solicitor, I called Kealey – and he sorted flowers for the wife. On that occasion in Zurich he stumped up the cash for our flights, to get us home, no questions asked.

What a crack it had all been – even if Kev wasn't quite as made up about it all.

That crazy adventure had all started with us simply wanting to honour our military heroes on the streets of Luton, and we'd ended up on the roof of the Fifa World HQ.

I suppose people will want to know exactly how that journey began.

9: THE DAY THAT CHANGED MY LIFE

I HAVE NO IDEA how the English Defence League's story will end. Whether it will grow as a street protest movement, whether it will rattle along as it is, or whether it will just gradually fade away and die like many such organisations, torn apart by a mix of far right elements it just can't shake off and MI5/Special Branch infiltrators poisoning it from within.

No? You don't think that latter scenario could happen, that it's the stuff of Hollywood? Don't be simple.

I can tell you everything about how it started however – and how the EDL never would have come into being but for the actions of the Bedfordshire Police. Take a bow boys, you played a blinder – and might ultimately have done the entire nation a service, despite your determination to stamp on the basic right of British people to protest.

People can thank our very own boys in blue for all of those marches and demonstrations up and down the land – with more than a little help from the politically correct idiots who run our town halls.

It all began on the day of the Luton homecoming of the 2nd Battalion of the Royal Anglian Regiment, recently returned from Afghanistan, when between them the bureaucrats and police managed to inflame an entire town.

It's easy to blame Sayful Islam and his extremist friends who screamed and spat their hatred in the faces of our troops that day – but it was the police and politicians who allowed and I would say even encouraged them to do it. It didn't have to happen.

And even then, when those outraged ordinary Luton people then said they wanted to express their support for our troops, it was the police who turned a peaceful, well planned gathering, into a violent riot. So, well done lads.

I went into Luton on that morning of Tuesday, March 10th 2009 with Kev. He's actually my mum's cousin and a good bit older – and generally more sensible – than me. We would hardly leave each other's side throughout the EDL years, apart from when one or the other of us was sat twiddling our thumbs in a jail cell. Or sometimes both of us.

It was probably a brave decision by someone to march the soldiers through Luton given what we had going on in our midst with the Muslim radicals, but the authorities did their best to keep the affair low key. There was very little publicity about it in the local press and scheduling it for a Tuesday, as opposed to a busy shopping day like Saturday, was probably intended to make sure that it wouldn't attract big crowds.

But the homecoming parade itself was the right decision, no doubt. We send these lads off to fight in Iraq and Afghanistan and all kinds of worldwide hellholes. If they can't march back through a British town in recognition of their service, then we really have lost the war. Despite it being a Tuesday, a great crowd turned out.

The streets were lined three and four deep and when the soldiers arrived it was from the east end of town, the direction of the airport. They marched through the pedestrian precinct then up and around the town hall and down to form up in parade on St George's Square to receive the homecoming salute.

It was a simple mark of respect, of honouring our troops, but it turned into a fiasco. It was a lovely spring day and me and Kev walked round to find out what the plans were, which way the troops were coming, that sort of stuff. We were standing by the town hall and noticed groups of Muslims starting to congregate, two or three people at a time, and then a group of some 30 women wearing burkhas.

It was Kev who remarked about how many police there were. We saw officers go over and talk to Sayful Islam outside the town hall about a half hour before the soldiers arrived. Then as the troops came marching through, the police ushered Sayful and his supporters, about 15 of them, inside the town hall – we thought they must be having some kind of meeting. But then as the regiment came past us and went up the left side of the town hall, to descend round the back and into the square, we heard this big commotion and ran up to see what was happening.

The police had taken Sayful's group through the building and outside via a back door, then placed them where they were perfectly positioned to shout their abuse at the soldiers. They had placards calling our troops 'Butchers of Basra' and saying 'Anglian soldiers go to hell'. And the police had simply guided them to a vantage position where they could hurl insults, while guarding them from people who were understandably pissed off by it all.

Members of the public were absolutely outraged, but the police were formed up with their backs to the Muslims, protecting them. One old gent, probably aged about 75 or 80, was shouting and gesticulating at Sayful Islam and his group – and the police threw the old chap on the floor.

As the soldiers marched on to the square the police then escorted Sayful's cretins back through the town hall and across to where a bigger group of Muslims were gathered, in their usual patch in the Arndale centre.

There were more and more Muslims turning up to join that group and, as word got around, there were more and more Luton people coming to have a go at them, blokes coming off building sites, turning up in their work clothes.

It was a bit of a stand off, with everyone shouting and bawling. One of the chants going up from our side was that 'Bin Laden's mother is a whore' which would come back to haunt Kev Carroll at least, some time later.

There was one funny moment, when one of the lads disappeared into Marks and Spencer's and reappeared a few minutes later on the roof of the Arndale, loaded up with about 25 packs of bacon, which he started throwing down at Sayful's mob. That got the biggest cheer of the day.

There were four people out of the group supporting the troops who were arrested over that confrontation, but it was fully two months later, when we were due to stage a demo of our own, that the police arrested big Kev – mostly as a way of disrupting us. A couple of days later they arrested five of Sayful's mob as well and charged them with public order offences. I suppose they were trying to balance things.

The Muslims got conditional discharges for threatening behaviour, although they were clearly puzzled at the fuss, because the police hadn't objected to their placards when they saw them. They probably had a point.

The Bedfordshire police chief expressed 'disappointment that a small number of people chose to cause a disturbance'. For fuck's sake, what did he expect? Couldn't his officers read those placards? Did they think people wouldn't be offended by our troops being called baby killers and butchers?

AS OUTRAGEOUS AS that was, what happened next changed everything. Here we were in a town that had given the world Al Muhajiroun and Anjem Choudary, and which had been the staging post in July 2005 for Germaine Lindsay on his way to kill 26 people on the Piccadilly line.

Most accounts reckon that Lindsay was radicalised in Luton's mosques along with his wife who was from over in Aylesbury, Samantha Lewthwaite. She's also known as the White Widow and was last heard of running round the middle east, the world's most wanted female terrorist.

People were really pissed off at what had happened. It capped everything that had been going on. We'd been given an opportunity to show support for our soldiers, for Luton people to stand up proudly, and the police had turned it into a party political broadcast for al Qaeda. Everyone you spoke to was furious about it.

One of the main Muslim extremists lived not in Bury Park but up in Stopsley, on Putteridge Road, right in the middle of a predominantly non-Muslim residential area. A group of us went up and strung English and British bunting and flags all over the road he lived on, which was our way of making a point, although later someone set fire to his car and sprayed graffiti on his house. I couldn't agree with that, but I can't say that I cried myself to sleep over it either.

At that point I was getting ready for what was supposed to be my stag party – to Cancun in Mexico with 30 of the lads. However the bride-to-be got pregnant and we had to postpone the wedding, but everyone had paid their deposits so we went for a bit of a lads' session anyway. When we got back there was due to be a St George's Day parade in town, but the police and council cancelled it, 'Due to tensions' as they put it. That was bullshit, and everyone knew it.

In response to that and given what had happened at the homecoming, I said that we needed to hold a rally in support of our armed forces. Everyone agreed. A lot of us know the local coppers, the Luton old bill. We knew that from their point of view they weren't happy with the way the soldiers' homecoming had gone either, the way they were directed to police the event.

It led to some real rumblings within the local force and as I understand it about 60 of them walked out at one point. Afterwards a lot of the Luton coppers came into work wearing Union Jack badges that said 'British police support British troops' and there was a dispute when lots of officers refused to take them off. Even today if you go to a Luton Town home football match, you'll still see some of the police wearing those badges.

We then got white nationalist outsiders coming to town, sniffing around. One poor bloke from Norwich turned up with a little homemade banner saying 'I support our troops'. He was just standing there, harming nobody, making a speech, but the police took him away 'for his own safety'.

We were watching all of this going on, and word went out that the police had been told to stop groups of white and black youths congregating around the town centre. I was told by one copper that when Sayful Islam and his friends were called in as driving around town, senior officers said not to interfere with them.

He said rank and file officers were angry at being told to police different communities differently, although I reckon that's probably been the case for years in more towns and cities across the country than you'd care to mention. It's why so much resentment exists between Muslim and non-Muslim communities, not that anyone's in a rush to accept that as being reality.

At one police briefing they apparently put up a big picture of me on screen in the station and the officer in charge described me as a 'leading far right racist'. One of the coppers put his hand up and interrupted. He'd known me since school and told him that no, whatever ever else I was, I was not a racist, and not far right either.

You have to realise that a lot of those ordinary Luton coppers were blokes from within our own families and communities. They knew what was going on. They were frustrated at the way they were being used and – as some saw it – abused, by their own senior staff.

And so, after that, they brought the Metropolitan Police in to deal with Luton's 'public order issues'.

THE WEEKEND after they cancelled the St George's Day parade, we arranged the first demonstration of the UPL – the United People of Luton. It was for the May Day bank holiday weekend, on the Sunday. I had some leaflets made and we distributed them around town, so the police were aware of what was planned. Even that wasn't as straight-forward as you might think. I was dropping leaflets off in pubs and social clubs and at one, Crawley Green Social Club, they stopped me, saying they couldn't take a 'political stance'. Political? In another pub, the Chequers, some geezer started giving me shit about racist propaganda and I told him to look at who was handing them out – two of the lads were black!

This wasn't about marching on Bury Park, not about any protest other than a simple tribute by Luton people to our troops. The leaflets were clear. We just wanted to parade through the town centre, to the war memorial, to have a minute's silence and a round of applause for our soldiers. That was all. How difficult did that have to be?

You wouldn't believe how difficult, as it turned out.

I'd rented a transit van which was stuffed full of placards that had been made by Kev and we parked it up in town overnight, behind the pub, Brookes. However as people were making their way there, police were stopping them, putting a camera in their face and making them say their name and give their date of birth. It was literally police state stuff. They made me take my shoes off, went through my pockets – went through everyone's pockets – basically a strip-search.

I'd noticed one bloke in the pub who I didn't know and asked him where he was from. He said he'd come from Barnet and that 20 of his National Front mates had just got off a train. I said, 'Look around this pub you mug. You are in Luton and you are not welcome. In fact, we might just kick YOUR heads in.' I don't think he could believe it, but he got up and walked out. The police must have known who he was, because they nicked him straight up.

And then as we came out of the pub the police said we were not allowed to march anyway – I think they'd underestimated how many people there would be, because there were about 300. And these weren't football hooligans by the way, these were ordinary Luton men and women, just wanting to pay their respects.

We handed out the placards anyway and set off through town, but the police had effectively drawn a line, ironically right where Sayful Islam and his terrorists spout their shit.

A copper on a horse barged my uncle and knocked him down busting his ankle. My black pal Little Craigy was carrying a placard saying 'NF Go to Hell' and a mounted policeman coshed him in the face, knocking his two front teeth out – and then everything went to hell.

At that the police removed the horses, but they kettled everyone in the square and wouldn't allow anyone to move, in or out. They kept people there for three hours. Women – including my auntie – pleaded to be allowed to go to the toilet but the police wouldn't let them. Men had to stand guard and screen their wives while they crouched and pissed in the street. It was a total disgrace.

Could you imagine the police doing that to Muslim women? Could you imagine our police treating any Muslim demonstration or crowd like that?

I'll tell you the answer right now – no. Not a chance. But it was okay to treat black and white men and women of Luton like animals.

Six of us actually got out of the police cordon. A friend got us into a building and out through the back door, so we were able to wrap around and come back from behind the police lines. That's when we had a confrontation with the group of National Front members who had turned up.

They were outside the town hall handing out flyers, so I just went up, grabbed the flyers, threw them in their faces and told them to get out of our town.

I don't think the police knew how to react to that – they looked confused. The thing is, a bunch of Muslim taxi drivers who were watching from nearby started applauding us. I lost my head with them as well – I told them, 'That's what we do with our extremists, do it with yours!' The police moved the NF gang on.

After three hours the police started letting people from the main demonstration leave in small groups.

IF PEOPLE WEREN'T pissed off already, after that it would only have taken one match for the town to explode. No one could believe what we'd been subjected to. There was always going to have to be another march because things simply couldn't end like that. We planned the second one for the next Bank Holiday at the end of May. I rang the police myself and told them, 'This town is going to blow up unless you lot get your act together'.

I heard about lads making petrol bombs, which they had stashed in a van parked up Farley Hill, just outside town. Some of the young tearaways wanted to riot, to start smashing and burning things. The Luton Islamic Centre got attacked at that time and word got around that it was us – that it was me, Yaxley – who did it, but it wasn't.

I went round the different estates meeting people, trying to talk some sense about things, making the point that we had to be better than that. And I told the police in no uncertain terms that unless they let us get to the memorial, the whole town was going to go up. People were raging.

Do you know what their answer was? Their solution to the discontent? They went round swooping on the houses of the lads they'd identified from the first UPL demo, arresting them and making it part of their bail conditions that they could not enter the town centre, 24 hours a day, seven days a week, for three months.

That was their idea of calming things down. Morons.

They came after me, went to my mum's, but luckily I wasn't in at the time. I ended up effectively going into hiding, to make sure they couldn't hit me with one of their restraining orders. So if you don't think that balaclavas are a good look, that they appear intimidating, paramilitary, and as if people have something to hide, I'd have to agree with you. In a free and democratic society, where there's freedom of speech and people are allowed to gather and protest, they wouldn't be necessary. In my experience however the only people who have that privilege in this country are left-wing and Islamic extremists.

On the day of the second UPL demo, something happened that I couldn't have imagined. Rival factions and gangs, lads who hate each other, all came together under this one banner. Blokes I've had major dramas with put their rivalries, put everything aside ... today we were all Luton, we were all England. We met up at a pub called the Sugar Loaf, then went onto Oliver's. I'd had 100 t-shirts with the slogan, 'No surrender to al Qaeda' made and brought about the same number of balaclavas.

Why? Because lots of the lads there, exercising their democratic right to protest, had effectively had that freedom cynically removed from them by the police, not out of any desire for justice, but to simply jackboot them down. To silence them. The lads who were banned by the police from the town centre turned up anyway. So I told them – from the minute we leave the pub, don't take the balaclavas off. That way the police don't know who's who, and so long as we don't break the law, everyone should be fine. The balaclavas might look bad, but they shouldn't be necessary.

There was trouble early on, when we were at Oliver's. Cars full of Muslims came by and started shouting abuse and a few bottles got thrown back at them. It was a completely different atmosphere from the first march, because this was just men and there was a sense that the police weren't stopping us today.

There were probably 500 lads and we assembled at the far end of Park Street. From there however, things went differently, because instead of meeting the police head on, everyone charged the other way – went round the town centre and came in from the far side of Luton. It turned basically into a sprint to get to the war memorial. Once we got there, we stood and held our two minute silence for our soldiers. We'd won our little personal battle – but the day still had more ahead of it.

After the silence everyone was walking back through the middle of town, but by then groups were fragmenting and confrontations were breaking out. A couple of chicken takeaway shops which locals suspected were a front for selling heroin got attacked and some windows were broken.

Some people charged onto the flyover and the police were fighting lads here and there. It was chaos, mostly, but I got out of the way. This was just a few days after my son was born – I was going out to wet my baby's head that night and could do without the grief.

But what had happened over those few weeks in 2009 had brought a lot of things home to me, not just with regard to what has happening to my town, but to my country too. It wasn't just the threat to every aspect of British life posed by Muslim radicals, but what looked and felt like a conspiracy of the British state to not only allow it, but encourage it.

Meanwhile paranoia had quickly set in amongst the local police. We initially planned a third UPL demo for the August bank holiday when Luton were playing against York City. An online petition to hit the town centre extremists with an ASBO had gathered thousands of names and we wanted to hand it in to the council at the town hall – except they wouldn't accept it. No one was playing ball, letting us have a voice or a presence, however peacefully we wanted it to be.

The issue was getting bigger by the day. Luton Town moved their York match forward to the Friday night, then the Home Secretary banned marches in Luton for three months. The police had been looking for me earlier, but when I went to the station voluntarily they said I was no longer needed. The banning order took care of all that.

We ended up cancelling the third march, but the police, via Chief Inspector Rob Bartlett, rang and then visited me at my mum's. He didn't believe we'd called it off, despite me telling him that if they were straight with us, we'd be straight with them. Since then I've had a decent relationship with Bartlett and when we later staged the Luton EDL Homecoming, we stewarded it ourselves and kept the troublemakers away. People turned up wanting to cause trouble and we stamped it right out.

When Bartlett came to my mum's he actually said that he didn't think this was going away – as in the protest movement. He still didn't believe me though, that the pending demo had been called off.

On the actual day of it, I got a call telling me that Kev Carroll had just been nicked – for swearing at the Islamic extremists at the original soldiers homecoming. They had sat on that charge until they needed it to screw with him. It happens all of the time. I thought it was hilarious because it was nothing serious, he wasn't going to jail or anything, and Boy Scout Kev had got to 40 years of age without ever being in a minute's trouble only to be arrested for swearing.

I was on the phone to an uncle when he said to hold on, the police were at the door. They were there to warn him to stay away from town. Then I got a call to say there was a full-scale riot kicking off. The Muslims were tearing the place up, even though we'd all stayed home.

Because the police were on the streets in force anyway, the Muslims of Bury Park thought it meant we were on our way. It ended up with a full on riot with the Bury Park mob ripping up paving slabs to throw at the coppers. Google it and see for yourself. It was worse than anything in the EDL years, but it got zero press – as usual.

I drove down there and as I was turning round the police stopped me. I asked what was going on and this copper said nothing! It looked like the battle for Baghdad airport and PC Plod whistled a happy tune and said, 'Nothing!'

But here's another example of what I was up against. I was in a car that I'd recently bought brand new, on finance – and they nicked me there and then on suspicion of driving a ringer. They seized my car and I ended up being taken in to the station to be booked just as Kev was coming out. That was the start of a bit of a pattern, as it happened. They even raided my mum's house looking for dodgy number plates, even though I'd bought the car brand new.

We were supposed to go to Center Parcs the next day but the police kept my car, even the baby seats, and didn't let me have it back until Wednesday. There were no charges because it was all bullshit, but they'd succeeded in ruining our holiday. Mission accomplished. Arseholes. It was almost as if they were provoking us, me, into carrying on, into making a stand against them. If so, I figure they lost.

I've asked myself many times, would the EDL have happened if the police and the council had calmly escorted our first demonstration to the war memorial and let ordinary men and women pay their respects?

I don't know. Maybe it would. But after what we experienced that summer of 2009 there wasn't a decision to make. Someone had to speak up about what was happening and it might as well be me. I just couldn't foresee how fast it would grow and how far it would reach. And I certainly couldn't have imagined that I would effectively be declared an enemy of the state just for speaking a few unpalatable, inconvenient truths.

One thing is for certain though. The minute we sat down and decided we'd started something that had to continue, my life changed forever. As did other people's to greater and lesser extents, and especially my family's.

10: BIRTH OF THE EDL

WE WERE BUZZING after the second UPL demo. We seemed to have touched a public nerve and woken people up to some of the appalling things going on under their noses. We were getting messages of support and people were putting things on internet messaging boards that indicated there was more to this than just a bunch of Luton people standing up to be counted.

The internet has revolutionised how public movements can explode. One moment, one image, one message, can go round the world in minutes. If it resonates with the public, it can be massive overnight. That was pretty much the case with the creation of the EDL.

We'd paid £450 for a video of the UPL march, which proved to be a stroke of genius in terms of making the EDL actually happen – that along with the football fraternity, with the video posted on football club messaging boards all around the country under the tag 'Luton Protest'.

We started a Facebook page called British Citizens Against Muslim Extremists and a basic website called 'Save Luton' with a petition to tackle the extremists preaching every week in the town centre. We wanted them hitting with an ASBO, because they were constantly attacking our mums and wives and girlfriends and daughters.

The media got interested in what was happening and some journalists were trying to find out who was behind it all, which led to a couple of red herrings being thrown their way. They found the house where the website was registered and took a photo of a guy, Matt Varga, who leaned out the window and said, 'Yeah?' to some dumb question or other, which they took to mean yeah, it's me, the guy behind it all. Not the brightest bunny in the hutch, Matt! Mind you, they didn't much help themselves.

Then we sent my mate Keir to meet the journalists and say it was all him, because Keir didn't give a shit about anything. I was petrified of people finding out my involvement at that stage.

How things developed from there was quite strange. We were messaged by someone called Dave Shaw – his profile picture was a massive three-Lions England tattoo on his back – and he said that Millwall fans and concerned locals were taking to the streets in a similar fashion.

A few of us went down to London, plus a lad from Bristol, another from Newcastle, people from round and about, all getting interested because of what had happened in Luton.

Except there was no Dave Shaw and no protest. It was a fake profile, a barrow-load of bullshit. But there were 30 of us in a pub, talking about what to do next, with the police sitting outside because already they were monitoring what was going on. We set off through Whitechapel singing England football songs, with the intention of walking to Whitechapel mosque and with the police for an escort. But by the time we got to the Blind Beggar pub on Whitechapel Road there must have been a thousand Muslims waiting. The police got us out of there, sharpish, thankfully.

By now I'd met Chris Renton. Chris and his brother Jack, from Bristol, set up the first EDL website. I only got a computer to get on Facebook and set this group up, so I didn't know much about that side of things. A car full of lads came from Bristol and we sent some black lads to fetch them in to the meeting – they thought they were getting set up. Time and again over the years, we've had to hammer that message home. There's nothing racist about us, lads. Get used to seeing non-white faces.

We kicked about a few names and finally decided on English Defence League. And we decided on the logo, the Knights Templar. In fact one of the things that helped establish our identity was when the Daily Star ran pictures of us and someone was wearing a tee-shirt saying 'EDL, Luton Division'. After that I started getting messages from everywhere.

Along with me and Kev, there were some good lads, great characters. Les Gearty was mad as a box of frogs, but he was as dependable as daylight, always there. Poor Les died recently, but because he didn't drink he effectively became my driver. There was Gillies and McGovern, Kev Mac and the Northern Irish lad Davy Cooling. There were also other family members including my mum's brother Rob. I never knew how clued up he was on some of the issues with Islam across the world. Rob's been there for me throughout, and he was a rock for my mum when she fell seriously ill. I always looked up to him and my older cousins, Fannin and Gary, who were prominent on the football scene.

From the start there were Edders and Kim, Kev Comer, Steve Ambry, Matty P, Andy, Rachel and Steve Currian, Andy Henderson, Fozzy and Dekka, Southbank Singh, big Stu and the rest of the Lanesfield crew ... they were all top people, the heart and soul of the original EDL.

Next up, I saw that the Islamic Forum of Europe was holding its conference at a central London hotel and we thought it would be a good idea to turn up and give them some grief. About 15 of us walked into the hotel lobby wearing EDL hoodies.

I don't know what we thought we were going to do, but when we saw there were about 2,000 extremists – including so-called moderate preacher Abdul Qadeer Baksh – we sat quietly in the corner. The police turned up and walked us out which, all things considered, was one of the very few times in my life I've been glad to see a uniform.

By now the message boards and Facebook were buzzing but there still wasn't anything fully formed in terms of organisation. Hate preacher Anjem Choudary had staged a public radicalisation in Birmingham as part of some kind of

Islamic roadshow, where he converted a young British lad called Shaun under a banner saying 'Jesus was a Muslim'. We looked around, read the papers, watched the news and, quite unbelievably, no one was talking about it.

It was as though it hadn't even happened. Could you imagine the reaction if we did that in the middle of Luton, converted an Islamic kid to Christianity? The army would have to ring that ISIS lot and ask to borrow extra body bags for the fall-out. But he was a Muslim, provoking us, and that was all right. Well, it was all right for some. Not us.

The next date for Choudary's public party piece was in Wood Green, in north London, so a bunch of us went down in the back of a van, all balaclavad up, with banners calling Choudary's wife a benefit cheat. It was a bit wild and random and after trouble kicked off one kid got hurt when he was hit by a bus, but he was okay and we managed to close down their stunt. It worked because after that they took their roadshow dates down from their website. We were having some kind of disruptive impact at least.

It was off to Birmingham after that. I'd read about a gathering of about 200 lads in the city staging a protest, saying basically, 'We want our country back' – so that was the next stop for us, the newly formed EDL.

There was a bus full of lads from Luton on that occasion, which was the first time the police decided the best tactic might be to bore us to death, to see how much fun we thought it was being made to wait in a car park for two hours outside the city – then be brought in and made to sit in a pub. All dressed up and nowhere to go.

I remember the lead copper saying, 'You are never ever going to get Villa, Wolves and Birmingham firms in the same pub without starting a war'. We'd been messaging all of them about turning out, so the police knew what was going on. And yet sure enough, those lads were all in it together and I was quite chuffed, because if nothing else we'd hit a nerve bigger than age-old football rivalries. If I had to analyse it, I'd say that rather than there being a common enemy, we had a common cause – our country. Everyone who lived in an area with a big and growing Muslim population was watching their community, their neighbourhood, their town, changing before their eyes.

We knew there was going to be shit going down in Birmingham that day because a Muslim counter-rally was announced after their chief imam called on them to come out in force and oppose us. I say that we knew it was happening. We knew, but we didn't see, because the police just kept us there for hours until eventually they said they couldn't get us out on our march. At that about 150 lads burst out of the back of the pub and it was mayhem. People were running wild all over the place.

The police brought in double decker buses to ship us out and apparently some geezer in a green bomber jacket who was getting on one of the buses gave a Hitler salute towards a group of journalists. To this day I reckon it was a plant. The Unite Against Fascism lot used that image against us for years. I didn't see it, others did – Sappy was going berserk, because his daughter is mixed race. They got a slapping and kicked off the bus. We weren't having that.

Every street we passed was littered with debris. Rampaging Muslims were putting windows in, attacking cars, going crazy. The police couldn't stop them. Cars full of Muslims were pulling up and attacking the buses, throwing whatever they could at us. The windows were shattered – we had to kick them out – but it was the images of that day that effectively put the EDL on the map.

YOU CAN CALL IT stubborn or awkward, you can call it bloody minded, but we hadn't got to have our march. So we announced that we'd be back three weeks later. Either the streets belonged to every Englishman as a matter of principle, or this war was already lost. What you won't have heard in all likelihood, is that I offered to call that march off if the police thought it was going to lead to more mayhem. We really did want to do things by the rules.

I spoke to the police anonymously and I asked if they wanted us to cancel. It was a senior female officer and she insisted that no, if we still wanted to demonstrate, they would ensure that we could. She told me, 'We will make sure you get there. We promise you.'

I think the fact that the Muslim community felt they could decide who does and doesn't come and go, and where, was a red rag to a bull on this occasion. The police didn't like us because we were trouble that they could do without, but ultimately – for some senior officers at least – a line is crossed when they're told who's in charge. This wasn't about us, the EDL, it was about them, the police, showing quite literally who was the boss.

When we returned I must have spent about £1,800 getting a bunch of placards made. The theme was mostly 'Muslims, no problem – extremist Muslims, big problem'.

In the event I think we had more placards than people. Again, the local Muslim community and the extreme left were whipped up into a frenzy and were going mental, mostly thanks to the former Respect Party MP Salma Yaqoob, who was also a Birmingham city councillor.

But the police were absolutely steadfast. They were letting us demonstrate. We got to stand by the Bull Ring, but there were no speeches or anything. Just us with our placards and a Jewish lad with his Star of David flag while the locals were going berserk all around. This woman Yaqoob was calling on them to smash the BNP and at one point they all got down on their knees, and then they jumped up and charged. It was madness.

The police put us in an underpass and kept us there for quite some time until they could get us out. And again on that second Birmingham visit we had an issue with a couple of Nazis, but again we gave them the boot.

What summed that demo up to me was something we saw in the newspapers the next day. We were on the bus being escorted away while all these Muslim and left-wing gangs were running riot, and there was a picture of a white kid, just some passer-by going about his own business, in the wrong place at the wrong time, getting a kicking on the floor by part of their mob, who robbed him for good measure. But the headline on it said, 'A fascist being attacked by anti-fascists'.

What does that tell you – quite apart from the fact that the idiot who wrote it hadn't the first clue what was actually happening? It made it clear, as we quickly got used to, that that is the default media position. We get called bigoted – but it's the mainstream media that's either bigoted, bone idle, or both, if you ask me. They've made their petty minds up and written the answers they want before they've even asked the questions.

Meanwhile, the EDL marched on. In time I would have problems with the infiltration of all kinds of elements, but I have to stress that for the most part, the EDL supporters were a great group, patriots in the purest sense. Probably 30 per cent were women. There were ex-services people, gays, Jews, blacks, a real cross-section. It was a reaction to what was happening all across the country, but also the complete refusal by anyone in authority to acknowledge it.

So the EDL were rough and ready, unsophisticated? That didn't make them any less real. Just before the 2010 election I was furious when David Cameron came out and said, 'There's none sicker than the EDL'.

Here's the thing. We get an Islamic atrocity and Cameron and Co are falling over themselves to emphasise that it's a minority, always a minority. Why couldn't they say the EDL had a problem minority? But no, it's fine to label an entire organisation, all of those ordinary people, as 'sick'. We were still building momentum though. We made and posted another video saying to people – your fellow countrymen are being attacked. What are you going to do?

Manchester was about a month later, which we targeted because there was a church in Longsight the local Muslims were turning into a mosque and they were bulldozing all the headstones. There would be an outrage if anyone else was doing it. This was as close to sacrilege, an attack on Christianity as you can get, and all the world outside was hearing was a big, 'So what?'

But by then we were picking up momentum. From there being 150 people at Birmingham, when we got to Manchester there were around 2,000 people supporting us.

I was wearing a niqab-type of face veil underneath my hoodie. I still didn't want to be a public face and on that occasion a bright young 19-year-old kid came along to do a speech, which was quite good. But that was the beginning and end of him – his mum threw a wobbler and he quit because of all the shit he got. The police turned nasty there and lots of lads were bitten when they set the dogs on us.

We were off and running though. A memorable early demo took place in Dudley, the future stomping ground of would-be Prime Minister Afzal Amin. There had been plans that I mentioned earlier to build a £20 million mega-mosque in the town dating back to about 2001 and the locals were up in arms over the vast scale of this thing. Big? It could have virtually housed the entire local Muslim community at that time, let alone provided them with extra prayer space. And it wasn't as if Dudley didn't have any mosques anyway. However that mosque was never about worship, it was about a big political statement. These cases usually are.

The police wanted us to sit down and talk to the Dudley Muslim Association, which I was fine with. But my main question to them was this: who was stumping up £20 million to build this monstrosity? And they kept saying, 'Local donations'. Local donations? £20 million? Wow. And this place is in one of the supposedly 10 most deprived communities in the country?

The original plans would have seen it dominate even historic Dudley Castle, so it was a natural place for the new EDL to go and protest. But first, we drove up the night before the demo and had a bit of fun.

We got onto the roof of the derelict buildings on the site of the planned mosque and one of the lads, a Northern Irish kid, Leon McCreery, set up camp on the highest point – and then we rigged up a PA system and that night started broadcasting the Muslim call to prayer. Over and over again. Well, if people were troubled by how much of a nuisance the five daily calls to prayer would be if the scheme went ahead, then it was only right that someone give it a test run for them.

What's more, with me on the phone to Leon, I could make speeches which sounded like I was up there with him. We were going all through the night until the police went up there armed with tasers and hauled Leon and another kid off to jail. They even remanded them in prison for a fortnight, until I paid £4,500 of my own money to a top lawyer to get them out.

When we followed that up with the demo, we were approached by a Russian man and his daughter, whose family had been affected by a terrorist attack in their homeland. They wanted to come with us, to make a point of their own.

When we marched, his eight-year-old daughter walked out ahead of the mass of protestors, carrying her Russian flag. It was a really moving sight and when we reached the demo point, they made little speeches of their own, in Russian, remembering their victims.

There was the usual trouble with local Muslims and UAF and we discovered that a police officer was smashed in the face with a brick by a local youth, who was promptly arrested. The imams marched a crowd down to the nick and demanded that the kid be released ... or else. And he was.

When I asked the police why, they said they had to make a 'judgment' about what best served the public interest. Not just there, but in other towns and cities with big Muslim populations. And their judgment was that allowing an arsehole to get away with smashing an officer in the face with a brick was in the public interest. I asked who ran that town? I didn't get an answer. I didn't need one.

THERE WAS a big turn out for Leeds at the end of October 2009, less for Nottingham and London in December, then a big turn out for Stoke in January, where things went tits up. That turned into a proper riot and if I'm being honest we weren't ready for it, we couldn't cope. A bunch of young blokes we hadn't seen before used it as an excuse to have a ruck with the police and after that we knew we had to talk about having our own stewards.

There was almost always a specific reason for going to a particular town or city, from local protests over a new mosque or sharia court, or anger over some horrendous grooming crime, to something as outrageous as that cause that took us to Manchester – plans to bulldoze a graveyard full of headstones. On a handful of occasions perhaps out of 70 or so demos while I was running things, we'd visit somewhere because of the strength and size of the local membership, to support them.

At Stoke I wrote a speech for my mate Gilheaney. We kept being called racists despite our black, Indian and other ethnic members. I thought if we had a black bloke speaking, the media couldn't ignore it, but they did anyway. I wrote a speech for him which started with Martin Luther King's 'I had a dream...' and Gilheaney rang me up, howling laughing. He said, 'You are fucking having me on!' I thought it was a bit of good banter and he took a bit of persuading, but credit to him, he got up there and did it.

At Dudley we had a dreadlocked black lad called James willing to get up and speak along with a Sikh girl Sareeta, who supported us. They were getting a bunch of shit from one of the football hooligan crews. One of them said, 'What the fuck is this?' when Dave and Sareeta came up. I told him that if he didn't like it, he was at the wrong demo.

It didn't help that the police kept stitching us up, which is what happened at Dudley towards the end of January 2010. There were 400-500 of us at Tipton, away from the main demo and the police said they were bringing buses to take us in, but they didn't. So we started marching and the police formed a line and drew batons and we ended up with a running battle for about two miles. We got up to the top of this grassy hill and came face to face with all of these Muslim police officers standing with the Muslim protestors, so we never actually got to the demo. It was chaos.

We went back to Dudley again, and we had stewards that time but it all kicked off once more. Police put all these big fences up to kettle us inside, but as soon as a bottle got thrown over the top at us by the far left and the local Muslims, everyone kicked off. It was out of control.

Not every EDL demo went to plan, especially in those early days, and our visit to Cardiff, to help spread the message in Wales, was a grade A balls-up.

An 18-seater minibus of us went down to support a locally organised protest against a sharia court in the city and I was a bit out of my comfort zone from the start, because I was with just a couple of my mates, Chesney and McGovern, and I really didn't know the rest of the lads who weren't from Luton. If I'm being honest, I thought I was with a bunch of wankers.

The demo was being organised by a lad I only knew as Marshy, a Cardiff City football hooligan who said they were all turning out to support us. Marshy reckoned to be pulling the EDL together in south Wales in the early days. Marshy, as it quickly became clear, was a complete and utter arse wipe. Even his own so-called friends couldn't stand him.

The Cardiff City fans turned out all right – purely and simply intent on serving us up, battering these English characters into the middle of next week. And they were accompanied by a gang of tooled-up Somalian geezers.

These were the early days remember, so the police weren't at all clued up about managing things where we were concerned. But my eyes weren't deceiving me when I saw these lads carrying sticks and bats and whatever, right in front of the coppers in the middle of Cardiff.

Whatever the local rivalries and issues, I guess their hatred of the English trumped everything.

I remember little Chesney had a pair of blue shorts on. He was only about 18 and there wasn't much of him, but I can still see these blue shorts flashing here, there and everywhere as the trouble kicked off. I'd doubted the crew I was on the bus with, but that was one show where there were 17 blokes more game than I was. When everyone made it back to the bus I apologised for thinking they were a set of wankers. We got out of Wales as fast as we could.

That was the end of the Welsh adventure as far as I was concerned. Patriots were still welcome, but it became clear that the Welsh Defence League was a far right gang based out of Swansea and we wanted nothing to do with them. Welsh people were still welcome to join the EDL.

Some time later, about 50 of us – mates, not EDL members – went down to south Wales, to Newport to support the boxer Joe Calzaghe in a world title fight. As soon as the locals heard our accents that was it, they wanted a ruck.

Strange people, that lot. They need to get over themselves. Meanwhile we were trying to get organised as things grew and took on a life of their own, but it was proving harder and harder.

For a brief while we had about a dozen people from around the country, trying to agree a structure and a campaign plan, whatever, but it just turned into a mass argument. It was getting nowhere so I said just drop it, we're going where I say. And that seemed to settle that. There really wasn't a plan.

KEVIN CARROLL FRONTED things up for the BBC documentary Young, British and Angry which came out in June 2010, just a year after the UPL marches had started the ball rolling, and after we'd had some big turn outs, over 2,500 at Bolton in March, 2,000 at Dudley a fortnight later and another 2,000 at Newcastle in May. At each of those there were an estimated 1,500, 1,300 and 1,000 Muslim and UAF counter-demonstrators.

The first time there was a picture of my face was at that latest Dudley demo. I'd had some EDL masks made but during the speeches mine must have slipped or got knocked and the photographer clearly had a long lens, but he or she managed to catch most of my mug which was printed in the Wolverhampton Express and Star.

It wasn't a massive deal but I was actually quite enjoying the mystery of it all. The police knew who Tommy Robinson was because behind the scenes they were putting my entire life through the ringer already, but as far as the world at large was concerned at least, I was still the 'International Man of Mystery!' It was great banter, a buzz I suppose. But the pressure was coming on from all angles.

I'll go into all of the financial shenanigans which led to my prison sentence over my brother-in-law's mortgage, but while the Pakistani gangs around Luton still didn't know who the real Tommy Robinson was, at that point the police absolutely did.

They nicked one of my mates, Andrew Wallman – his nickname was Mandy and he had his troubles with the law, no doubt. When they raided him they found three guns and £140,000 in cash. As I understand things SOCA, the Serious and Organised Crime Agency, talked to him about a possible deal after they'd seen me going into his place.

Mandy's missis came to see me at The Parrot pub in Farley Hill and told me the law wanted to stick the blame for the guns on me. They'd seen me going in the house and they'd seen a big picture of a group of us on the wall, then they put two and two together and came up with 37 or something. What they didn't know was that I was going round all the lads in town, collecting a few quid from everyone for a local girl with a serious illness.

If you go to school and do stuff in and around Luton for long enough you will know people like Mandy, you will know at least some people with questionable backgrounds and activities, and I did. He got 13-and-a-half years for that, but he told them to fuck off in terms of trying to fit me up. We don't do that to each other in Luton.

Word was starting to get around though about Tommy Robinson. I didn't make the Bolton demo because I got a call from my mum while on the bus on the way there. Some massive white guy had knocked on her door and said to tell her son the devil was coming for him. I made them drop me off and bolted back home to make sure mum was okay.

DURING THIS PERIOD when things were taking off so rapidly for the 'upstart' EDL, the BNP leader Nick Griffin came out and accused us of being a government front. He said that no group could be this big, this fast, and with such a massive public profile, without state backing. Griffin had a conspiracy theory that it was all a covert operation meant to give the government an excuse to bring in martial law. What a joke of a bloke, #hawkeye.

I was interviewed at Granada Studios in Manchester and went in wearing a burkha under my coat. Muslim women wear it so that men can't perv after them. I was doing it to stay alive. On another occasion for an interview at Center Parcs I wore the EDL hoodie with the veil underneath.

I still wanted someone else to grab leadership of the group and run with it, take it to the next level, whatever that might be. I didn't want the aggravation, but more than that, I didn't think I could do it or was the right person to do it. We had created a massive street protest group virtually overnight from those humble if angry beginnings in Luton, but I hadn't a clue how to develop that.

And then there was me, and the baggage I brought. I'd had a few years of madness with the football lads and the late nights. I didn't have a clean past what with the prison sentence for the fight with the off duty copper, and I didn't think I could either cope with the limelight or do the EDL and the cause the justice it deserved.

Paraic O'Brien, who did a BBC Newsnight profile on us early on, challenged me to reveal myself. It got to the point where the anonymity was starting to become a bigger story than what we were actually trying to achieve.

The truth is, we weren't prepared for how quickly things took off. The numbers turning up at protests kept growing and our online support shot up to about 15,000 in no time at all. That brought its own troubles, because the bigger we got, the more interested our enemies were in shutting us down. We kept getting hacked and attacked from all directions, the Facebook page would be got at, our website taken down. It was non-stop aggravation.

The day before my wedding in July 2011 was the day that the Norwegian maniac Anders Breivik went on a killing spree. That night our Facebook page came under fire at a time when we had over 100,000 supporters. It was pivotal to how we operated, because it got the word out to everyone, so simply. If we were going to do a demo anywhere, or wanted to announce anything, it was just click, press a button and hey presto, it went everywhere.

As for who was behind the sabotage? I don't know – the usual suspects. Left wingers, Marxists, Islamists, your guess is as good as mine. The government even, I'm sure they could quite easily do it, although on one occasion the hacking was tracked back to someone in Lebanon. The day Anders Breivik went on his shooting spree, straight away our Facebook page went boom, straight down. We had to start all over again – about three times in total.

The Facebook group got to about 180,000 at one point but when my identity was finally made public, the reaction at home was everything I feared.

A nephew of Nigel Khan, one of the town's most notorious characters, put a picture of me on Facebook saying, 'Wanted – Big Reward'. This was during the period when their mosque had been attacked and everything was being blamed on the EDL, which was not surprisingly one of the reasons I didn't want to be known.

But here's the thing, this character, this relative of Khan, was well known for going out boozing. He had a wife all head to toe in a burkha – a white girl mind you – and a kid at the Luton Islamic Centre's madrassah, and he was going out on the lash with all the gangsters.

So by way of getting back at him, I made a Youtube video with a picture of me and a Union Jack and then him with a Pakistani flag, then lots of poppy seeds and pictures of people injecting heroin. I Google-earthed his house, the gym he went to, then published the whole lot on the Faceboook group as being the man who had set himself up as the face of the EDL's opposition. His arse went, completely. He rang my brother-in-law, begging me to take it down. He's my age and I still see him around town and, funnily enough, we talk, we get along well enough. Funny old world.

ALL THE TIME that the EDL was spreading and taking off around the country, we had big issues bubbling away on the streets of Luton. None of that was going away.

I've always been a thorn in the side of some of the troublemakers locally, like Abdul Qadeer Baksh.

I first came across him when the EDL started and all sorts of trouble began kicking off in Luton. There were fire bombings of buildings, cars being torched, and EDL slogans being sprayed on people's front doors, on the Labour party offices, all over. Sure enough, here was Qadeer all over the news condemning these Islamophobic attacks on his community and saying Luton Muslims were living in fear.

And I remember thinking, 'You're talking shit mate'.

I'd already had to move out of my home when we started the EDL, and there was a lucky escape when they went to firebomb my house – but did next door by mistake.

My car was torched but whoever did it sprayed EDL on the front door – of the wrong house. I went the next morning to apologise to the bloke who'd been caught in the crossfire and I had a photograph taken of myself by the graffiti, which happened to be the same yellow paint that had been used in the other attacks round town. That struck me as being a bit strange.

It was one of about 26 fire bombings that happened all around Luton and the campaign was working too, because people were turning against me. I got a phone call from an older black lad, who was on the football scene, about another car getting torched and he thought the young EDL lads must be going round causing havoc. Most of the graffiti was this EDL slogan being sprayed everywhere, with occasionally a swastika on the side of a mosque. People were turning against us, thinking we were attacking people indiscriminately, except that I knew we had nothing to do with it – not that anyone was willing to listen.

I had a meeting booked with Gavin Shuker, who was the local Labour MP. His offices got vandalised and sprayed with EDL and he used that as an excuse not to meet me.

Then the police called us down for a meeting and they told us they'd caught who'd been doing it. The senior officer said they had solid evidence on six of the cases and that the suspects were Muslims. I thought, 'happy days' – but the copper went on and said that when they'd raided these characters, they'd found evidence of things a lot worse than anything like a graffiti or arson charge, and that they'd be going away for a very long time.

I asked for assurances that they'd make it public, which the officer agreed, but you can guess the rest. The police statement simply said that the attacks were not committed by the English Defence League. And that was that. No big publicity announcement that these were Muslims attacking their own community to try to paint us in a bad light.

If the police had nailed us for it, the news would have been all over every newspaper and television station in the country. But there was – there still is – a conspiracy of silence when the criminals are Muslims. I don't believe that Rotherham and Rochdale and the growing list of public scandals have changed much at all, unless it's a case that the police simply can't avoid it, and are forced to front it up.

I had a meeting with Abdul Qadeer Baksh. We were interviewed by the local radio station in the middle of Luton about our upcoming EDL demo, and Qadeer said we needed to get together. Me and Kev went to meet him in a hotel in town and he turned up with two people carriers full of big, bearded militants.

It was a bit of a show of force I suppose, though they were actually quite polite to us. These lads looked like killers – they may well have been, come to think of it – and me, Kev and a lad called Danny Wilson simply strolled in. Just the three of us. These bodyguard types lingered about and when we sat down the first thing Qadeer said was that sharia would not come here in his lifetime and probably not in his sons' – but he said the generation after that, when 'the people will it', sharia will be here in Britain, and we won't be able to prevent it, that nobody can stop it.

And I laughed and told him thanks for confirming why I started the English Defence League – because we would fight that until the day we died.

We got on reasonably well in that meeting ironically, Qadeer and I, but our views and visions for the country were complete opposites. I talked about the problems our women were having, scared of the Muslim gangs, and he said he'd talk to the people responsible. It's amazing that he admitted that he even could.

Kev and I told him – there were too many incidents of Muslims attacking people just trying to go about their lives and that for every action there would be a reaction. This was no way forwards. He needed to pass that message back to his community.

Did it make a difference? Not that I could ever tell.

WHILE THE EDL was causing headaches for towns and cities and police forces up and down the country, the authorities in Luton at least succeeded eventually in cramping my style. I've admitted that I'd been in more than enough rucks and brawls up and down and around England's football clubs. I'd grown out of all that so called 'buzz' though by this point. However when the police picked me up and landed me with a football banning order, it was one occasion that I hadn't done anything wrong whatsoever.

It was a Tuesday night game against Newport and while there was some trouble, I wasn't involved. I was having a singsong and a chant and suddenly, boom – arrested. But it was over an unrelated incident from months before. At interview there was no mention of trouble at the football. I was bailed for eight weeks at which point it had turned into a Section 4 Public Order offence – suddenly I was supposed to be the ringleader of a 100-man mass brawl.

No arrests. No CCTV. In the age of mobile phones and videos being loaded online, not a single example of this supposed mass brawl, just these two coppers saying I was 'directing' it.

I told the court I was singing, I was probably even calling the Newport fans a bunch of Welsh sheepshaggers, but I had nothing to do with any trouble. Not that you have a prayer with magistrates anyway and I was found guilty.

I appealed it, but my bail conditions kept me out of town on Saturdays, and one-mile away from the ground at all times – which was all of Bury Park. That was the point of it all. When the appeal eventually came to Crown Court, one of the coppers said he saw me throw the first punch and that I was directing the violence. The judge had to remind him, that that wasn't in his original statement and he had to withdraw it. It was even reported in The Guardian that this copper was lying on oath – and yet the judge still refused to overturn the decision and I got a three-year football banning order. Mission accomplished.

As part of that I was banned from travelling to England football games and the rules covering that situation are that six days before a match you have to surrender your passport at the local police station.

One time I drove down to do the necessaries and I had my son in the car with me, but when I got to the Luton cop shop there were lots of Pakistani gangsters outside – geezers from the Gambino gang, and I was with my son. It just wasn't safe to go in.

We went home and I drove back down to the police station the next day and explained to the lady officer that

I'd tried to attend, but couldn't for fear of what might have happened. I thought that was being sensibly cautious.

No big deal, eh? Think again. Two months later they dragged me out of bed and arrested me for breaching the football banning order. It went all the way to court at Luton Magistrates and when the policewoman was called as a witness her evidence was that it had happened exactly as I said. The judge was gobsmacked. She simply said, 'What?' and dismissed the case. The police must have nothing better to do, honestly.

I sometimes think the local cops, when they're bored, sit around dreaming up new ways to piss me off. The night before my wedding in 2012 I booked a really nice restaurant, Billy's in Harpenden, for 30 of us, close family and friends. I got a call that afternoon from the owner saying the police had been in and warned her about these violent extremists and how she was asking for trouble. She said she would have to cancel. I drove straight over there and the woman saw me and said, 'You? You and your friends are always here – half of them are black!' I said, 'I know love. That's the police for you.'

Our evening went ahead, but ruining our wedding – that would have been their idea of a good laugh.

WHILE ALL OF that was going on with the EDL and at home in Luton, the outside problems of people wanting to resolve me as an issue – ie, kill me – was picking up pace.

I've mentioned the six Osman warnings. I got the sense eventually that these threats played into the police's hands, firstly in terms of inconveniencing someone – me – who was a pain in the arse to them, and then in hopefully succeeding in driving the target of the threats – me again – into becoming fearful and going into hiding. I dare say the third outcome, of one of the madmen managing to chop my head off, wouldn't have been too unpopular with the police either.

The first incident came just before our EDL Homecoming demo in Luton. I was out having a few beers and got a call to go down to the police station. A copper read out a letter saying that members of the Bury Park community were angered by my recent actions and appearances on television that had inflamed tensions, and members of that community meant to cause serious harm to the health and safety of me and my family.

The officer said the police couldn't protect me round the clock and I couldn't break the law to protect my family. So they advised me to stay out of the public spotlight and to stay out of Luton for the foreseeable future. At that, I asked the officer for the letter – and he looked like he'd shit his pants.

So he promptly disappeared for half an hour and when he came back and gave me the letter, they'd redacted it all. Blocked out all reference to Bury Park and the Muslim community. I just started to laugh. I said, 'There's the problem pal, right there. You know exactly who wants to hurt me and my family.'

Later that evening three officers turned up at the house. My wife was pregnant with our second child and they insisted that because the threat wasn't just to me but the family, that she had to be told about it. They just loved doing that, causing as much upset as possible.

I still don't know if the threat was credible or if this was the police trying to put the squeeze on me, and what's more, put the squeeze on me through my family. I've had death threats via social media by the hundred, by the thousand, and the police haven't done a single thing about it. Not once. But this time it seemed it suited them.

That night I asked the copper if he'd ever sat a Muslim woman down and told her that a non-Muslim planned to kill her. He couldn't answer. He wouldn't answer. Because of course he hadn't. It doesn't happen.

The last Osman warning in my EDL time was in 2013 and on that occasion the police quoted, 'a named individual' making credible threats and I said to them, 'So you know who it is – what the fuck are you doing about it?' They just look at you lamely and say they can't do anything about it. Seriously? Do you believe that?

The one that got most public attention was the Al-Shabaab threat, not long after they'd carried out the Kenyan shopping mall massacre. This time counter terrorism officers turned up banging on the front door at 3am. I told my wife to wait upstairs.

At this time, towards the end of the EDL (for me) they were still cranking up the pressure ahead of the mortgage case coming to court, saying they were considering putting my wife on trial too.

I wondered if the Al-Shabaab threat was just another part of them winding up the pressure, getting me to crack. The police officers said: 'We have intercepted a terror video from Somalia. You are pictured and named. Then we have seen an Al-Shabaab tweet saying that you must be killed at all costs.'

This was at the time a Somali terror suspect with links to them did a runner from the East London mosque dressed in a burkha. Mohamed Ahmed Mohamed made fools of the security forces at which Scotland Yard said, 'He is not considered at this time to represent a direct threat to the public'. No, but his lords and masters had just told him and all his mates to chop me up.

Despite the geezer doing a runner, his lawyers still got legal aid to fight a case arguing that he shouldn't be on a Home Office control order. Six months after escaping in disguise he even won the case. All those human rights lawyers, stuffing their pockets with taxpayers' cash, to defend a terrorist who's so convinced of his innocence that he did a runner in a burkha. Unbelievable.

I was due to appear in St Albans Crown Court after the Al-Shabaab threat and at least they took that seriously. I might have been considered dispensable while everyone else named in the video got reasonable protection, but they put the court on lockdown, with counter terrorism officers, bomb squad, the lot. The press were even told they couldn't report that I was in the building.

The Al-Shabaab threat – or Al Kebab as I prefer to call them – wasn't just directed at me, but also the Quilliam Foundation executive Usama Hasan, plus Mo Ansar. They got 24 hour protection from Special Branch or Counter-Terrorism or the Thunderbirds or someone. I got a letter.

Maybe I was supposed to fold it into a paper plane and poke it in the eye of the suicide bomber coming to get me and my family. Short of something better to do, I got a mate to come round and film me drawing a pirate map with an 'X marks the spot' on it, and pinned it to the front door for any terrorists looking for me. Wankers.

11: WE NEED TO TALK ABOUT KEVIN CARROLL

PEOPLE IDENTIFY the EDL primarily with Tommy Robinson understandably but none of what happened would have been possible without my cousin Kevin Carroll, co-founder of the EDL, first class carpenter, builder and five-star bloke. Kev considers himself to construction what Obi-Wan Kenobi was to The Force in Star Wars. The man.

The thing is, we are chalk and cheese in just about every way two blokes can be. We're literally a Little and Large double act, because I'm this little geezer at 5ft 6ins and he's huge, at 6ft 5ins. I'm a bit all over the place, disorganised, random and unpredictable. But if you go pick Kev up from his house, he'll walk out of the door, then walk back in again to check something or other, then back out, then back in. OCD all over. When we're out and about I can tell you exactly what he's going to do before he does it.

He's a proper boy scout. If I go pick him up when it's snowing, he'll come out of the house with a blanket, a spade, four litres of water ... you'd think we were going up Everest, not down to Tesco. Talk about 'Be Prepared'. If you were ever in an emergency, you'd want Kevin Carroll with you. He'd be great on one of these desert island survival programmes.

Anyone with a connection to a group like the English Defence League is going to be pigeon-holed as a violent, right-wing halfwit, as though they eat, breathe and live some kind of all-consuming hatred. That is so not the Kevin Carroll that I know.

Oh sure, he can stand up for himself. He isn't just big, he's always been big on fitness, physically fitter than blokes half his age. A formidable bloke all around. You still wouldn't mess with him. But he's as soft as a brush at heart. He absolutely loves animals – some of the lads call him Dr Doolittle. On one site that he was running he found an injured bird, scooped it up off the floor and brought it to the hut. He fixed its wing, nursed it back to health and kept it in there until it was recovered and strong enough to fly.

That's Kev all over. He's nobody's idea of a fighter – at that size he's never had to be, although he used to do a bit of boxing when he was younger – but I think he'd throw a wobbler with anyone who hurt an animal.

You go up to his house and into his back garden and there he is, feeding four or five foxes. Wild foxes and they all come to his house. He's not right, if you want my opinion. But I love the man to bits. More than anything though, Kev's a people person. He has a presence. At EDL demos, if the crowd was getting edgy, he could get up there and take command of the entire place with a word.

He is a proud, born and bred Lutonian, through and through and although he was never involved in the football hooligan scene, he was a Luton Town fan. He was deeply affected when he lost his beloved nephew Liam – Limo-Gimo as Kev called him – in 2007 at the age of 14 after a long illness. Liam was the mascot for Town's first home game that season and he said it was the best day he ever had. He passed away that same afternoon. It was as though he'd hung on just for that.

Kev was one of those blokes who epitomised what the 'old' Luton was about, a seamless mix of black and white communities. He could roll into blues nights at the Five-0 club and he was respected by blokes in the West Indian community like Johnny Ashton, Des P, Hyron, Everton B, Jester, Ash ... all top lads.

Last December he lost a good friend who we both knew and respected. Lenos Wilson was one of Luton's greatest sons. Lenos was a volunteer running the Non-Violence Alliance. When gang trouble broke out among younger members of the black community – and we're talking about repeated shootings – Lenos would bring in older lads to go out on the street. He and Kev were very close. These were men who wanted their town to be a safe and happy place for everyone.

But Kev has also, like me, become more and more concerned with what's happening around us with radical Islam over the years. That's the one thing, the one subject at least, about which we most have in common.

We had a big job when we were contracting for Little Legs and the hut which was our site office ended up like a shrine to everything that's going on with Islam globally. One entire wall was plastered with stories ranging from the attacks on the soldiers in Luton and the activities of radicals like Abu Hamza and Omar Bakri Mohammed, to atrocities around the world.

The soldiers' homecoming brought things to a head for Kev. He'd never had a criminal record or been arrested until that day – and then eight CID and uniform coppers dragged him out of bed at 5.50am. He had his moment in court though. He said, 'I am 40 years old, I have never been in trouble in my life, and you're now prosecuting me and giving me a criminal record, for calling a group of Muslims, who spit hatred at our soldiers, a bunch of wankers.'

I heard the tape of the police interview and you have to picture the scene of Kev and his brief sitting with these officers and a laptop on the table from which you can hear Kev singing, 'She's a whore, she's a whore, bin Laden's mother is a whore...' The copper says, 'Is this you?'

Kev replies, 'Woah, woah, woah, hold on a minute...'

And then there's a long pregnant pause. And finally Kev says, 'She hasn't made a complaint has she? Because if she has I haven't got a problem with her, just her wanker of a son.' Everyone cracked up, even the coppers and the brief.

I don't think he could believe it. And it was absurd. He was the first one arrested, before the police bothered picking up any of the Muslims who caused all of the trouble in the first place. It was as if they only nicked them in order to justify hammering a few of us, given their belief that a third UPL demo was in the pipeline.

Kev was taken to magistrates court and fined as a result, but boy did he get his money's worth. It was hilarious, the courtroom was in stitches, although I don't think the magistrates saw the funny side of things. I was wetting myself on the back row of the public seats.

The prosecution bloke was getting all serious while reading Kev's interview. The police accused him of calling the protestors, 'Fucking wankers', when again Kev replied, 'Hold on a minute – officers, are we not all agreed that that bunch of people are fucking wankers? The whole, entire country is agreed on this matter, and now you want to prosecute me for saying it?'

The way he spoke in his interview was golden. He's a clever bloke, a witty bloke, and he just belittled the whole process, made it all sound so ridiculous, which of course it was anyway – but the police and the courts don't like that. Not one bit. They found Kev guilty and fined him, but it didn't end there. He appealed and the case went to Crown Court, by which time everything had moved on because now the EDL had come into being and things were starting to move quite quickly.

I was forced to take a long, hard look at myself when Kev went back to have his appeal against conviction heard.

THE APPEAL WENT to Luton Crown Court and about 200-300 EDL supporters came to give Kev a bit of backing. I bottled it that day. Because it was in Luton town centre, and because I knew all the local Muslim characters would be there, and because they all knew who I was, I didn't show up. I didn't want everyone knowing it was me behind the fledgling EDL. In a way, it was cowardly I suppose. I remember being pissed off with myself for not going there to stand by him. I told Kev I was ill and I left him to front everything up, which he did in man-size fashion. I remember watching video coverage of it the next day and thinking, 'Fucking hell Kev, you've got balls'.

He walked out of court and all the EDL supporters and the media were there. He gave a speech about the case, about the police taking him to court. All the EDL supporters walked through the town centre and I remember watching it on the news. I knew pretty much everyone there, on both sides of the divide. There was a big Muslim presence too. It wasn't organised in the sense of a confrontation, but their community can just gather those numbers in a matter of minutes and I think that's what happened in response to the EDL support for Kev.

Suddenly the police were faced with coming up with some form of containment strategy in the middle of Luton, so they effectively locked off the middle of the town, separating the two groups. I remember watching it and thinking that everyone I knew was there – and I wasn't. I'd let everyone down, including myself, but especially Kev.

When the BBC got in touch about the rapid growth of the EDL and said they wanted to produce a documentary 'Young, British and Angry', Kev was the first person to step up. That played a big part in establishing the movement and if he hadn't done that, perhaps things wouldn't have continued growing the way they did. Meanwhile I'd been hiding behind false names and balaclavas and there was Kev, brave and bold as you like, facing the world.

Still with Kev's character and the courts, I should mention the one time that things turned out well for him, and which highlights a lot of what we were regularly up against with the police.

There was a well publicised incident 12 months later, on Armistice Day, when hate preacher Anjem Choudary's group calling themselves Muslims Against Crusades – as opposed to the also outlawed Al Muhajiroun – planned a poppy burning protest in London during the two-minute silence. A group of us went to London and I travelled with Kev and another of the lads, Keir. We got off the train and the police were immediately into everyone. They stopped and searched and then arrested Keir, but we managed to dodge them. The protest was at the Albert Memorial, but about 300 of the lads met up at a pub in King's Cross and we went across town from there.

Choudary had made public that he was going to disrupt the two minute silence and if I'm being totally honest, with all that had gone on over the past couple of years I couldn't believe that the police would actually let him.

Let him? They might as well have cheered him on.

They had Choudary and all his radicals penned in, but then we found that the police had reserved another pen for us. I told them we weren't going in – it wasn't our protest. We were just there to honour the occasion.

You can imagine how much difference my opinion made. I approached one copper and asked him what all this was about, letting these haters disrupt what was supposed to be a solemn, respectful event. 'It's freedom of speech mate,' was the best he could manage.

At that I just slipped off on my own. These fanatics were screaming, 'British soldiers burn in hell' and I just had to at least try to do something about it. They were waving the black terror flag which now symbolises ISIS. I climbed up onto a ledge about 40-feet above the crowd, making my way past the police cordon. It was all a bit Tom Cruise, Mission Impossible, but when I climbed down, a bunch of security blokes were waiting for me. Except where they then placed me was right in the middle of the police cordon.

I couldn't stand quietly by and watch these traitors insult our war dead, completely disrespect the country they were leeching off. So I put my hood up and ran and jumped over the barrier straight into the middle of Choudary and his fanatics. Somebody had to show them not everyone was happy to stand silently by. What's more, the fact that fat little old Tommy could manage to hurdle those barriers still gets me a drink in some pubs! Check it out on Youtube under 'Tommy Robinson poppy burning'. Pretty impressive athletic ability for a little fat geezer, if I say so myself!

There was a bit of a fracas, but once the police followed me in and dragged me away they stopped the protest, so I suppose I succeeded in achieving something.

But then I was arrested and charged with assaulting a police officer, which once more was complete and utter bollocks. I was only saved from a probable 3-4 year prison sentence – given my previous offence – because a tv cameraman had the entire incident on film. When they hit me with that charge he let me have the footage. Yet another case based on police lies, thrown out of court.

Afterwards, as I was sitting in the police station looking out of the window a van pulled up – and getting out was Kev again. I couldn't help but laugh. They'd arrested him for affray or violent disorder; some such bollocks. They said he picked up a metal crash barrier and threw it at the police, which I must say was completely out of character for him. He'd have his day on that one though. Then they took him away for a strip search for good measure, which would completely ruin his day.

That night when they let us out and I got home, my missus had her nan round and she wasn't impressed. 'Again,' she said. 'You've been arrested. Again.' And I said, 'They were burning poppies, what were we supposed to do?'

She said, 'It's too late, they've taken over.'

I just couldn't get that, I couldn't understand that. I told her that if everyone had had that attitude in the 1930s we'd all be talking German.

That incident at the Albert Memorial and the charges they tried to make stick contributed to a bigger picture with all of these repeated, picky little something-or-nothing arrests like the time in Bury Park when they tried to do me for possessing a motor that was supposedly a ringer, but never was.

None of it made much sense until I got taken to court for an incident at a demo in Blackburn. On that occasion I got in a scrap with a far right idiot who had no place being there, and when it came to court the police produced a dossier to try to have an ASBO – Anti-Social Behaviour Order – enforced against me.

They were building all this bullshit up to try get me banned from not only attending EDL demos, but from associating with the group at all. An ASBO, with almost limitless scope to restrict an individual, would have solved all their problems in one go. Thankfully the judge saw it for what it was, an attempt to silence freedom of speech and freedom of congregation, and refused it, point blank.

They were building all of these things up in order to keep me away from any form of public protest. We were not breaking the law, but we were seriously inconveniencing the police. So what better than an ASBO? It's what we'd petitioned for after the UPL demo, to try to have the Muslim extremists stopped from preaching in town.

If you break the ASBO, you can be away to jail which makes the law happy either way – whether or not you've committed a crime worthy of being locked up, which I hadn't. They'd already 'got' Kev for swearing at the Luton homecoming parade and I think they reasoned that they'd knock something together on the poppy burning too – except that it didn't work out too well on that occasion.

I'd noticed that every time we were in court, there was one police officer, a Detective Constable Hearing, who was apparently involved in public order issues for Scotland

Yard. Every time I was in court – anywhere – I'd look and this bloke would be sitting back there, watching.

I used to wonder what he was doing, but it was part of a co-ordinated attempt to make our lives as difficult as possible. For instance when they put Kev on trial for throwing that metal barrier, it was scheduled for the same day that I was in court for the incident with the far right idiot at Blackburn. It meant we couldn't be there to support each other and any EDL support for us would be split too.

They'd put Kev through it over that charge – five court visits over 12 months, with a 2-4 year sentence hanging over his head. On the day of the trial, both of his defence witnesses bottled it, texting to say they wouldn't be coming to give evidence. His heart must have been in his boots.

In Kev's case, five officers were called to give evidence. They stood and took the oath and said one by one that he had picked up a metal crash barrier and thrown it at them. Except the meatheads hadn't done their homework very well this time. They hadn't sat down and fabricated their statements as expertly as they might usually, because Kev's barrister ripped them to shreds.

In court, on the Bible, the evidence of every single one was different. One said that Kev picked the barrier up over his head; one said he threw it to the side. Etcetera, etcetera.

The female judge actually gave them a bollocking, and she threw the case out.

No luck there then – so then the police raided his house and arrested him on a poxy minor charge about public order bullshit, the same as they eventually did to me.

When my case for assaulting a police officer at the poppy burning came up, my solicitor told me to not even bother attending court. We had that video footage of the entire incident and yes, I jumped over the barriers, but in no way did I assault a policeman and the video showed all of it. The case was thrown out as my solicitor predicted.

A happy ending then? You'd think so, wouldn't you? But it takes more than truth and a court to keep a determined copper down. Four weeks later they came and arrested me again over the same incident and this time charged me with a public order offence, like Kev. They said that when I jumped the fence I caused distress and alarm to those Muslims burning the poppies. They also arrested a couple of the Muslim protestors too.

The courts fined the poppy burners £50. They fined me £350 for upsetting the poor little sensitive sweethearts.

Good old British justice, eh?

AS MUCH AS A lot of the focus around the EDL has been on me – good or bad – Kevin Carroll was front and centre during those early days. Later, when things started falling apart for me personally and the EDL generally, Kev was right there for me, as he always had been. He might not have been though. Not at all. I've mentioned my half-a-dozen Osman warnings for death threats, but there was no warning letter on one particular occasion when Kev had a close shave – just a knock on the door.

I got a call from Kev's wife. Someone had been to their house in the middle of Farley Hill and banged on the front door. Kev looked out of the window and saw someone walking away. It seemed this person had thrown something at the door and left, so Kev waited a minute, then thought he'd go see what was happening.

He got in his van and drove to the end of the road and there was a bloke walking with his hood up. Kev pulled over and asked him if he'd seen any kids messing about, as anyone might. But when the bloke turned round, he was clearly a Muslim. And he put his hand inside his hoodie at which point Kev thought that something wasn't quite right.

He started to walk towards Kev, who immediately shot off in the van, racing back to his house, and as he pulled up on the driveway and got out, he saw and heard his wife screaming at the window.

The Muslim assassin was running after him – and by now it was plain to see that he had a shotgun. Kev legged it away from his house with this geezer chasing him, but not getting close enough that he'd be in range for the shotgun. If he got within 20 yards, then Kevin was in some serious shit. You can picture this big middle-aged bloke running like Linford Christie with a would-be killer after him.

Kev jumped over a fence trying to get away, smashed his foot, broke his toe in six places and popped his right knee out. So he was cursing having hurdled this fence with his leg in agony, while on the other side of the fence the Son of Bin Laden couldn't both climb it and carry the shotgun at the same time. Afterwards, all Kev could go on about was his toe. You should have seen the size of it. He looked like Shrek with a bad case of gout. We laughed our arses off.

On the serious side, his wife had rung the police and they sent armed officers and automatically sent some to my house too. It was about midnight and I had my whole road swarming with armed cops, who, I could tell, didn't believe a word of what Kev had said happened.

This was a few days before our biggest demonstration to date, the Luton Homecoming of 2010, and I could tell they didn't believe it. But when they got round to their door-to-door inquiries on Kev's street they got four independent witnesses to verify it. It was about 24 hours later that they realised the shit was actually serious.

At that point they called both of us to arrange a meeting with senior officers and offered to give us new identities and put us in a protection programme. But of course that would mean relocating our families and they said we'd need to completely cease contact with the EDL. They told us we could never be involved with the organisation and would have to keep quiet forever and a day.

We were in Kev's when they came to make the offer and the police were sitting there when my mobile phone rang, and I answered it on loudspeaker. It was Muslims and they were saying stuff like, 'You fucking dead, you fucking pussy'. The police chief was sitting there and I simply told him that I got that every day.

Kev and I told them we weren't interested in a new identity, that it wasn't happening, which was obviously a big disappointment, if only because it would have made a lot of their problems go away on a local level.

In the event they put an armed guard on our houses for a week and, after that, they left police cars on our drives for about a month. On one hand it was good to have the police there, because I can't say I'm overly impressed with some of the ways they have reacted to threats against me, but on the other hand you can imagine how the neighbours took it.

Where I was living at the time, in this quiet little cul-de-sac, no one knew who I was. My daughter had just started nursery, and the woman who ran it lived in our road. My wife was hysterical over it all. You can understand why.

They put out a witness appeal for this bloke with the shotgun but all we got were accusations from the far left that it was all made up for publicity purposes, that it didn't happen. They should have seen Kev's toe!

After that, the police put fireproof letterboxes on our houses and gave us a range of security measure like panic buttons – but the bastards still managed to torch Kev's van on another occasion.

Kev, being the boy scout he is, had CCTV set up all over his house. He was just sitting at home when two Muslim lads set fire to the tyres of his van, directly outside the house. He actually thought the house next door was on fire and the CCTV footage shows him come hurtling out in his dressing gown with a fire extinguisher. He thought he was going to have to pull old Mr and Mrs Smith or whoever out of their blazing gaff, but he ended up running round his own van in his dressing gown putting his own burning tyres out. We howled laughing when we saw that, which a lot of people might think is ridiculous – but it's one of those things. If you didn't laugh you'd go mad, or you'd have a breakdown.

It was only when Kev checked the CCTV later that he saw they'd first tried to pour it through his letter box, which luckily was now screwed down. They were trying to burn the house down with people inside.

People are always giving me shit for using a false name and I tell them, they have not got a clue. If you knew Kevin Carroll in Luton, then you knew exactly where he lived, and that bloke did it all with his head up, without hiding.

I'm the one more likely to fly off the handle, which may or may not be a bit of the 'little man' syndrome, but Kev has ... I don't know, a presence? If you're in his company, he can impress you without having to be all mouth like some people. He had a massive presence with the lads, with the EDL followers as well. He was never one of the football crowd, because he never needed that in his life. He was, he just is, a pretty together bloke.

Once I finally got my head around what this thing needed to be, what had to be done with the EDL, it became a completely solid thing between the two of us. It was a great combination. Kev didn't need the ego trip of being leader. He was just about the cause, the idealism of what we were doing.

When I see him now, Kev will occasionally look at me and shake his head, and say that it was all completely mad – as though he needs someone to name-check him and say, 'Yes brother, you were completely off your head'.

But he was the man you wanted at your side, in anything. When we got nicked in Switzerland for the FIFA protest, we were together. He never flinched, if the point we were making was right. There probably was a madness to it all at times, when everything seemed to be getting out of hand, and it appeared to be bigger than us.

But I always knew that if I was going to get killed in and amongst the madness, then Kev was willing to get killed and vice versa. We sort of bounced off each other and kept one another going. He was the sensible one, such as you can have someone sensible in the middle of all that madness.

When it all went down, when I got locked up and literally thrown to the wolves in the prison system, there was only one man in the world I'd have wanted with me. But it turned out that he was also going through completely unnecessary shit on the outside.

Kevin Carroll is a top bloke. And boy is he funny. Even if he has a completely fucked up toe and a dodgy knee.

12: ME AND THE MEDIA

A LOT IS MADE of the names I've used over the years, about the attempts to maintain anonymity, to keep some measure of privacy – it's been a long time since that was a realistic goal though. But given what my family have been subjected to since, is it a surprise that I tried?

There's usually a story or a reason behind the stunts we pulled in the early years of the UPL and EDL – and stories behind the various names I've used over the years too. All I can say now is that they seemed like good ideas at the time. Clearly, some weren't as clever as I'd imagined.

It's tough enough having predictable enemies, whether they are radical Islamic extremists or far-left Socialists, the Marxist headbangers from UAF. At least with that lot you know who the enemy are. In terms of establishing the EDL as a mainstream protest group however, our biggest enemies were the supposedly impartial British press and our own government and lawmakers. From that day, pretty much to this (with a few honourable exceptions) the media coverage of the UPL/EDL and even my current situation has been at best lazy and ignorant, at worst politically motivated and malicious.

From our point of view, going back to that first demo as the United People of Luton, we met up and we had our placards and signs, prominent among which were ones that said 'National Front go to hell.' Sure, we were opposed to what Muslim extremists and gangsters were doing to our town and our children, but there was very clearly never any sympathy with or any time for the far right. I know, I keep going on ... but maybe if I say it enough times it might sink into some thick skulls eventually.

I thought that it was so, so clear what we were about – and then when I picked up my local newspaper, the Luton

News, straight from the get-go, it called us all far right extremists. And I thought, 'What the hell are these people on about?' I just couldn't get it.

All we wanted to do on that first demo was walk through town, to hold a minute's silence. That's all we tried to do – show that most ordinary Luton people supported our troops, as opposed to wanting them to burn in hell.

With the benefit of experience I realise that it was a simple knee-jerk reaction by a bunch of amateurs. Straight away we were being called far right extremists. They'd either forgotten about all the anti-NF signs or, more likely, they'd chosen to ignore them. It was as though it didn't matter what you were saying or doing, that's who 'they' had decided you were. Pigeon-holed and labelled – far right. Racist, extremist. Thug, for good, lazy measure. That would apply equally to our mums, wives and our grandmothers, no doubt.

For sure, we were a bunch of mostly blokes who resembled a crowd of football hooligans a bit too much for some people. I get that. And with good reason too – because we mostly were. But we were standing up as patriots, as working class and rough and ready as we were. There wasn't much that was complicated about it.

We objected to the Islamification of our country and, given what we're still seeing happen not just around the country but around the world, is that really such a bad thing? Is making that point some form of disease? Is it a criminal act in itself? It would seem so, even though we weren't attacking anyone, blowing up anyone – and certainly not beheading anyone.

It appears to me that for as long as this island has been a nation state, the working class have been very much appreciated when it came to giving them a gun, shoving them in a trench and sending them off to die on the orders of the snooty and superior upper classes.

However when that same working class sees alien ideologies taking over its communities, when its own families are being racially victimised, and when entire areas are effectively being ethnically cleansed of non-Muslim people, the working class are suddenly the bad guys for standing up and speaking out against it.

Am I missing something? Please, educate me if I am. I'm all ears – and I have never refused to debate these topics with people, even when I've walked in with my eyes open, knowing that I'm about to get ambushed by the metropolitan liberal elite. I can usually see a 'let's gang up on Tommy' set-up coming these days, but it wasn't always the case.

I wasn't much of a newspaper reader back in the days of the UPL and the start of the EDL. I didn't watch News at Ten, Question Time or Newsnight, a programme that I'd soon find myself being invited to appear on.

At the time I remember wondering what it was all about, all this mud-slinging at us, this stereotyping. I thought maybe they were just mistaken, that we'd been ... I don't know, unlucky. That our message just hadn't been sophisticated enough. But no, I don't think we could have done anything to affect the prejudice. They were just lazy, the vast majority of the media – and not very clever either.

The wake-up call wasn't long coming. The first real shocks for me came with a couple of different experiences. For starters, I didn't know about right wing and left wing newspapers. Really. I had no idea. I didn't know about the Guardian basically being the PR-wing of the Communist Party. I didn't have any interest in it.

I mention the Guardian because I was asked by them first, when it all started, to go and have a meeting, to talk. It was one of the very first interviews I did, and I brought my mates Isaac – he's Little Craigy who got his teeth knocked out by the mounted police officer – Benji and

Dorsett. It was in Luton at the Brache Restaurant – a nice place. It becomes a bit of a theme in my story, but basically that was the start of my mindset that at least we were going to get a free meal out of the arseholes who wanted to use us, if nothing else.

I went to the meeting at a time when no one yet really knew who I was. So I turned up with my three pals – and they were three black lads. Now you couldn't miss these boys, especially Dorsett, who's about 6ft 5ins. He's younger than me, but growing up in Luton he was probably one of the handiest blokes around town.

I didn't know who or what the Guardian was about, so I was talking about everything that was going on in Luton, just blabbing it all out, all the social problems, all the street radicalisation, everything – the reasons why we were doing what we were doing. And then the newspaper article came out and I was looking at it, thinking, 'What the fuck, what's this geezer on about?'

And he basically, again, called me, called us, racists. He completely did not mention the fact that I'd turned up with three black men who were clearly my close friends. These blokes weren't my minders, they were my mates.

I just couldn't get it. I couldn't understand it because they were blindly lying. And that was my first experience of the Guardian, my first experience of the national press.

Then when I started speaking to other people, telling them about how I'd been stitched up, they couldn't believe it – not the Guardian! You didn't talk to the Guardian!

I didn't know what they meant. I couldn't understand how there could be a bona fide, highly regarded national newspaper dedicated to smearing people, to smearing anyone who had an opinion that didn't match theirs.

Talk about being wet behind the ears!

This was in the early days. It was rather like a fast-track apprenticeship in understanding the world beyond Luton.

It still seems perverse to me, the way that taking pride in the cross of St George and the Union Jack suddenly makes you at best a far right bigot, at worst a violent Nazi.

I sometimes think these left-wing anti-Brits must stare and stare at our national flag, thinking that if they do it long enough they'll eventually see a swastika emerging from it. How did our country ever get to that point, where simple patriotism and a respect for our heritage, values and tradition, could be deliberately warped into something nasty and perverse?

I was having to grow up fast in terms of understanding the media agenda, from my hometown paper to the national press. Again, if you watch the UPL demo online, you hear everyone shouting, 'We are Luton town'. Everyone was from Luton. That's what it was about.

But the newspaper, the politicians, they all made statements saying that outsiders came into Luton to stir up trouble. There were no outsiders. Me and my pals were running it, we knew who was there. And afterwards we sat round asking each other, 'What do they mean outsiders? We're all from Luton.'

Having lived through so many similar experiences since, I don't think it was a particular plot against me or the EDL. I really do just put it down to shit journalists and lazy attitudes of a great number of not very intelligent people – with politicians first and foremost. In a race to the deep end of the stupid pool, they and the journalists would probably drown hand in hand. A dead heat if you like.

In those early days we were made to feel we were not even part of the fabric that made up the town. I remember watching the head of Luton's Labour council, Hazel Simmons, announcing that all of these outsiders were not welcome in Luton. I actually had to stop and wonder what she was going on about? What did she mean, that we were not welcome in Luton? All we were trying to do was rally public support for our troops because of what the council and police had just let happen to our soldiers, in front of the watching world. So we had the Luton News, the Guardian, and then the picture in a national tabloid from the Birmingham demo – the one of, 'A fascist being kicked by anti-fascists' – and I think that was the worst.

From there things got progressively worse. Predictably, disappointingly, stupidly worse. It was like an infectious rash. Once one newspaper, politician or television station said it, the next one along had to find something shittier to say about us, some more extreme way to describe us. I have been called a Nazi so many times in the media – usually by The Sun, even when I kicked Nazis out of the EDL, literally having to fight and get myself in even more trouble, trying to keep them away. And then even when I left the EDL, they still called me a Nazi, a fascist, a racist.

So if your question is, can I trust the press? My question back to you is this – would you? At least when I am interviewed live the words are quite clearly mine, even if I make a complete bollocks of saying what I mean.

Well, I say that. It might be true of a news interview, but when you let someone into your confidence, to try to form an impartial, measured view of your life, as I did for the Channel 4 Proud and Prejudiced documentary, you leave yourself at the hand of the videotape editors. And they can be much worse than the ignorant bastards on the Fleet Street newsdesks.

I TOOK TOM COSTELLO basically into my family for more than a year, let him become a part of my life while he filmed and produced a Channel 4 documentary which I thought was meant to be about what was happening in Luton. When it emerged it was titled Proud and Prejudiced.

I've been hugely naïve I suppose in dealing with the media over the years, but I'd like to think that shows that I don't feel I've got anything to hide. I wear my heart on my sleeve, too much at times, and I say what I think. You'd like to believe that that measure of honesty would be respected, but it hasn't generally worked out that way for me.

I often passed Tom Costello off as a friend, a family member even, and I took him everywhere with me – just so that he could make a name for himself, in essence. Because that's what he did. He puffed his pathetic chest out while shitting on me from a great height.

Tom graduated from Oxford and in fairness I knew from the start that he was very left wing and had been involved in anti-capitalist marches and stuff. But I liked him, and I really took him in. I gave him open access, so much so that I invited him to my wedding. I thought a man that intelligent would be open to seeing another viewpoint and I didn't think I had anything to hide.

He'd spend a day or two with us every couple of weeks and we'd be on the phone regularly. He actually said that his peers, in private schools and at Oxford and Cambridge, had no experience whatsoever of a life like this.

He said they wouldn't be able to understand the sense of community that we had. Tom came out with us one Friday night to the pub, with the lads, and he said he'd never experienced anything like it, that he'd had a great time, in a community where everyone knows each other and looks after each other. He was 23 or 24 and had never stepped out into our real world.

The very first time he came on a demo I went into an off-licence and came out with a litre of 'vodka' which I necked then screamed, 'Now I'm ready to demo!' That was the Tommy Robinson caricature he'd come to see. I think he was getting a hard on over it. I told him later – it was only water in the vodka bottle, Tom, you muppet.

I wanted him to see a 360-degree picture of life in Luton so I rang up Bingo, a Pakistani Muslim who is involved heavily in their gang stuff and I asked him what was happening, what was going on. He asked where I was, I told him the Bird and Bush pub and he pulled into the car park with a couple of other Muslim lads.

I told Tom we'd get in their car and I would introduce him as my cousin, from out of town, and whatever he did not to mention that he was a journalist. So we got in the car with these Muslim hard cases and we were laughing and joking with them for about an hour, having a crack about the EDL.

Tom sat watching and listening to it all, and when we got out of the car he simply couldn't believe what he'd seen and heard. That Tommy Robinson was mates with these Muslim lads. It was a way of showing him that I grew up in this town, that I could do that all day with Muslims – some Muslims – but that we were always going to differ on our opinion of Islam.

Another time I was in a car with Bingo when a police car pulled up, and this copper shone a torch in to find me sitting in the car with three Pakistanis. You should have seen the police officer's face. It was a picture.

I showed Tom so much of what was going on. When we went to Blackburn and it all kicked off with the Nazis trying to hang on the EDL's coattails, he got back on the bus and he was white with fright. Lots of the lads were covered in blood – from fighting the National Front – and he was the one who was scared shitless. He said, 'I can't believe you're fighting the far right, you're actually fighting fascism'. He was completely thrown by it. I simply told him, 'That's right Tom, because we're not fascists'.

ALL THE WAY through the production of that documentary, he told me there would be no voice over, that it was literally going to be compiled from the real-life footage they had gathered. When it came to editing it, he called and said that I came across as 'too good', whatever that meant, and there were a few issues to discuss.

Tom booked hotel rooms and took a few of us out on a piss-up on the company bank card. It was a proper bender. Except that the deceitful bastard had hidden cameras in the room, so he could get me off guard and get some soundbites painting me in a less than favourable light. Strike one. Then he told me they were putting a voice-over on the documentary after all, so of course it turned into a complete hatchet job.

All the way through, Tom said the documentary was about Luton and its problems, but it was nothing of the sort, it was this fabricated conflict featuring me and Sayful Islam as opposite sides of this prejudiced spectrum – Proud and Prejudiced. Such as I could laugh about it later, I said that I was the Proud one, Sayful was the Prejudiced.

Through friends of friends I got to see it before it aired. I phoned Tom Costello about a scene where I was walking through town at 1am, steaming, and I was wearing a CP Company coat, which was hooded with goggles – I looked like a frog. And I was joking, saying 'ribbit, ribbit'. A load of beer and a shit joke. But when I saw the documentary they'd inserted sub-titles suggesting I was saying 'Breivik' – and then cut the piece in right after a segment about the leader of the Norwegian Defence League coming to Luton. I had met him and we'd talked about what was happening in Norway, with that maniac Anders Breivik. Tom must have gone to some lengths to try to screw me on that.

I told him he was a cheeky bastard, and asked him what he thought I'd said. He said 'ribbit'. It was the only thing in the whole programme they put a sub-title on.

The little shit was pathetic, saying none of it was his fault, and that I came across too well, that leaving out the part about burning poppies was nothing to do with him, blah blah blah. Pathetic little arsehole.

And then to cap it all, when the documentary aired, Channel 4 sent him away on holiday 'for protection' – in case I was pissed off with him. He was having a right laugh, getting a free holiday, because Channel 4 thought I'd come looking for him. What a bunch of pathetic drama queens.

Too right I was annoyed, but these people live in a dream world. They get shit-scared of their own shadows. No matter, I would get to confront the weasel anyway.

I heard there was a talk at the British Film Institute in London about Proud and Prejudiced, fronted by Costello. I managed to wangle three tickets and one of my mates went in with a camera, posing as a journalist.

My disguise was a beauty though. Me and my pal Benji, a big Ghanaian lad, went down to Bury Park and I hid in the car while he went into a Muslim clothes shop to buy a burkha – the full mashings, face veil, gloves, everything. He said he was getting it for his sister.

So, I dressed up in that gear and me and Benji headed off in a taxi, and as cars pulled up alongside us, I'd be flipping them the finger – a Muslim woman in the full rig. You should have seen the look on the other drivers' faces – a little Muslim lady giving them the finger. They couldn't see me pissing myself laughing behind the niqab.

I walked down Oxford Street five steps behind Benji, as though I was his missis, muttering 'Allahu Akbar' or 'get fucked' to passers-by from behind this niqab. I was laughing my arse off behind that veil. We breezed straight into the BFI event, past security, and I sat three rows back from the front while Costello did his speech.

The room was full of up and coming journalists, and I sat watching this bloke acting like he'd been under cover in the EDL for two years. He talked about a friend of mine, Jim McDaid, who served for 14 years in the military, a proper, stand up guy, a decent bloke. And here was Costello saying that Tommy had a bodyguard with him all the time, who always carried a gun. And I was sitting there thinking, 'You bullshitting little prick'.

He was up there, bigging himself up, loving the limelight, while I sat in my head-to-toe burkha, behind my niqab, biting my lip. Then it came to the Q&As and Benji put his hand up. He asked, 'Is Tommy Robinson a racist?'

Costello paused then replied, 'Yes, clearly he is a racist'. At that point I just stood up and ripped the niqab off, and I put my hand up to Benji, standing next to me, who grasped hold of it.

I said, 'A racist Tom? How fucking dare you, when you've spent all that time with me? You've seen the way I live my life, you've met all my friends!'

The whole room held its breath. He'd been tearing Tommy Robinson apart for an hour – and Tommy had been sitting quietly listening to it all. The little prick was pathetic. 'Tommy, can we go outside and chat?' he whined.

And I said, 'Let's chat here, let's sit here Tom and chat about what you've just told these people.'

I said to Benji, 'Am I a racist bruv?'

Costello started saying that I was out of order, but the only one being naughty in that room was Tom Costello with his self-serving fantasies.

When he came outside we went into the hallway and this security guard had the nerve to say that he knew all along that it was a man under the burkha when we went in. He probably did – and he was too scared of causing offence to do his job and stop me. That could have been a massive security breach, a real threat, but the burkha trumps everything in modern Britain. Costello couldn't stop saying sorry and going on about how badly he felt.

But what I wanted to know was why he never said that almost all of Tommy Robinson's mates are sons of immigrants, and that everywhere he goes, black men shake his hand? Why wouldn't he say that actually Tommy

Robinson has got lots of Muslim friends? He didn't have an answer. He couldn't stop saying sorry.

I'd invited him to my wedding and my family members had told me not to trust him because he was a journalist. But I did trust him. And I ended up looking like a complete wanker for doing so.

ONE OF THE frustrating things about dealing with the media was experiencing the universal cowardice of people who completely agree with the stand the EDL was taking, but daren't speak up themselves.

When I was interviewed on ITV's Daybreak, people followed me outside to shake my hand and encourage me to carry on with what we were doing. But would they ever admit to doing that, to voicing their support? Never.

I did a BBC show and afterwards an older lady approached me and said she was so sorry for what was happening to me. I was waiting to meet another journalist and she said exactly the same, that they were all behind us. It was heartening to an extent I suppose, but one of these days all of those people are going to have to make a decision about exactly how much they care, how much support they're willing to give in public.

At least when you're on live television, you live and die by your own words and efforts. I don't mind being put on the spot and grilled by people like Jeremy Paxman and Andrew Neil. I respect those people for challenging you robustly. That's their job. I might not be as articulate and well spoken as them, but I can put across my views clearly enough. I can stand up for myself.

On one occasion the BBC had me on Radio 4 during the week, and because it was live, I got all of my points across. Talk about the shit hitting the fan! The Guardian, all these left wing groups and newspapers, they had a mass pant-wetting moment. They were completely disgusted that I wasn't properly challenged on my views. Someone published 10 points about things I should have been put on the spot over. It was stuff like my different names, my criminal record – nothing at all to do with the points I was raising, just a personal onslaught aimed at me.

As a result of the backlash Andrew Neil invited me on his Sunday Politics show and put those 10 points to me. He also had picture after picture of EDL supporters with their arms in the air – they were chanting – and what he said was, 'Nazi salute, Nazi salute'.

I just sat there and told him to show me one video of someone doing a Nazi salute. Not a photo, a video. Anyone with their arm in the air could be stitched up like that. When I got home I tweeted Andrew Neil pictures of Barack Obama doing a Nazi salute, Katie Perry doing a Nazi salute – even one of him, Andrew Neil doing a Nazi salute, and I asked what he had to say about it? Not much, in truth.

Some time later he interviewed one of the leaders of the Muslim Council of Britain and in fairness he tore him to pieces. I do think that's something that has changed recently, because a few years ago those characters got a soft ride everywhere they went.

I was incredibly nervous when I went on Newsnight with Jeremy Paxman. It was following a bunch of Unite Against Fascism tweets and they were frothing with excitement at the prospect of Tommy Robinson being destroyed by attack-dog Paxo. Sadly for them it went alright and the next day the Daily Mail said, 'The articulate young leader of the English Defence League made Jeremy Paxman look average'.

I felt pretty pleased with myself about that, I have to say. And, in typical style, I bent the BBC's arms up their backs for a slap-up meal for me and my pals before the show. When they invited me on, I told them I wanted travel for four, plus a meal at a restaurant called the Meat

Company, opposite their studios. They said they couldn't do that so I said fine, see you later, and I hung up.

There was a bit of a stand off, but they wanted me in the studio, so we got our meal. It's about £60 for a steak at that place and we maxed it. Well, they got enough out of me.

When we went into the green room my mates were all getting on the booze, and I was so nervous that I wanted to hit the bottle with them, but Paxman came in for a chat and told me not to be nervous – because this was my first big thing. He was really nice. At least he was until we went on air.

At one point I thought he was trying to belittle me, so I asked if he knew anyone addicted to heroin that had been peddled to them by Muslim gangs? Did he know anyone who'd been murdered by Muslim gangs? Any young girls, or family relatives, who had been sexually abused or raped by Muslim gangs? I told him, on every point – you don't and I do. I told him that I didn't expect him to 'get it', but I did expect him to listen.

And at that he sat back. And afterwards, as soon as we went off air, he said, 'Do you know what, when you said that' – and everyone in the studio was there – he said, 'I can't begin to think about it. Neither can any of us.'

He was very fair. And what I took most satisfaction from was that all the left wing lunatics were absolutely raging, because they'd thought I was going to fail miserably. I was learning, learning on the job.

NOT EVERY TELEVISION experience was a winner though. Tom Costello stitched me up on Proud and Prejudiced and I got ambushed on the BBC3 Free Speech programme by a couple of clowns. One of them is an incredibly ignorant woman Saira Khan, whose career was 'made' by being on The Apprentice, and some rapper geezer, Akala. It was all pretty much a let's-get-Tommy party,

LONG JOURNEY:
From the mean streets of Luton (above), where me, Keir and our friends had to hide behind balaclacas on the UPL demo, to addressing 40,000 Pegida supporters at their anniversary rally in Dresden in October 2015
© GETTY IMAGES

FLYING HER FLAG:
A young Russian girl leads the EDL's first Dudley demo, carrying a national flag to commemorate atrocities her family had suffered

WELCOME TO LUTON BIRTHPLACE OF THE ENGLISH DEFENCE LEAGUE

BROTHERS IN ARMS: Me and Kev Carroll - the bravest, most loyal bloke you could meet

POPPY PROTEST: Being arrested in London after disrupting Anjem Choudary's poppy burning. If a tv cameraman hadn't secretly given me footage showing there was no assault on a police officer, I'd have probably got 3-4 years. They tell big lies, YOUR police

AMERICAN FRIENDS: With Robert Spencer, Kevin Carroll and Pamela Geller

TOP OF THE WORLD: On the roof of the Fifa HQ in Zurich, protesting at England not being allowed to wear the poppy on their shirts

IN FLAMES: An attack on my car and a neighbour's house, plus the burning of a swastika for the national media

DISTORTION: 'Anti-fascists attack a fascist' said the press (left) when Muslims rioted in Birmingham. Note the guy jumping at the kid's head. Not a great photo (below) but that's me in the burkha with Benji, before confronting Tom Costello at the British Film Institute

M25 SHOWDOWN: The back of our Luton van was opened to be greeted by what felt like half of the Metropolitan Police

NO SURRENDER: Addressing the EDL 'troops' in a combat jacket presented to me by one of our heroes who served in Afghanistan

ENGLISH DEFENCE LEAGUE

TOWER HAMLETS TRAVESTY: The police allowed Kev Carroll to be assaulted on camera, before a senior female officer stopped us and ordered our arrest for 'obstructing the police'. The charge was thrown out ... again

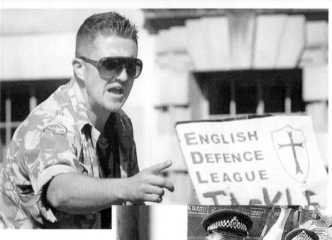

VOICE OF REASON: When the police co-operated with us in organising and stewarding EDL demos we largely managed to avoid confrontation and trouble – something the UAF rabble-rousers always looked for

TOWERING TURN-OUT: EDL protestors pack the length of London's Tower Bridge

IN DIGSUISE: 'Rabbi Benjamin Kidemon' greets the crowd in Tower Hamlets – before stripping off the hat and fake beard to address the crowd

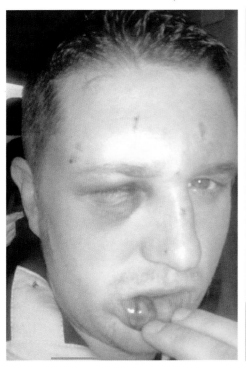

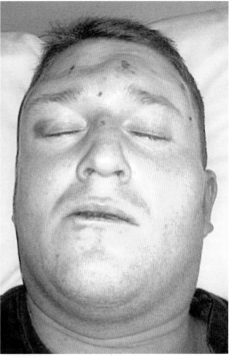

THE PRICE OF FREE SPEECH: A number of times I've been attacked by Muslim gangs just going about my daily life. And that's without the state trying to have me killed when in their 'care' as at Woodhill prison

FLOWERS FOR LEE: Paying tribute to Drummer Lee Rigby at the Luton staging of the nationwide Walk for Lee

MOVING ON:
Usama Hasan (above) is
a very intelligent and
well-meaning member of the
Quilliam Foundation. This
was the occasion of me
and Kev quitting the EDL

WAR OF WORDS:
A disagreement in Newcastle
with Mohammed Ansar while
filming When Tommy Met Mo.
Everything had to
revolve around him. A joke

LUTON
LOONIES:
Sayful Islam
(far left)
and his fellow
dress-wearing
coward, the
ginger convert
Ibrahim
Anderson

PART OF THE UNION: Being interviewed at the Oxford Union – finally

WELCOME HOME: Being attacked by Muslims in Luton (below) while trying to show a Times journalist around the town

THE BOYS: Out with the lads for a few drinks on Remembrance Sunday, November 2015

Welcome to Luton
↑ Walkway to Town Centre

which mostly consisted of everyone calling me a racist and then refusing to answer a single question I put to them.

One 'reasonable' member of the audience suggested they put me on an island and bomb it with anthrax – and everyone cheered. And the guy who said it? Apparently he worked in schools in Newcastle, educating kids about Islam.

But do you know what? More than a quarter of a million people watched that on Youtube, if not live, and the last time I looked there were 8,000 comments attached to the clip, overwhelmingly in favour of my position. I suppose, if you look at it like that, letting the far left scream their hatred works as good as any message of ours. They show themselves up for what they are – they're the extremist bigots, not us.

Before I went in for that BBC3 Free Speech show I met the producer from Question Time, and he asked me what I was expecting. I said I knew exactly what was going to happen – that the whole place was going to gang up on me and that I'd come off as the victim ... so let's go!

They sat me in the audience, and when I came off, he asked how it went and I said that it was exactly as I wanted it to go – because every normal person watching that at home would be frustrated and angry about the stitch up.

It's almost a price worth paying, to be subject to the abuse, and at other times get hit or punched on camera. Because it doesn't just prove a point about the nature of these so-called 'peace-loving' lefties and Muslims, it takes ordinary people into a world they don't know. It shows them what's going on out there. The biggest task we have is to open people's eyes to what's going on, whether that's on our streets, or rooted in the prejudice of the establishment.

After that show I was walking through Luton town centre, just going to get a jacket potato for lunch, and a woman came up and said she was frothing, completely angry at that 'Free Speech' programme.

Mission accomplished, I thought. These peace-lovers are full of their own hate, and they can't even see it.

MOST PEOPLE WOULD agree that the beginning of the end for the BNP and their leader Nick Griffin was when he went on the BBC's Question Time before the 2010 election and got absolutely shredded by Sayeeda Warsi.

There was a simple reason that he looked and sounded and came across as a racist prick – because he is. The nasty, stupid things he's said about the Holocaust. Trying to defend the Ku Klux Klan. He is a racist, so it's not difficult to let him embarrass himself in public as one.

But that's the difference with all of the things they try to trip me up on – they can't find anything I've said that comes close to equating with Griffin's rubbish. It doesn't stop them trying though. The only things they can catch me out on are the mistakes I've made in my life, or the way I've acted or the trouble I've got into, but that shouldn't take away from the points I'm making. It still does though.

I grew in confidence with public speaking as the years went by, mostly because I knew my subject inside out more and more. For me it was about life experiences, but the interviewers trying to provoke an argument, or have a decent debate, usually didn't understand it and you ended up trying to debate someone else's preconceptions.

I've walked into the old office of the local newspaper where I knew most of the people, and they've told me that mostly they're up against their own bosses.

I got dragged out of my car once and battered by a gang of Muslims and as they were kicking shit out of me, they were shouting, 'That's for the mosque'. We had succeeded in stopping a new mosque getting built. When I told the paper what happened, they said there was no evidence it had anything to do with the mosque. I said I should know – because it was my head they were kicking.

And do you know what they did? They took a social media post put out by the far right North West Infidels saying that Tommy Robinson had been beaten up by Luton football hooligans, and used that for their headline.

I'm sorry, but anyone in Luton would laugh their head off at that ridiculous idea. But the North West Infidels said it was true, so my local newspaper, even though I'd told them what happened, even though there were witnesses, took the word of a bunch of Nazis who hate me.

When everything started taking off with the EDL I didn't realise how much the press had an agenda. I was only 26 and very naive. I thought they at least tried to tell the truth, to provide fair reporting.

I had been pleasantly surprised in the EDL's early days when the Daily Star appeared to give us a fair shake. It was a refreshing, if brief, moment in time. When we burned a swastika flag, they ran a headline saying 'English Defence League fight back'. They ran a poll in the paper asking if people would vote for the EDL as a political party, and 99% of the thousands of people who responded said yes.

Things changed quickly enough though. When we went to the FIFA headquarters in Zurich and me and Kev got on the roof, I rang the guy at the Daily Star and he said, 'Mate you could be on the fucking moon with an EDL flag, and we'd not be allowed to run it'.

The Daily Star got a ration of shit at the Leveson Inquiry when one of its reporters resigned and squealed to The Guardian that it had an anti-Muslim agenda. I thought that was bollocks and they were just doing a fair job. That's not tolerated though, in our modern media police state.

I was told later by a journalist that the left-wing National Union of Journalists instructs its members to always refer to the EDL as extreme and far right, to always paint them in a negative light. When I first heard that I thought it was pure horseshit. I couldn't believe such stuff goes on, but if in fact it doesn't, you wouldn't guess from seeing the coverage the EDL continued to get.

Descriptions like 'far right' or 'extremist' quickly became the bog-standard prefix for using the words English Defence League or EDL. Not that I have any statistics to back this up, I'd probably guess that the majority of EDL supporters were traditionally Labour party voters more than anything else. They couldn't vote EDL that's for sure, because we were never about politics or getting elected. We just wanted to make a point.

STICKING WITH THE media stuff, Stacey Dooley's BBC3 documentary in 2012, My Hometown Fanatics, made for interesting viewing. From the public's point of view, to see Stacey being abused and accosted by Muslim men and women on the streets of Luton was a real eye-opener.

From a personal point of view, it was disappointing how many things were not said – like the fact that Stacey's ex-boyfriend Barry converted to Islam while he was in prison. Or that Stacey grew up in Farley Hill and saw what was happening first hand – and that she was booed and jeered and ran out of The Parrot pub crying when she went back there as a tv celebrity.

It probably wouldn't have served much of a purpose, career-wise, for the girl to put all that out on public display. And let me say, I wish Stacey all the very best. She's a Luton girl who's done well, so good on her – even if another thing she didn't acknowledge in the documentary was how close we were for a while when we were both a lot younger.

Neither did she refer to her old friend Caroline – the same gorgeous girl and talented singer that I wrote of earlier, who was taken away from her family and turned effectively into a burkha-wearing Muslim sex slave.

It would have been good to see Stacey talk to Caroline's mum and get her perspective on Luton's problems, although

I doubt that a lot of people in those positions would be willing to go on camera. But Stacey did say that the Stephen Lennon she knew was no kind of racist, so I suppose I should be thankful for that at least.

The shock on Stacey's face when she went to film a Muslim anti-police protest march told its own story, but the bruising encounters when both the women and men then turned on her revealed a greater truth about the realities of towns like Luton. Right there, live on film, fundamental Muslims embarrassed not just themselves, but probably all of their white liberal apologists who like to pretend this kind of thing doesn't happen.

They only just stopped short of calling Stacey a whore – and good on her for giving them a serving back – but they were spitting their hatred at her. Condemned by their own words. Stacey said it was shameful that they took their children along to share the hatred, to indoctrinate them into this separatist, hateful ideology at as young an age as possible. She even got it first hand from Anjem Choudary who was quoting the Koran, saying the only law that he and they are answerable to is sharia, and that she was already halfway to hell fire herself.

Stacey walked around both Bury Park and Luton town centre wearing a niqab and she even persevered until she got to meet me. I got a fair crack from her – it was funny when she said that she'd never heard me mention 'good Muslims' in public, and I replied that not only did I always say it in interviews, but that the producers cut it out every time – and that hers would cut it too. It was left in, so hats off to Stacey.

We ended up with a crowd scene in the middle of Luton, surrounded by a group of young Muslims and I think she was starting to worry about her safety. It's funny. If the abuse Stacey Dooley got happened to me, then the verdict would be that I was asking for it. If a pretty investigative journalist like her gets rounded on by a bunch of medieval Brit-haters, then people are shocked.

In the final analysis I think she bottled it at the end of the programme, talking a bunch of wishy-washy rubbish about a tiny minority of people being a problem, and that we all just need to love and respect each other.

Yeah right, Stace, babe. Didn't you see the love in those protestors eyes? In Anjem Choudary's eyes?

Still the Youtube video of that show has been seen by over three million people, so at least someone's starting to pay attention. I saw her on another television show, The Wright Stuff, not too long ago and suddenly she was Stacey Dooley from St Albans, not Luton.

No shit. Good luck to the girl though.

I'M NOT SURE that television producers are blessed with the biggest sets of balls. After Lee Rigby's murder I was called and asked to appear on Newsnight, Daybreak and a couple of other programmes and, me being me, I put it out on social media that I'd be on the telly. That was a mistake. Every single one of them cancelled. Like someone had pulled a switch. Was it their bosses? Possibly. Was it left wing fanatics threatening to come and ransack the studios if they gave me the time of day? Probably. Pretty pathetic though, isn't it?

I sensed that there was a slight shift of public attitude after I left the EDL, more of a willingness to listen to the words I was actually speaking – in some quarters at least – rather than just hammering lazily away at the 'far right' EDL. After one Sunday Politics debate with Muslims4UK founder Inayat Bunglawala, another guest Esther Rantzen actually came out and said some positive things about the points I was making. They did a snap poll of viewers, asking if 'we' should be listening to people like Tommy Robinson and the EDL and the replies were a resounding

95% in favour. I laughed. With 5% of the population being Muslim, that pretty much gave me 100% support!

But Bunglawala is just another chancer, if you ask me. He was an extremist spokesman for the Muslim Council of Britain, then pow, he suddenly saw the light, reinvented himself as a so-called 'moderate' voice and suddenly left-wing organisations couldn't throw enough attention and influence at him.

This was a man who once praised Bin Laden, which everyone seems to have conveniently and suddenly forgotten. Well, I don't forget and I like to keep reminding people. Leopards, changing spots and all that.

As such, since leaving the EDL I would say that yes, more people seemed finally willing to listen to me than during the four or five years previously, and that I made more progress in terms of having a voice outside the group than I ever could have had while still in it.

But I was still left regretting one big media opportunity – the chance to take our message to the American mainstream. I really screwed that up.

13: WHAT'S IN A NAME?

I WAS BORN Stephen Yaxley, although almost everyone calls me Tommy these days, even many people I'm close to. If I'm walking through Luton and people recognise me, even from our old days at school, at the football or whatever, they'll shout, 'Hiya Tommy'. Some people from way back will still occasionally call me Yax, but not many.

When I was at the football I had another nickname – Tyrone. Any guesses? The short fat geezer off Coronation Street. I was supposed to look like him, so I got Tyrone.

I already had a bit of form with making up names, going back to the time the Daily Sport did a photoshoot with some strippers – sorry, glamour models – and a bunch of the football lads. We were taking a convoy of 14 stretch limos to an away match in Coventry and these girls came with us. In fact one of them was from Biggleswade, and I put her on the phone with a Biggleswade lad I was in Bedford nick with – and she ended up marrying him!

I organised it all with the Sport, but when it came to the interview I gave the reporter my mate's name, Steve Dann, 26, a bricklayer from Stopsley. It just came out! Steve was standing next to me in the picture but when it came to the interview it credited him with everything – he rang me up and said his missis was going nuts. It was only a joke, a bit of mischief. Some folk just can't see the funny side.

If I was going to do one thing differently about starting the EDL today, it would be to make clearer, more conscious decisions at the start. To plan a bit better.

We knew we weren't 'far right' in the sense that people portrayed and as I said when questioned by Andrew Neil, a bit of clever photo cropping and you could have Jesus looking like he was giving a Nazi salute instead of a blessing. My point is that when people walk and chant, they raise both arms in the air. It's the easiest thing in the world to make that look bad. Anyone who has ever pointed at something above waist height can be made by the papers to be giving a Nazi salute. They get away with it time and again. And there was never a shortage of people wanting to make it look bad, to suit their pre-conceived ideas.

The whole balaclavas thing, in the early days, was a big mistake. I spent a year trying to stay out of the limelight, but that was never realistically going to last, and in the meantime it made everything look a bit paramilitary.

I can rationalise it given what the police were doing to some of the Luton lads right at the start, but it looked as if we had something to hide, and it looked as if we were bringing menace to people's streets. It made a rod for our own back, if connecting with ordinary people was meant to be the point. The truth is, we didn't really think that deeply about it.

There was a reason for the balaclavas. I'd seen how the police will target and victimise anyone they can identify from my experiences at football. We'd seen that, especially after that Luton-Watford game some years before. With the EDL we were not going out to start trouble, to start fights, but we were always plagued, followed, abused and attacked by the far left and Muslims and you never knew when you might have to defend yourself. Any anonymity you could get in that instance had to help ... or so we thought.

I'd been to jail once and although I wasn't afraid of it, I was in no rush to go back. But neither was I trying to do anything that would mean I'd have to. Before, even when I'd tried to disguise myself reading the leaflet out at the home game with Peterborough, my identity had got out and I'd received all kinds of threats from the local Muslim gangs.

With the UPL and then the EDL, I possibly foolishly thought that I could keep some sort of anonymity, hence the balaclavas and the fake names. It ended up creating the wrong impression and eventually there would be few places that I could go without being recognised, but I wasn't to know that at the time. There never was much of a plan behind what we were trying to do with the EDL.

AFTER THE UPL march I was interviewed on Radio 5 Live by Victoria Derbyshire and I was just trying to divert attention away from me, while still talking about the issues, so I used a different name. That time it was Wayne King. I struggled to keep a straight face if I'm honest.

Here's a female BBC presenter talking about 'Wayne King'. I guess they didn't expect people to tug their rope so blatantly, so to speak, when such a serious subject was being discussed. The national newspapers used that name too. Some of those interviews are still there online. Useless bastards, they couldn't even see someone was taking the piss out of them.

We started getting requests for interviews and at first it was a bit of a laugh. It was literally me, Kev and a few mates and we were kind of bigging things up. I said that we'd formed a committee, that we had representatives from all across the district, blah, blah, blah, making it sound a lot more than it actually was. We'd set up a website 'Save Luton' and a Facebook page, so people and the media were getting in touch with us through that.

At that point we didn't realise what a nerve we'd hit with people and how far it was all going to go. We'd started off standing up for our own streets, but there was a mood in towns and cities all across England that showed a lot of ordinary people wanted to do something about a problem that clearly wasn't confined to Luton.

The next name I used was Tommy Robinson, which was another attempt to give some stick to a bloke with a bit of a reputation. It was the name that stuck though.

It was the idea of an uncle who influenced me quite a lot when I was younger, but who has turned into a poisonous and manipulative individual. He has issues, I know that. And if you're interested, no, we're not on talking terms. I think he was probably jealous of Tommy Robinson, who wrote a football hooligan book called 'MIG Down' in 2006.

Tommy Robinson wasn't his proper name either, but he wrote about me in his book. I was only young but he said I was a 'natural born leader'. He used my name though, Yaxley, which was annoying. It annoyed my mum and my family more. It would have been nice if he'd asked how I wanted referring to, because he gave the older MIG blokes different names, but with us youngsters he dropped all of our real names in. If he'd asked, I'd have opted for Tyrone.

Between the UPL and the EDL, I was basically plucking names out of thin air and as Tommy Robinson wasn't a real person anyway, I had a go with that. It might have only lasted a couple of weeks or a couple of months, but once it got out there in the public domain and became associated with the EDL, it just stuck. And that was that.

I should have shown him a bit more respect in hindsight. He looked out for a lot of us younger lads, back then.

But suddenly I was Tommy Robinson to the outside world and, increasingly, within my own world. It was 12 months before my real identity was exposed but by then everyone in the EDL had come to know me as Tommy. To everyone and almost everywhere, I was Tommy Robinson.

I think of myself as Tommy a lot of the time. The tag, the name stuck, but who I really was and what I looked like stayed under the radar for a year or so.

When my real identity eventually emerged, even my mum was in the dark and I had to go and explain what was going on. You can imagine the shock. Up until then, even with the EDL taking off on a national scale, the Muslim lads I knew in Luton and a lot of my old friends – few of them knew it was me behind the thing. How my identity was finally exposed though was a sign of other issues to come for the EDL, of hangers-on and of hard core extremists who wanted to drag the movement in directions we really were not comfortable with.

PAUL RAY IS a nutter. A 100 per cent, bona fide, right wing fruitcake from Dunstable. He contacted us when we were the UPL and we spoke to him once, but he never came to a demonstration, not the UPL nor the EDL.

He then disappeared from public view, apparently because of a bunch of reported threats against his life from Muslims. The next thing, he surfaced in Malta, where he had teamed up with a joker called 'Nazi' Nick Gregor.

If this all sounds a bit far-fetched, hang about, because it gets better. Nazi Nick Gregor is a German character who was reputedly the most feared Nazi in Europe – in recent years obviously. He once did a documentary with the Ulster loyalist paramilitary Johnny 'Mad Dog' Adair and reportedly used to be his bodyguard. There were stories about Nazi Nick smuggling diamonds in Africa, Nazi Nick the gunman – all sorts. There was speculation about him being a mentor for Anders Breivik who committed the Oslo massacre. And suddenly we had this local headcase Paul Ray hanging out with Nazi Nick in Malta.

We were about 18 months into the EDL, by which time my face was in the public domain, but the world still knew me as Tommy Robinson. Then one evening, out of the blue, I got a phone call from him – from Paul Ray. He spoke and then the German bloke came on the phone and said, 'You've got until midnight to hand over control of the English Defence League; the Facebook group, the website, everything. If you haven't done this by midnight, then your address, your real name, your family's addresses – everything is going to be put online'.

The last thing he said was, 'Tick tock, tick tock ... the clock's ticking mate'.

We weren't going to play ball with these idiots. Midnight came and went and sure enough Paul Ray posted something online – a video publicising my real identity, and saying that I'd kidnapped his mum. If anyone was in any doubt about how mad he was, that must have had them shaking their heads in disbelief. Kidnap his mum? What a complete nut job.

I have to admit that at that point I was basically shitting myself, because of the backlash I thought must be coming. The days of walking round Luton unchallenged were gone because once the Muslim brothers knew who Tommy Robinson was, that it was their old 'mate' Yax, things were going to change for good.

Were my initial fears founded? Absolutely – and some, because I was suddenly a target. That said, I suppose it wasn't just inevitable eventually, but possibly for the best. Once the mask was off and there was no more hiding to be done, it took things onto the next level. There was a certain sense of freedom despite the baggage it brought.

After that I met Kev and one or two others to discuss what we did next. We couldn't just bumble on as we were, doing half a job, we had to decide to commit or jack it all in. Me and Kev shook hands and said, 'That's us, we're in, for good or bad, win or lose'.

You couldn't just put one toe in the water and hope that it wasn't freezing. It was straight in at the deep end. We agreed that whatever got thrown at us, no matter what happened, we wouldn't shy away, we'd just front everything up and deal with it.

That changed everything essentially. I hadn't been doing TV interviews or putting myself visibly out there, but what quickly became clear was that once I did, support for the EDL rocketed. Our message got across much better. People were far more likely to pay attention to someone talking to them face to face and not from behind a mask.

By that time I'd become Tommy Robinson in my own life, to all intents and purposes. That was the name now fixed to the EDL persona and steadily that became me, to the point where even Kev started calling me Tommy.

Where I am now confuses things somewhat. Occasionally if I go into Luton and see some of the lads from way back, they'll still call me Yax. But we've had to move houses so many times and when I walk around in my normal life – such as I have 'normal' – no one calls me Tommy. That's a different bloke. I'm known as Stephen, Steve. It doesn't make for a straightforward day to day existence. I might be trying to do a bit of ordinary 'Stephen' stuff but I can't stop people seeing Tommy.

I went to one of my last probation meetings in Bedford and I'd just come out when a car pulled up. It was a Muslim lad and he started mouthing out of the window, but I just ignored him and carried on walking. At that he spun the car round and shouted, 'You're fucking dead!'

I stopped, walked over towards his car and told him to get out. But as I did, a bloke at a cash point nearby who had seen what was going on went absolutely nuts with the lad in the car. The kid didn't know what he'd walked into and completely bottled it. The stranger came over, shook my hand and said, 'Alright Tommy?'

I was fine and walked over to Argos. I'd been there about 10 minutes, got to the front of the queue and who walked in? Yeah, the Muslim bloke. You should have seen his face when he saw me. I said, 'You little coward, you're alright shouting out of your car window, aren't you?'

He shit himself. Everyone in Argos was listening and he just stood there, falling into his own arse. I wasn't going to do anything, I was just showing him up for what he was. And at that point another two Muslims came into the shop

– and so suddenly he was Genghis Khan again, mouthing off, giving it large. I just laughed. I said to everyone in Argos, 'Look what he's just done! He just melted, five minutes ago, and suddenly he's grown a pair of balls!'

It all came to nothing. He was just a coward like so many of these big mouths are. And that's the whole 'Tommy' thing, everywhere I go, where people recognise me, it can be abuse from someone like that character or someone random who wants to shake my hand, shake Tommy's hand. When I'm at home with the kids and their friends, or their parents, it's Steve or Stephen and I'm comfortable with it all – although with a growing family I can see the day when some really difficult conversations are going to be required.

My daughter heard me on the phone a while back, and I absent-mindedly said, 'Yeah hello, it's Tommy,' – and she came over all confused and said, 'You're not Tommy!' So I looked at her confused face, and I said, 'Darling I'm talking to granddad Tommy!'

We went to Alton Towers and as we were driving out the bloke on reception said, 'Alright Tommy, how you doing?' And I shook hands with him. 'So my daughter said again, 'Dad you're not Tommy. Why did he call you Tommy?'

My eldest daughter doesn't even know what the name Yaxley is. We went to a Luton football match a while back and a friend's older daughter said, 'Yax, I saw you on TV!' and I just nudged her dad, who sort of gave her a look and thankfully my kids were oblivious. All of which would be bad enough – and yes, I can hear you all tut-tutting – but that's only half of it, because then she heard me on the phone to the dentist, and I used the name Paul Harris. I was in the kitchen and I said, 'It's Paul.' And she said again … well you can imagine.

In fact, I imagine most of you are thinking, 'Paul Harris? Who the hell is Paul Harris?' But yes, Paul Harris. That happens to be my legal name – and no, not witness protection or any of that stuff. The state has been trying to get me killed, not keep me out of harm's way. That's a privilege that seems to be reserved mostly for people who want to blow the country up.

Strictly speaking, Paul Harris is my actual name – although that's another completely mad episode.

But the whole confusing and convoluted tale is going to have to come out with the kids sooner or later. With the internet and Google these days, it's only going to take one incident to get my eldest one poking about.

That's something me and her mum really need to explain because I don't want her first understanding of my background to be all the lazy, label-happy media stuff, all the online hate and the one-sided versions.

She needs some kind of guidance from us. I want her to understand a little bit more about what brought her dad to the place he is. And yes, I know that's going to mean me being honest about things I'm not proud of either. I never said it would be easy.

But she also needs to be old enough to understand what's happened in towns like Rochdale and Rotherham, like Luton and Tower Hamlets and across the world in fact, places where Islam is not the peaceful religion it likes to sell itself as, but the brutal, medieval, murdering machine that it represents to so many millions of oppressed people.

I expect there's a middle ground between discussing those barbarities and enlightening her about daddy and his colourful background, but I'd like to think she'd see my speech to the Oxford Union before she tuned into some of the wild hatred of a bloke who's simply trying to understand what's happening to his country, to share that disturbing prospect, and perhaps do something about it.

I consider myself an ordinary bloke who wants his kids to grow up in a fair, democratic and tolerant country. But I'm also an ordinary bloke who thinks the odds on that aren't particularly bright, not the way we're going. So yes, I know that some time quite soon I'm not going to be able to shield or hide from her what daddy's last few years have involved, and in time her little brother and sister too. I'm just not sure that the age they're at right now is quite the right time for that grown up conversation.

I mean, if I've managed to confuse you lot with the stories about these names, what would it do to those poor mites? Then again, none of it was exactly a plan. The fact is that such as I have regrets, it's about the problems I've caused members of my family, albeit unintentionally.

On one occasion I was doing a local radio interview with Zulfiqar Khan, who's one of Bury Park's pretend moderates. My mum was a support worker at a local school and one of her colleagues was Khan's daughter. The school was unaware she was my mum, and she had to listen as all the staff were gathered together that morning by the head and asked to pray for Khan, because he was debating the far-right extremist leader of the English Defence League.

Can you imagine how my poor mother felt about that? Subsequently when she got ill, mum had fantastic support from the school, above and beyond the call of duty. That day however, I was understandably pissed off.

When he and I started, the first thing I asked was whether he wanted sharia law in Britain or not. A simple yes or no. He wouldn't answer, but I wouldn't carry on until he did, so I kept on – hoping the staff at my mum's school were listening – saying he had to answer first. Eventually he admitted: 'And what if we do want sharia law?'

Thank you. And all I wanted was to not have to break British law in order to expose the people who would replace it with a medieval, third world ideology. So which of us had extreme views exactly?

Growing up I was christened a Catholic and my mum is still devoutly religious. She says her prayers every single night, but I've lost all faith in the Catholic church. I don't have religion. In the early days of the EDL I was talking to a deacon in the Catholic church, about everything going on with Islam. His answer to everything was the Lord's prayer, 'Our Father, who art in Heaven, forgive us our trespasses, as we forgive those who trespass against us...'

That was it, the answer to all the strife on the planet. We had to forgive those who trespass against us. The answer to radical Islam was to forgive them for chopping us to bits, as they took over the world. Here comes the machete, aimed at your neck '....forgive them their trespasses...'

I told him, mate, it's a bit more complicated than that. You're in for a nasty surprise as and when Islam decides which religions are acceptable in 'their' British state. What happens when there's none of your lot left to forgive them? That's heaven?

I spend a lot more time studying Islam these days and so far I haven't managed to discover any nation states where Islam is the dominant religion and other faiths are given equal standing or respect. Clearly lots of people believe that Britain will break that mould and we'll all live in a happy-clappy, multi-faith society. Good luck with that.

After that radio show with Zulfiqar Khan some of the teachers who 'knew' about me told mum they thought I'd done really well – but of course they couldn't say it publicly, not out loud. That's taboo in modern Britain.

Whatever I am and have been, my mum has been a saint. She's been going through some really serious health issues, but over the years she's helped so many youngsters with problems. I've been in pubs in town, in supermarkets, out and about, and mums and dads have come up and said their son or daughter wouldn't have made it through school without her. She came home with a young girl one Christmas and just announced that she was moving in. That she was going to be living with our family.

The girl was called Jamie-Leigh and she had a tragic background. Her mum threw her out and because she was 16 and in the last year at school, Social Services were putting her in a hostel. Mum wasn't having that – so she brought her home to live with her family.

She's a super lady. I'm not sure what she ever did to deserve having trouble like me for a son.

WHATEVER ELSE THE impact on the national psyche of Tommy Robinson and the EDL has been, the real and significant impact has been on my family.

We try to go about our lives normally, although obviously I'm mindful of sensible things – like not putting myself in stupidly dangerous situations. It isn't easy, especially when the supposed forces of law and order have it in for you too.

I was having a beer in the Sugar Loaf pub, watching a Man Utd vs Man City game when an uncle phoned to say his son was being followed. It was that ginger-haired extremist whose mug is always on the telly, Ibrahim Anderson (he converted while inside for armed robbery). He and his mates had seen the lad, recognised him as being with me at a children's birthday party, spun their car around and started following him towards the family home in Wigmore. Me and Keir jumped in my motor and set off.

This was panic stations. A bunch of well known radicals were following my cousin at a time when I was already Islam's Public Enemy no.1 – not long after the police had stopped a gang of terrorists on the M1 with a car full of assorted bombs, guns and other weapons, which had been intended for the EDL demo in Dewsbury.

What were we supposed to think was going down?

My uncle was waiting by the bushes in their garden with a baseball bat, and as the first car full of Muslims pulled up onto the drive he jumped out and started smashing their windows in, at which they reversed away up the road.

That's when me and Keir came racing round the corner. I actually had a box of balaclavas in the back that had just been returned to me by the police having been confiscated previously, so me and Keir pulled one on and jumped out.

The five of them had got out of their car but when they saw us they shit themselves and set off running. I was chasing the big ginger geezer and I caught his legs. He was yelping like a bitch. Right then the police came hurtling onto the scene which was probably just in time, because within seconds more and more cars full of Muslim blokes were turning up.

There were probably about 25 of them, by which time the police had me handcuffed against the car. They pulled my balaclava off at which point the Muslim mob, seeing who it was, went completely berserk, baying for blood. The police didn't know what to do except call for more help.

Almost all of this is on video and as I was being arrested I told the police what had happened to start the confrontation. I told them that the Muslim gang had weapons and that they had started the trouble. I was shouting my head off, which was when about eight of their mob started coming down the road towards us. The police had to get dogs out to move them back.

The Muslims were shouting, 'You're fucking dead, we got your faces, we got your faces, you're fucking dead!'

I was arrested even though I'd done nothing except scare them off wearing a balaclava, but we had to wait for another 10 or so police cars to come and clear the road to get us out of the mob's blockade at the end of the cul-de-sac.

My uncle and cousin were arrested too, and then the police got a remand extension to hold me in the cells even longer, even though the only charge I could possibly be up on was criminal damage over one of their cars – and I wasn't even there when it got smashed up. Thirty-six hours later I was still locked up.

They finally took me in to interview and I was smiling, firstly because I hadn't done anything, and secondly because I was sure they must have nicked those arseholes. The police began the interview and I asked straight out, 'What did you find on them?'

And I could tell straight away from this female officer's face. I said, 'Hold on, you didn't even search them, did you? You didn't even look for their weapons?'

She said they'd no reason to search this gang of about 25 of Luton's most radical, violent Muslims, who were howling like madmen in the middle of a housing estate.

I was speechless, I swear. A month before they didn't bother searching a car full of extremists for two days, and then purely by accident they found guns, bombs and IEDs and now their spiritual brothers were at our houses baying for blood. And the complete imbeciles of Luton and Beds Police never even searched them – while I was being held for 36 hours on a shitty criminal damage charge I hadn't committed!

I told those officers when they arrested me outside my uncle's exactly what was going down, who was involved, and that it was all on video, recorded on a mobile phone.

What do you think their priority was – searching that raging mob? Of course not. They wanted to find that mobile phone, the one that was filming their incompetence. The police went looking for that and tried to seize it. Thankfully my cousin slipped it to a neighbour because as soon as I got out of the police station I uploaded the video which showed me telling the cops exactly what had happened and how this mob was after us, all tooled up. Instead, the only three people arrested were me and two family members, while this mob was screaming all kinds of obscenities.

Why weren't they arrested or searched? Because the police are cowards. They don't want to provoke a commotion with 'the community' and they know that while decent non-

Muslim people will generally put up with their shit, however unjust, if they so much as say 'boo' to Sayful Islam and his cronies, they'll have a full scale riot on their hands.

You might say that the police were looking for that video evidence in order to obtain evidence to press charges, but you'd be like the legion of Politically Correct people who are one of this country's biggest problems. They see only what they want to see. The police could have had that video evidence and brought charges any time they wanted, even after it was posted online. They just didn't want it – except to suppress it. They never do.

It can't have been more than a week after that incident that I was out shopping in Luton with the family and I saw Ibrahim Anderson's sister taking photographs of my wife and kids on her phone. I asked her for it, then I told her to give me it, and she ran into Clark's shoe shop.

I followed her and she picked up a boot and started hitting me with it. A black chap intervened and I told him that her brother was one of the biggest terrorist supporters in the country and she was trying to photograph my children. I took the phone off her and took a few pictures of her and her kids, and asked how she liked that?

And then, with my sensible head on, I rang the police and told them what happened. As for the other ruck at my uncle's? As usual they spun it out for eight weeks, and then they dropped everything. Like they do.

14: THE EDL - 2

THERE ARE A LOT of things I would do differently if we were to start the EDL over again, but you have to understand that this was an ad hoc street movement in the purest sense of the word. We posted dates of demos and protests on Facebook. We acted on a whim – my whim usually – in response to being offended at some piece of politically correct madness or other.

It was innocent in a lot of ways, naïve in others. There was no goal, no motive, other than to shout our opposition to what was happening to our communities, our towns, our cities. Our country. Tommy Robinson was never hoping to be Prime Minister, unlike Dudley North's Conservative candidate and friend of some decidedly dodgy characters, Afzal Amin.

But, and I'll go to my grave insisting this, it was never intended to be racist. We despised the BNP and other far right groups every bit as much as Sayful Islam's bunch. We were anti-Muslim extremism, not anti-Muslim people, but that shouldn't mean we couldn't criticise some of the things happening in their community. They could do a lot more to help both themselves and so-called community cohesion.

I don't think that's right wing or racist, is it? If we're supposed to all be in this together, it would be nice for them to make some kind of effort, to pull their fingers out occasionally, especially the so-called silent majority.

Here we are towards the back end of 2015 and there doesn't seem to be a week goes by without another story of sexual grooming by gangs of Muslim men, another council or police force living in denial of it, or another family or group of young men running off to join ISIS.

We recently had a family of 12 from Luton heading for Syria. Good riddance, I say. Hot on the heels of that, the children's charity Barnardo's said they warned the authorities in Aylesbury as long ago as 2008 about Muslim men raping young white girls. Back then the EDL went and highlighted the very same. And now I've just read an apology from some clown at Buckinghamshire County Council saying they are appalled at the crimes. Almost as an afterthought he says oops, sorry, but they know more about the crimes now than they did at the time.

I won't hold my breath waiting for an apology, or bother with a 'told you so', because you only have to raise these issues in public and there's a queue of people to Land's End and back who want to hit you over the head with the lazy 'racist' label. That's anyone who dares mention the subject. When it's Tommy Robinson, magnify that by a thousand.

I don't know if it says more about the haters' prejudices or just their stupidity. Probably both. If this country becomes the Islamic state that its followers dream of, it will be down to the non-Muslim British people who effectively paved the way for it with their soppy, we-need-to-show-more-love-and-tolerance capitulation. Boy, will they be in for a real surprise, come judgment day.

Can you really imagine one big, multi-cultural, loved-up melting pot where we're all brothers and sisters?

I think not. Not if the evidence of every Islamic state in the world, down through history, is anything to go by.

Why should the UK be different? We tolerate the complete subjugation of half the Muslim population – women – by their medieval men and there is neither a single sign of that changing from within, nor of our Human Rights liberals even daring to mention it out loud. Yet these people dream of a loved-up, one nation future? Madness.

Those Brit-hating Unite Against Fascism turncoats might not be the first lot on their knees if and when sharia is the law of this land, but their turn would certainly come, have no doubt about that.

What we soon found with the EDL was that there was a huge swathe of British people every bit as concerned at all the signs as we were.

After Manchester and Leeds in 2009, then Stoke, Bolton and Dudley in early 2010, with thousands of people turning out to support us, the EDL was off and running.

We criss-crossed the country from Plymouth to Newcastle, responding to appeals from local communities and new branches that were springing up here and there. People wanted to protest against another mega mosque, others saw their young people being attacked or poisoned with drugs. We went to help them complain about it.

An EDL Youth Division started up under a young mixed race London lad, Joel Titus, but we lost him after he got in some football bother. Although it was nothing to do with us, he got a 10-year ASBO to stay away from the EDL.

None of it was easy or straightforward. From the very first visits to Birmingham it had been a battle to keep the right wing fringe away. We were being sustained by a mass of great people, true patriots, but as the movement grew so did the problems.

The key thing we should have done first was formalise a membership, secure the data of all the people who were the groundswell of the movement in those early weeks and months. We never had an income stream to speak of, a way of funding our activities. As often as not it was me or Kev putting our hands in our pockets to make banners, to make t-shirts and hoodies, to hire a bus, put diesel in the van.

WE DID HAVE some structures and support mechanisms, based around individuals who made massive contributions to getting the EDL up and running.

One person who deserves special mention is Helen Gower, who is as close as I could ever get to a surrogate mum and a guard dog, all in one. Even now, most days I'll get a phone call from Hel, reminding me that I'm doing this, supposed to be going there, should be talking to so-and-so. I can't thank her enough for what she's done over the years.

She started helping out with the online stuff via another bloke who was key in those formative days, Guramit Singh. Guramit was the EDL Sikh leader and when we started he was saying things that even I wouldn't dare come out with about the bloke I always refer to in interviews as the false prophet. He really pushed the boundaries with the points he was making out on the street, in the public domain.

In one speech he wrote, referring to the saying about Mohammed and the mountain, he came up with something like, 'Now the mountains are coming to you … and on top of the mountains are the English Defence League!' Brave stuff. Helen was helping Guramit within a support group we set up to handle all of the online stuff, because there were so many videos needed posting, so much information coming in that needed sifting through.

Another bloke was known only by his nickname, 'Nemesis'. I know, a bit out there. But a lot of people only wanted to be known by nicknames or pseudonyms for understandable reasons. He was really talented though and produced some top class articles and blogs.

He said he'd been studying counter-jihad stuff for years and his work was quite high-brow, intellectual. I found it interesting that here was a really smart bloke who held mostly left wing views and who hated Nazis and racism – but for those same reasons he saw the dangers of Islam.

His advice on all kinds of subjects was always solid, but no one knew who he was or where he lived – just that he had a shitty job in a call centre. I admit that I wondered if he was an MI5 plant. He only came to a demo once – you won't find a picture of him anywhere – and then he simply said he couldn't come again, because of issues with his domestic life and his situation as a single dad.

Some people came and went like that, but Hel was a constant, and has been throughout. She started helping with all of the EDL stuff, but got closer and closer to what I was doing, I suppose more of a PA. Here was a quite elderly lady, who was going through a terrible time with her husband who'd had a serious accident, but who was there for me every step of the way.

If I was debating someone like Mo Ansar, Hel would do all the background and research and provide me with everything I knew to make the case, argue the point. When I left the EDL she stayed on for a while, but I think eventually she couldn't stand the petty politics. Quite a few people turned on Hel, which sadly became the way of things. She really was a guard dog though, doing background checks on problem individuals, on the people coming and going within our scene, always asking difficult questions, probing, which you can understand didn't always go down well the people concerned.

I'd have 40-year-old blokes getting all worked up and throwing their toys out of the pram. I was like, 'You're going to quit the fight against Islam because a 70-year-old lady has got arsey with you? Grow up.'

Early on we were called to a meeting of what I can only call London intellectuals by Alan Lake, a very bright chap who was supportive of us. People tried to make him out as a millionaire financier of the EDL but that was nonsense. He introduced us to a group of people at a house in Barbican and they were talking strategies and 'out-manouvering the police' and discussing counter-jihadi stuff. It was a bit over my head back then, if I'm honest.

I was intrigued when the evangelist Christian minister Colin Dye asked to meet us in London and said he'd been talking to a leading figure in the Baptist church, who told him he'd been asked by the Queen herself 'how long her country had' – in reference to Islam – and he'd replied 'no more than 60 years ma'am.' True? I don't know, but neither do I know why these people would lie to me.

The longer we went though, the more the internal aggro became the biggest issue. You wouldn't believe what becoming a Divisional Leader could do to a bloke's ego.

A lot of these people were neither trained nor cut out for a leadership role on the tills at Tesco, let alone a complex protest group. I'd get calls from members around the country saying they were being bullied. FFS, as they say.

For me it was increasingly about the cause, beyond everything, and it was difficult coming to terms with the fact that for a lot of the supporters it was about having a beer and a day out on a Saturday. For a lot of them the EDL became basically a club, a place for people who hadn't had a community of mates before. I'd been there, done that, got the tee-shirts and the hangovers, but the further we went, the more my head was just into the cause.

Helen Gower was dogged in trying to protect me – you knew if you crossed her! – but I think she got tired of the bullshit eventually after I left, and threw her hat in with me. I really don't know what I'd do without her. There were times when I felt the pressure getting to me and I'd look at some of the things Hel was having to contend with at home with her husband's declining health, and I'd wonder what the hell I had to worry about.

Helen sadly lost her husband earlier this year. She's remained my absolute rock throughout though.

THE ENGLISH DEFENCE League wasn't just about a cause spreading around Britain however, because suddenly we were attracting attention not just from home but abroad too. We were being noticed by people in the USA, while there were also groups springing up around Europe.

That brought a whole bunch of problems of its own and you only have to mention Anders Breivik to understand the potential for disaster that was lurking on the continent. Attention and support that we might be flattered by, could easily turn out to be courtesy of a collection of Nazi nutters. I didn't have the time to deal with every single approach.

We set up a European Freedom Initiative headed up by Steve Simmons, originally from Luton. Steve tried to coordinate this umbrella function for like-minded groups springing up here and there. He would try to root out the good and bad and pull people together, people that I could then go and talk to if required. It wasn't very sophisticated but it seemed to be a way of reaching parts of Europe with similar problems. We travelled abroad on a couple of memorable occasions to demos in Europe and Scandinavia and things were very different over there, for sure.

Fifteen of us went to support Geert Wilders at a Dutch Freedom Party rally in Amsterdam. That was a learning curve. We arrived and the police said they'd lead us to the rally. They led us straight into an ambush.

Apparently the Ajax football fans are all ultra-left and the local papers had been painting the EDL as neo-Nazis. Suddenly we were facing a mob of Moroccan blokes with their hands reaching for back pockets, saying tonight we would be getting our throats cut.

We backed off and got to the mini-bus, at which point this crew set about it – and suddenly our guardian angels arrived out of nowhere. They said they were British military. I've no idea, but they were very big, very handy blokes, in a military-style vehicle and they cleared the attackers in seconds. They escorted us round to the demo point, where we arrived in a bus without a window in it. God knows what the Dutch crowd thought. That's what you call making a first impression.

THE EDL NEVER had any cash to speak of, but it wasn't because there wasn't the opportunity to get financial backing. Just as I had a lot of interest and support from American conservatives who follow what happens in the UK really closely, so I had an approach in early 2010 to talk about tapping into cash.

Someone contacted us through the website saying they could arrange funding on a significant scale for the EDL, so we arranged a meeting at a hotel in Newcastle. This bloke said he could get huge amounts of money for us from overseas – except that he wanted 30% as his cut, his arrangement fee if you like.

The figure he originally came up with was £5 million, which he seemed to think was little more than loose change. He explained how it would work, where the money would be transferred from and to, with accounts held in China making its way around the world and back to us.

The source? Believe it or not, none other than Tony Blair's old pal, Colonel Gaddafi, the Libyan dictator. They wanted us to use our EDL rallies and demonstrations to say that the British military should not be going into Libya, that we should not be invading or getting involved. We were told we could access money from pretty much every country in the middle east on the same premise – that governments across the region were all doing it. I remember one phrase this geezer came out with. He said the cost of one missile can be millions, so five million was nothing in the greater scheme of things.

Looking back, I reckoned that it was only what George Galloway was doing, cosying up to Saddam Hussain in Iraq. After the Newcastle meeting I went on the internet and found pictures of Gaddafi with the BNP leader Nick Griffin. More recently I've heard the same of Paul Golding from Britain First – that he has been offered money from Russian President Vladimir Putin. That's not to say he or anyone else took it, but it opened our eyes to what was going on out there in the big wide world.

Was I tempted? Stupidly perhaps, no I wasn't. It felt like treason. I didn't like what our government was doing, but I certainly didn't like what dictators were doing in other countries. It felt like I would be taking money not only from Muslims to combat what their cousins were trying to achieve in our country, but more than that, from one of the bona fide bad guys. As much as the money could have propelled us on, I wasn't comfortable being funded by people I considered dictators or terrorists.

In hindsight, people couldn't have thought any worse of us than they already did. We might as well have taken the money and told our critics to do one, because what's another death threat between enemies? It wasn't as if the money did Gaddafi any good, when his house of cards collapsed and the rebels dragged him out of his rat hole and executed him.

I suppose I kept thinking that one day people would waken up to what we were really about, listen to our words, to what we were saying, as opposed to their own rhetoric, that we would eventually be seen as the good guys.

Idiot, eh? It would turn out, after the execution of Lee Rigby, that we couldn't even do a charitable deed without having the money thrown back in our faces. I'll talk about that more a little later.

IT WASN'T AS IF we didn't keep trying to make the anti-Nazi, anti-racist point ourselves, in the face of everyone just branding us far right.

In the early days we invited Paraic O'Brien from the BBC's Newsnight, plus the Daily Star, to a press conference at a derelict building in Luton. It was actually at the back of a building site me and Kev were working on, but old boy scout himself spent a week dolling this place up to look something decent. He also made a big swastika flag.

It almost went tits up from the start. Half of our lads were black or mixed race anyway and one of them, Dwayne, arrived with a couple of his cousins, up from London. He told them they were going to be on the telly, to make this non-racist point. But as they came up the steps Kev Carroll's head popped over the balcony – in a balaclava – shouting to them, 'No names!' And then they walked into a room full of blokes in balaclavas holding a swastika. On the Newsnight clip, just as Paraic O'Brien is coming up the steps you just see these lads bolting past him down the stairs. I think they'd got the wrong end of the stick, but I could see the funny side.

These were the early days, so we were still trying to keep our identities hidden, hence the ballys. It wasn't meant in any way paramilitary, but I can see how it came across. Anyway, we gave everyone a black t-shirt – except one of the lads, Black Kev, who got a white one. It was hilarious because he stood out like a sore thumb, but at least it pressed home the mixed race message. We read a statement condemning Anjem Choudary and burned the swastika flag too. I kind of cringed after O'Brien interviewed me, then asked my pal Tyrone why he was here, and Tyrone replied, 'What he says.'

Well, some are leaders, some are followers I suppose.

Keeping the extremists away would be a constant problem. Some time later, probably in 2012 when splinter groups were springing up around the place, I posted a video online, challenging them. It was specifically the North East Infidels in Newcastle mouthing off, getting all militant, and I told any of them who had a problem to come to Luton and sort it. Wouldn't you know it, but one of them did.

I was down in London watching the filming of Celebrity Juice, when I got a call from the landlord of the Duke of Clarence saying this geezer had come all the way down from Newcastle looking for me.

We shot back on a train and sure enough here was this lad Stevie Carroll, come all this way to sort me out – except that when we came face to face, he said he just wanted to talk. I said no, not until we'd done what he came for. So we went out back and then, after we'd sorted it out, we shook hands. At least he had the balls to front me up.

That sort of stuff wasn't the only internal problem we faced however. Early on I was asked to have a meeting with someone in Luton and a guy turned up in full Hells Angels colours with six or seven big lads, who all looked like doormen, all tattooed up.

He said his real name was Tom, but he was using the name Kev Shevesky from the Hertfordshire Division of EDL. He said he'd just got back from doing security for Geert Wilders in Holland. Interesting, but I wasn't sure. He'd been working his way around the area, going to EDL meet and greets, helping out, delivering leaflets, being generally very active.

This was before a demo in Stoke and he said he had plenty of lads there and should he tell them to start smashing up mosques? I said no, just tell them to go to the demo point. He was coming over a bit racist and I told him, look around the pub, some of my mates are black and Asian. One of his lads was wearing an EDL hoodie with the name 'Iceman' on it – and I'd processed all that EDL gear.

I'd also done a bit of homework on local Hells Angels, but he didn't seem too clued up about the scene when I mentioned one or two people. He also said that his dad was Polish so I said, 'Good morning how are you?' in Polish – and he went blank. He was very interested in all of our plans, where we were going, what we were doing.

It wasn't sitting right and I had a friend with a security company in Milton Keynes, so I got him to sweep the house and our motors – and sure enough we found a tracking device hidden on the works van. Next I looked in my records for the address of the bloke with the Iceman hoodie and went to the flat in Enfield where it was ordered from. It turned out that the half dozen bouncers had all been hired for the day by this Shevesky character.

After that I got Shevesky's mobile phone number and his address – and it appeared the house was registered to a security company in Holland. When I went round to the place it was all alarmed up, there was CCTV, security fencing, the lot. So I rang him up and he got all cocky, saying, 'We have loads of people into your movement, all over the country, we have infiltrated you.'

Was he a policeman? UAF? Far right? No idea then, no idea now, but I did manage to put the shits up him.

I drove down to his house one morning as he and a woman were coming out. She immediately bolted inside and within five minutes there were police crawling everywhere. So I told them that I'd seen this bloke looking at my kids and I wanted to know what he was up to – which settled things down for me at least where the cops were concerned.

Later he rang me, crying like a baby. Embarrassing. I said I had trackers on his car, knew everything about him, had pictures of his wife ... he promised to pack it in and stay away, but wouldn't say who he was working for.

Later I was told that he'd been part of the BNP security detail on Nick Griffin, but I suppose he could just as easily have been from the News of the World. Who knows? Either way, he disappeared and we never heard from him again.

There were others though. The police have a squad that specialises in infiltrating public protest groups like ours. I worked out some questionable individuals early on, but it got to the point where the pressure of watching everyone – and watching your back – was becoming intolerable.

I could cope with it from Muslim fanatics on the streets of Luton, but from people who were supposed to be on 'our' side? We had one bloke from Nottingham who used to introduce me to speak at rallies and demos ... and then we were told that he used to do the same job for Nick Griffin, so we got rid of him. It was a constant problem, this infiltration and association of individuals we really didn't want to be anywhere near us.

As time went on there would be constant internal whispering campaigns that we were joining up with the BNP, rubbish like that. Over my dead body, and on one occasion towards the end of my time with the EDL I had to rush back from abroad to a demo in Walsall because of rumblings, to lay down the law – no BNP. Never.

THE HIGHLIGHT OF early 2011 was the EDL's Luton Homecoming, the first time we'd been back since the UPL started the ball rolling. Having begun our street protest movement with the United People of Luton, and taken it around the country in the form of the EDL, it was a big day when we brought it back, on the first weekend of February.

It was five days before that demo that the bloke went to Kev's house with a shotgun and chased him down the road.

We all stayed overnight in the Hilton hotel in Stopsley where we were joined on demo day by an American rabbi, Nachum Shifren. He's a Californian, fundamentalist Jew known as 'the surfing Rabbi' who actually contacted us and made his own way over for the Luton Homecoming. He'd seen that Luton Council had supported a Palestinian group that held an event to boycott Israeli goods.

Rabbi Shifren is a very outspoken American critic of Islam and it seems he'd read a lot about what was happening here, specifically the time a group of Jews attending a Holocaust memorial service had to be kept safe inside Luton town hall because Sayful Islam and his crew came to abuse them. The former synagogue is now the radical Luton Islamic Centre ironically. Most of the local Jewish population has been driven out of Luton, but at that time Orthodox Jews often needed a police escort when they were out in public. It drew Rabbi Shifren to us.

Anyway he turned up, knocking on our hotel door at 8am and half the lads were all still steamed up, wearing the previous day's clothes. But the thing was, because it was the Sabbath and he was strictly religious, he couldn't get in a car with us to go to the demo in town. He had to walk – which was about four miles, all the way with a police escort. It was hilarious.

That demo was one of the biggest to date, with three or four thousand protestors. It went off really calmly, too. Not long before the Home Secretary Theresa May had banned one of our marches in Leicester, despite the fact that radical Muslim groups had been marching there for 20 years. We weren't going to cancel Leicester though, on principle. We just told our people, wherever you land in Leicester, don't let them herd us together, just go on the streets, get to the rally point however best you can. Pockets of 30, 40, 50 lads were converging from all points of the compass. It turned into absolute anarchy. There was trouble flaring up every which way you looked – but it was the police attitude that was the recipe for disaster.

Peterborough was next and their police told me they couldn't have what happened at Leicester. So I said, 'Don't ban us then. Let us help you arrange it properly.'

For Luton, with the now familiar Chief Inspector Rob Bartlett, it was the same. For the sake of the EDL as an organisation and especially as its leadership, we didn't want a riot. This was our town, where our families have to go shopping, to live, to mix. Why would we want to wreck it?

We told the police that we could handle potential trouble-makers, but if they got involved and heavy-handed it would be a nightmare. We arranged for them to let us use Charlie Brown's nightclub, we agreed a pretty short route for the march and we put all of the Luton lads at the front with a clear message to one and all – no messing about.

Some lads always wanted to kick off, because you can't weed out every single one of the idiots, but the Luton blokes were giving them a slap. The police watched and saw we could control it.

More importantly, we staged our demo without all of the Muslim agitators stirring things up. That big ginger prick Ibrahim Anderson had made a video saying that we were going to get it, but in the event none of them turned out.

There were some 2,000 coppers on duty and the reported cost of policing the demo was £2 million, which was so unnecessary. The council had been busy scaremongering, getting shops to board up their windows, terrifying people without reason. They even put on a fleet of buses to take all of Bury Park's young Muslims for a big free jolly to the Leisure World at Jarman Park in Hemel Hempstead.

In the event, things passed off as peacefully as we always wanted. And that was generally the way – if the police let us help them, and if they were willing to be smart about how they handled the local UAF and Muslim anti-EDL demonstrators, there didn't have to be a battle.

My message to whichever senior officer I was talking to was 'no line of sight'. If they could keep the left-wing mob away from us, we could control our lot. But once the bottles and bricks start raining down, with the police letting them get right in our faces, people were always going to react.

It happened towards the back end, at my last Birmingham demo, after the death of Lee Rigby. I was at the stage giving my speech, so didn't see all the trouble, but a bunch of people went to jail for the violence that day.

If I have one regret about where and when the EDL staged its rallies, it's that we never got to properly crack Tower Hamlets. It wasn't for the want of trying, but whether it was the Metropolitan Police or the Home Secretary, they were not letting us demonstrate in what was and still is a de facto Islamic caliphate.

I got locked up for just trying to walk through the place once with Kev, so staging a full-on demo was never going to be easy. The closest we got was at Aldgate, on the doorstep of Tower Hamlets, but it was when I was on bail for the incident with the far right idiot at Blackburn and I was banned from any contact whatsoever with the EDL.

I couldn't email anyone, phone them, fax them, send them a birthday card, blow them a kiss even. Nothing. I certainly couldn't attend that upcoming rally at Aldgate, but I could liaise with the police however, to try to ensure everything went off smoothly. Like I said, I'm a nice guy, all heart when I get the chance!

I told the Met liaison officer that we had a rabbi attending who would need safe passage in, because the London unions helpfully decided to strike on the tube lines serving the area. We got about 2,000 people there anyway.

That morning I went up to The Parrot to top up the booze I'd been on through the night, and the landlady stuck on this big bushy beard topped off with an orthodox Jewish hat. Once I put my black Stone Island coat on and a pair of shades, I was ready. I got some funny looks on the way there, particularly stopping off in a boozer for a couple of vodka and lemonades, while doing 'the robot dance'. When we got to Aldgate I phoned the liaison officer and sure enough the police escorted me and half a dozen members of the EDL Jewish Division through to the demo point.

I was introduced to the crowd as Rabbi Benjamin Kidemon – and I couldn't wait to take that fake beard and hat off, because I was sweating like a bitch. It was a hot day. You should have seen the look on the face of the Met liaison officer when the police realised they'd been made to look like a bunch of clowns.

Yes, I knew I'd end up in a cell, but there's a serious point. I was being denied my basic, human right of free speech. Any way you look at it, that's what was happening.

If they were going to lock me up for it, they'd be making me a political prisoner.

Once the police got their wits about them they came after me. Jim McDaid, our security officer, reckoned he'd already spotted some 'unfriendlies' in the crowd – you can see them on the Youtube video of the rally – and we legged it while the EDL lads got in the way of the cops.

We ended up going down through the basement of an Indian restaurant, up a fire escape and through a derelict building, before jumping on board a passing bus. I had a cameraman with me and I was pissing myself. We'd escaped the might of Scotland Yard thanks to a £2.20 bus ticket – and what's more the bus was going to Tower Hamlets, so we got off and went for a pint there.

The police rang me and told me to hand myself in, but I was flying, high on adrenaline and I told them, 'Catch me if you can'. 'Hand yourself in Tommy,' they said. 'Don't make us come after your family'.

They always have a way, don't they? I got picked up that night in Luton and they remanded me into Bedford prison. It was the first time I'd been back in a proper nick since that incident with the off duty copper all those years before, but it was far from the last.

After a night in the cells they put me straight into solitary confinement and I immediately went on hunger strike. In my mind they had turned me into a political prisoner and I wasn't taking that lying down.

I didn't eat for seven days and every night the EDL came and protested outside. The law must have tired of all the aggravation eventually, because they released me.

OUR ORGANISATION WAS never a political movement. Even if the EDL had become a political body, I doubt that I would have been welcomed for tea, biscuits and a cordial chat with someone like then Home Secretary Theresa May.

But neither was the overall aim simply about marches and demonstrations. That's why, in June 2011, I got one of her constituents to arrange a meeting at her MP's surgery at Maidenhead town hall and we just walked straight in.

There was a bloke who was probably her personal security officer, but I just sat down, got my laptop out and told Mrs May I wanted to talk to her about Abdul Qadeer Baksh and the Luton Islamic Centre. Baksh was and still is a radical – since discredited – but back then politicians like Theresa May were still giving him a seat at their table, involving him in their supposed anti-extremism schemes, and all the while a lot of other people – like me – considered that he was one of the bad guys, part of the problem, not the solution. It was quite funny, because when I sat down the Home Secretary didn't know whether to shout, shit, shower or shave. In the end all she did was sit back and say, all hoity-toity, 'My government has made its views clear on Muslim extremism'.

I showed her a video of a white girl getting beaten up by a Muslim gang, but she wouldn't look at it. And so I kept rewinding it and replaying. She eventually looked because she could see I wasn't stopping, but all she would say was, 'I can't comment'. I told her, 'No, but you would comment if it was a white gang attacking a woman in a burkha'.

I was there for about 20 minutes and she just sat as passive as you like, not sure what the hell to do for the best. She knew what to do the minute I stood up to leave though. Within an hour it was all over the national news that she'd been ambushed by Tommy Robinson of the EDL.

Well, she didn't want people to think it was a formal meeting or an appointment, did she? Heaven forbid she actually agreed to speak to a concerned citizen!

I'M SOMETIMES ASKED if the EDL achieved anything, or at least if it did during my years running it. We highlighted a lot of uncomfortable truths, that's for sure. We shone a torch into some dark corners the authorities preferred that nobody take notice of, and which they tried hard to pretend didn't exist. But it wasn't entirely or solely about noisy marches and demonstrations. Sometimes, the simple threat of us coming to a town or city to stage a demo was enough to get things done.

It was close to home for me, but when word went around Luton that they were going to turn a shop unit in the Arndale Centre into what was called a 'prayer room' but would in fact end up being a mosque, people were horrified.

I went round all the shops, asking the managers and owners if they really wanted this. Robbie's Bakery, which all of our wives and mums, aunties and nans used, was next door to it. They might as well have simply shut down on a Friday because no one would have gone to that end of the centre while it had a congregation of Muslim men going to prayer. They just wouldn't.

And it wasn't as if there weren't already more mosques nearby than you could shake a stick at. This wasn't about the convenience of a prayer room, it was about another symbol of a Muslim takeover. I spoke to the bloke who runs a Turkish restaurant nearby and he said it was just about the last thing they needed – and he was a Muslim!

I didn't find a single shop or unit owner who was in favour of it, so I went along to see the centre manager and he talked a load of bollocks about 'public consultation' and what have you, saying there were 'calls from members of community for it'. I told him straight: 'You do that and we will shut the shopping centre every Saturday if we have to.'

It never opened.

On another occasion some bright spark put a toilet in a shopping centre that was just a hole in the ground with two feet marks either side – like something out of Iraq or Saudi. I mean, medieval holes in the ground, FFS, in 21st century

England? I rang the shopping centre and told them they had seven days to sort their toilets, or the EDL was coming to town and the management would have to board up all the shops and explain to everyone exactly why.

Was it a form of blackmail? Of course it was. But it worked, more importantly. In the autumn of 2010 I wrote to 360 councils talking about the history of Christmas and the use of the word 'Christ'. I'd seen that the previous year at least half a dozen councils had effectively re-branded Christmas, changing its name to Winter Festival and similar such rubbish. We said that if they changed the name of Christmas the EDL would be paying them a visit – and we listed the costs involved to the police and local authority of trying to manage a full-on EDL demo.

Here's the good thing about proposing a stunt like that – they do the publicity job for you. The story hits the local papers with everyone (in officialdom at least) getting their knickers in a twist over our intended visit, but all they manage to do is build support for us. The Milton Keynes paper went ballistic, accusing the EDL of blackmail in this letter about Christmas. But here's the thing they just don't seem to get – it built support for us, not the opposite.

We were seen to be trying to protect our culture. Everyone gets annoyed when Political Correctness like this undermines the bread and butter of British traditions and heritage, but mostly people don't have a voice.

We might not have been everyone's cup of tea but we highlighted things that most ordinary folk agreed with. That Christmas, not one of those councils ditched Christmas in favour of a so-called Winter Festival.

I think that counted as something of a win for us.

THE PRESSURE KEPT building though, and it was like herding cats trying to keep the different splinter factions in line. Groups like the North-West Infidels and North-East

Infidels, wanting to go further and further to the right. Nightmare. Some of the Yorkshire lot were the worst. Things started coming to a head at Walthamstow in September 2012. I'd been liaising closely with the police because the threat level against me had risen after the planned massacre at Dewsbury a few weeks earlier.

We'd been to Dewsbury in the early days and been stitched up by the police, literally caged in the railway station car park. On the later occasion in 2012 everything went ahead pretty routinely by all accounts – I say by all accounts, because I wasn't there. We had some domestic strife going on at home and I was a mess. It was a rare time I'd missed a demo, which proved to be a lifesaver, literally. The rally ended early and everyone went home, with very little grief from the usual suspects. The UAF and some local Muslims turned out, but it sounded like it was all a bit half-hearted by them, and the police kept them out of range.

It was a good job because Omar Mohammed Khan, Mohammed Hasseen, Anzal Hussain, Mohammed Saud, Zohaib Ahmed and Jewel Uddin subsequently admitted preparing an act of terrorism. Five of them drove to Dewsbury with a car loaded with two shotguns, swords, knives, a nail bomb containing 4,578 pieces of shrapnel and a partially-assembled pipe bomb. When they missed the party they went to pray at the massive Markazi Mosque in the Savile Town area – Dewsbury's Bury Park – and they were spotted on CCTV. They would have gotten clean away with it but for their car not being insured. They were stopped heading home down the M1 and it was two days later before the police found the arsenal in their car boot.

At their sentencing a year later – they all got about 19 years – me and Kev went along to the Old Bailey and called out 'God save the Queen' when they got sentenced, which didn't go down well with their families, who were all shouting 'Allahu Akbar!' Tough shit. How many innocent people were they happy to kill that day? Because they didn't like our point of view?

After Dewsbury though, the police were on notice and we did our best to work with them. By this point it was quite a slick operation. I would arrange to meet the police and they would bring us in to the demo point – but at Walthamstow we were kept waiting and waiting. When I rang they said it wasn't safe to bring us in, which was bollocks.

They'd kept the main body of EDL supporters isolated, out of town, while they were busy with this howling mob of Muslims and UAF. Me and the security team drove straight through to the demo point where we were showered with bricks and bottles. The police switched our PA system off and wanted us to retreat back to the EDL lads who'd been standing out of the way for hours, but I gave a speech anyway, challenging the police to arrest me and calling both them and the mob a set of wankers.

And then, when we finally got to the main body of EDL protestors, they all turned on me, complaining about where the leadership had been all the time. One geezer was going on, 'I've spent £100 on this today, I want my £100 back.' I thought, 'I don't need this shit. I don't get paid for this.'

The police then arrested hundreds of EDL people for no good reason and took them to different parts of London, held them for a while – and then let them go in small groups, all wearing their EDL hoodies which I can only think was meant to endanger them, to provoke trouble.

Well, at least those lads could take them off. My face is my EDL hoodie. And I can't take that off. They wear their EDL hoodie for a day, then they go home, take it off and get on with life until their next day out. I'm stuck with mine, 24/7. There was a big backlash against me within the group over the next few days – until people saw the online video of what had actually happened, with a group of us physically under attack, being stitched up by the police.

But it was all building up, all getting too much. It felt like I was babysitting a couple of thousand people at a time and nobody appreciated it. But then again I was at a pretty low ebb all round, what with one thing or another.

What happened at Walthamstow brought a lot of things to a head. The pressure was coming on from all sides. The rank and file EDL support was always fantastic, but there was a select few people always intent on slandering me, spreading rumours, stirring things up in the background.

At the same time, parts of the organisation were wanting to go their own way and, in all honesty, I didn't know how to handle it. I wasn't a trained manager or organiser. We'd been running on adrenaline and instinct, not some sophisticated campaign plan.

At the same time, my family and my old friends thought I was going missing too. Because of EDL business I wasn't getting to friends' weddings or celebrations, and they thought I'd turned on them. A couple of mates, Flitton and Stoker, called and asked me what was going on. They said people who cared about me, good friends, just weren't seeing me any longer.

After Walthamstow there was a demo planned for Walsall and I was getting messages that if I wasn't there, things were going to implode, the organisation would split … people were telling me I wasn't interested, wasn't this, wasn't that – I was supposed to be everywhere at once and everything to everyone. There were whispering campaigns, people saying we had to align with this lot, get in bed with that lot. Lots of bullshit.

And then on the weekend of Walsall I went off on a stag party to Slovenia, deciding I was having a bit of 'me' time. The calls telling me that I had to get my arse back were incessant. Non-stop. If I didn't show in Walsall, that was that, the BNP were taking us over, this was going to happen, that was going to happen.

I'd been out on the piss in Slovenia all day Friday but it wasn't going away, and at about 2am I rang Helen Gower and told her to fix me a flight. I came back. I made it to Walsall and I asked the crowd straight out – do you want this organisation to work with the BNP? Put your hand up. There wasn't a single hand. I pointed to every non-white face around us and told them directly – you wouldn't be here, you wouldn't be here. And I signed off with, 'Up yours Nick Griffin, we will never align with you!'

I WAS STARTING to unravel, but I was still capable of being completely and utterly pissed off at the way we were being treated. I was raving about Walthamstow and what the police had put us through there. They hadn't let us protest, so I decided to give them something to get really worked up about.

I hadn't been sleeping, I was drinking and doing drugs and probably going in a direction that I would have come to regret eventually. After the abortive Walthamstow demo, then Walsall, I decided we'd have a day of action – except I didn't tell anyone where or when it was.

I felt that I couldn't trust anyone. We were leaking like a bloody sieve and Kev was busy with his new campaign to get elected as the Police and Crime Commissioner for Luton and Beds. He took it really seriously and got a good number of votes in the election too, but it meant that I was out front quite a bit on my own. The night before my day of action Chief Inspector Bartlett rang me up to ask what was going on – they knew something was up. All I told him was that it wasn't in Luton, so he need not worry. I'd always been straight with him and I still was. There was nothing for the local law to worry about.

We hired a big Luton box van and gathered a few lads from each area – Newcastle, Scotland, Birmingham, East Anglia, the South West, but on our way to the meet, driving through Bury Park at about 8am, one of the lads saw Sayful Islam. It was the first time I'd seen him face to face since he hit me through the car window when we were making the Proud and Prejudiced documentary.

I stopped the car at the traffic lights and legged it after him, and Mr Jihad ran like a whelping bitch. Yeah right, they love death more than we love life. I'm not quite sure what happened except that he must have tripped over his dress, fallen and bruised himself a bit when he fell. Apparently he lost his mobile phone and keys as well when I was chasing him. Shit happens, I guess...

Locals started coming out and it wouldn't be long until it was an unfriendly crowd scene, but I was howling laughing at this pathetic piece of shit, grovelling in the street. I chuckled away at that – right until the day went completely tits up.

One option I had in mind for our day of action was to go visit the East London Mosque, but I had someone on the ground in the neighbourhood and he told me the place was crawling with coppers.

We also had Abu Hamza's address in west London and had worked out how much benefits he was getting, how big a drain on society he was. The idea was that we'd go knock on his door, give him a seven day notice to vacate the property that belonged to a country he despised, and whose military servicemen and women he repeatedly called for the massacre of.

We were going to tell Abu Hamza, 'Leave or face the consequences'. Don't ask me what the consequences were going to be. I didn't think it through that far. Lastly I'd traced three addresses of people tied up in Operation Bullfinch, the Oxford paedophile case, all of whom were out on bail. Paying them a visit was a further option.

I changed the original meet at the last minute to a different pub in Hitchin and I still wouldn't tell anyone what the plan was, just that I'd reveal it when we were on our way. There must have been around 70 of us in the back of that lorry, packed in like sardines, all wearing balaclavas and sweating like so many fat birds in spacesuits. People were nearly passing out with the lack of oxygen.

Kev wasn't in the back with us, because of the Police Commissioner stuff. He was suited and booted, trying to look all professional, following on behind in my BMW.

I'd programmed the satnav to three addresses using back roads, but the driver reprogrammed it, which I didn't know because I was sweating my nuts off in the back. It took us down the M25, and that proved fatal to the plan.

The police were waiting for us at South Mimms services. I was in the van with the lads and had to crack open the back a bit because people were collapsing from the heat and lack of air – then Kev rang to say there were meat wagons flying up the M25, in serious numbers. And then the shitty van ran out of diesel. It just slowed and whimpered and coughed, spluttered and farted to a pathetic stop on the M25, like something out of a comedy sketch. It was about time too, because there were people in a seriously bad way in the back.

We threw open the door and Jesus, but there was just a mass of police about four deep, all with Taser guns aimed at us, these little red laser dots dancing about on our chests. Shit and double shit. Although at least we could breathe!

Police intelligence apparently had it that we were armed and dangerous and heading to attack mosques. The fact is we were all sweating like pigs thinking what a stupid idea it had been in the first place. We were just glad to take the balaclavas off and get out of the lorry.

We were all arrested on suspicion of whatever they could dream up on the spur of the moment, but then they transferred me to Westminster and landed me with an extra surprise – they were arresting me in relation to the assault of Sayful Islam earlier that morning. Like I said, the little grass just fell ... but that wasn't all. They also charged me for entering the USA illegally, over an incident when I tried to accept a speaking invitation, but used a mate's passport having already been refused entry due to Home Office interference. I was bailed for the Sayful Islam incident and the lorry, but then they remanded me over the American stunt.

Mum came down with members of family who had put up £80,000 bail to get me out – but the judge refused it on any terms and I was remanded into prison from then, in October, until January. Locked up for three months, over using a mate's passport – while Muslim rapists and paedophiles were getting bail? Unbelievable.

Since then, there's been a case of a British Muslim girl who used her twin sister's passport in order to go join ISIS. She wanted to fight jihad against us and kept her liberty. I wanted to speak up for Britain and got 10 months.

I was going to plead not guilty because I hadn't actually broken any laws in Britain, it was on the American side where I'd been a bit cheeky. However my solicitor told me that if I fought the case I'd be on remand until a trial date as far away as June. If I pleaded guilty, I'd most likely walk with time served on remand, which pretty much ended up being the case.

It was expensive from the point of view that they impounded my car, which Kev had been in. It cost me two grand to get it back, when I eventually got out. More importantly, that prison time turned out to be a blessing, if a painful one. It was, quite literally, a sobering 22 weeks of me taking stock.

PAMELA GELLER AND Robert Spencer are two of America's leading anti-Islamist campaigners, who'd been staunch supporters of what we were doing pretty much from the beginning. They both write hard-hitting blogs and highlight the dangers of radical Islam in the USA. At one point they planned on attending an EDL march to Woolwich, in memory of Lee Rigby, but Home Secretary Theresa May banned them from entering Britain.

So much for the land of democracy and free speech, don't you think? Here we are, a haven for Muslim hate preachers, people we can't even get rid of despite them wanting to blow the country up, and whose extremist messages we regularly give a platform on the BBC.

And what happens when two friends of Britain want to come and simply pay their respects to one of our fallen heroes? They're banned from the country. It's all arse-about-face if you ask me.

My increasing public profile led to me meeting a lot of different people and a group of US senators flew over to meet us in London. It was really encouraging. They said that unlike the portrayal by our own media and politicians, what they saw at an EDL demonstration wasn't thugs and hooligans, but the last line of resistance. They were viewing it from outside in – completely differently.

They invited me to the States to meet and talk to other like-minded people, to inform them about what was happen in towns and cities across Britain. They were clearly of the view that as bad as we were having things in the UK, the USA was next with its fast-growing Muslim population and not much of a stomach for tackling some of the many problems that brings with it.

I could spread the word about what happens when Islam takes a hold of and even takes over a community and we arranged to fly over on September 10th, in time for an event to mark the anniversary of the September 11th attacks on the Twin Towers.

Me and Kev and a couple of the boys flew out to New York but when we got to immigration I was told, point blank, that I was not being allowed in. Apparently we had been followed by security officers from London and what's more the Home Office had been in touch with the American state department and flagged me up as a dangerous individual, someone who shouldn't be welcome in the 'Land of the Free and Home of the Brave', as their national anthem preaches.

The boys carried on and had a bit of fun, but the purpose of the visit had been hijacked. I was turned right around and put on a plane home, so don't ever think that Big Brother isn't watching you.

What I did next though was dumb, totally. At least it was in the sense that I'm going to struggle if ever the kids want to go to Disneyworld in Florida. I was seriously pissed off at what we'd been put through, so I went down to Luton Register Office and applied to change my name by deed poll. I became Paul Harris – and as soon as I did, I applied for a passport. Legally, I suppose I still am Paul Harris.

But then, as a bit of a belt and braces exercise, I borrowed a pal's passport too, for good measure. Did we look alike? Not really. But what is it they say – if you resemble your passport photo, you're probably not well enough to travel anyway. So off I went again.

I flew Virgin Atlantic out of Heathrow to JFK in New York using the passport of Andrew McMaster. Kev came along with me but he flew into nearby Newark airport.

It all seemed to be going pretty smoothly, but then at immigration, after they'd taken my fingerprints, I was told to go and wait to be seen and they pointed to a room which I recognised from the last visit which went tits up. I knew what was coming, so I never went into the room – I bolted. I headed straight out of the airport, grabbed a cab and headed into town where I met up with Kev.

We booked into a hotel in Manhattan and I got to speak at an event staged to mark the September 11 atrocity, but also to raise concern over provocative plans to build a mega mosque near the site of the Twin Towers. The evening was a dinner for about 300 people and I was on after a New York senator. I spoke to them about who the EDL were and what we were about. I tried to explain the problems we in Britain faced with militant Islam and I brought a warning to the United States.

I told them that I wished someone had given us a warning in the UK 20 years ago, about what was happening to our country – and that they'd better believe it was coming to them too.

Kev and I stayed for two nights before we flew home, this time using a ticket I bought in my 'own' name of Paul Harris. It was stupid, it was impulsive, it was very expensive, and it cost me massively, in far more than financial terms.

Did I really think I would get away with it? I don't know, seriously. And I certainly didn't think the repercussions would be as punishing as they were. I mean, it wasn't as though I'd hurt anyone, was it? I'd just stuck two fingers up to the authorities, is all. I guess governments don't have much of a sense of humour when you're messing with them, trying to prove a point. They like to have the last word.

When it eventually came to court, the judge at Southwark Crown Court said it was by no means a 'trivial' offence and banged me up for 10 months.

Do I regret it? In a way I do, because I'd love to see America one day. But by getting me locked away, it woke me up to the chaos my life had become, and to what I was doing to my wife and children, to my mum and dad. So in that sense, it probably saved my life.

15: ENEMY OF THE STATE

YOU ARE ONLY supposed to do a maximum of 72 hours in solitary confinement, when you are imprisoned in the British penal system, before your case is referred to the Home Secretary for consideration.

I described earlier how I did that first stretch in Bedford prison as a young man, saying that I reckoned I could handle it. You find a group of blokes you can relate to, talk to, hang with. There are basic comforts, exercise, activities, a television to watch, a reasonable representation of a social life, I suppose you could say.

Solitary confinement, being what they call 'down the block' is very different indeed. When that case for illegally entering the USA arose, and because of the threats against me, I was usually asked if I wanted to 'go on the numbers', which meant, did I want protection? That in turn meant did I want to be sectioned with all the various perverts and paedophiles, kept away from the general population?

No I did not, thank you very much. If it meant risking my life in and amongst Islamic terrorists, so be it. I wasn't choosing to get myself locked away with those weirdos. I'd rather take my chances. It was an old fashioned Luton-pride thing, I suppose.

Down the block, you are caged in a room pretty much like a police cell, which is meant by definition to be for temporary confinement. A concrete 'bed' with a thin plastic mattress on it. A toilet. And that, my friends, is that. Once a day you can go for a shower, make a phone call, then walk around a square metal box with no daylight whatsoever for half an hour, because solitary tends to be underground.

It's a punishment, for someone who has not shown themselves fit to be treated like a normal prisoner. Is it designed to drive a man mad? It sure is. And if not, it's meant to take him as close to the limit as you can without resorting to torture. That's why there are strict rules about isolating people until they start trying to claw and eat their way through the walls – or top themselves. You're supposed to be limited to a 28-day stretch in solitary. I did 22 weeks.

The blokes who effectively 'live' in solitary confinement, because of being a danger to anyone and everyone including themselves, are not human beings in the way most civilised people would recognise the term. Before we dig deeper however, I need to put into perspective what my life outside of the EDL had become, and specifically the way the British state was dealing with the Tommy Robinson problem.

I'VE TRIED TO BE as honest as I can here, so far as memory serves, with the mistakes I've made, with the downright bloody stupid things I've done but which seemed like a good idea at the time. I often knew it was going to end in tears, like the stunt on top of the Fifa building in Zurich. They're not exactly going to give you a limousine ride to the airport and upgrade you to first class after an escapade like that, are they?

But sometimes making the point, fighting for the principle, has to be worth the minor inconvenience of a few hundred quid fine and a couple of days in a police cell.

I'm really not trying to paint myself as some kind of martyr, because that's not how I see things. I'm just an ordinary bloke who got sick and tired of being a second class citizen in his own town and in his own country.

I simply decided that someone had to stand up and ask the question – what we are doing? Are we happy what we're allowing to happen to a country that our forefathers fought and died to preserve for their children and grandchildren? Do we know what we're risking by totally ignoring the issues that were slapping me in the face on a daily basis? Do we even know we're doing it?

The moment we started the EDL, with me as the nominal head, the British state declared war on Tommy Robinson. Whether it was the police using arrest and detention as a way to either piss me off or disrupt EDL activities, whether it was taking apart my working life going back to the Year Dot, or whether it was prison governors and screws physically throwing me to the lions by putting me on an open wing amongst violent Muslim extremists, I've had the lot thrown at me.

The goal? To grind me down. To shut me up. That's all I can fathom. To make the point that the state can beat down anyone who thinks they can mess with it. If you can think of a better explanation for some of the tales I'm about to tell, then I'd love to hear it.

Sure, I've asked for trouble. And some. But to the extent of prison warders locking me in a room with three violent Muslim prisoners who kicked me into an unrecognisable mess? That doesn't happen in a civilised country, within a system like the United Kingdom's, does it?

Yeah right. Don't make me laugh. Not that I was doing much of that through broken teeth with my head slashed to the skull and my eyes swollen shut.

Just as I've tried to describe the journey of the EDL as an organisation, so I'll try to illustrate how, alongside it, the British state got to work trying to cut the head off it. The police came looking for me right after the first UPL demo and it didn't stop to the day I walked out of Peterborough nick on Friday July 24th 2015. Not even then actually.

A little while after the UPL arose out of the Royal Anglian Regiment's homecoming, in the very early days of the EDL, Kev and I were heading to talk to people from the Scottish Defence League in Edinburgh.

When the pair of us rolled up at Luton airport I was arrested by Special Branch on suspicion of criminal damage and a racially aggravated incident.

I hadn't a clue what they were talking about. They said they would be raiding properties linked to me and sure enough they took my mum's house apart. Apparently there had been criminal damage at a hotel in Sheffield, where we'd stayed after an early Leeds demo.

According to Special Branch, I had asked the girl on reception where she was from. She happened to be from Afghanistan and if anything I was flirting with her. The young woman was clearly a headscarf-wearing Muslim and we were 10 hoodie-wearing EDL members, so I made sure we were super nice. I told her that two of my best friends at school were from Afghanistan – Kamran and Imran.

Meanwhile the police said that a door fitting in the hotel corridor had been broken. It was a £30 fitting and they sent 15 officers from Sheffield, all the way to Luton, looking for proof that I had stayed there. They took my computer and arrested a friend who had booked the room. We had officers with machine guns at my house. They even seized my dad's business computer and kept it for three weeks.

All over a £30 door fitting? How do they even get a warrant for all of that shit? Tell me it doesn't sound like something out of Soviet Russia.

Our next demo after that was due to be Bradford where I was going to discuss sexual grooming by Muslim gangs – so the police bailed me to appear on the Saturday of that demo. My bail included conditions that I couldn't associate with more than three EDL supporters. You don't need to be Sherlock Holmes to work out what that was all about.

There were no charges brought, a pattern that would be repeated time and again, but the warning signs were clear.

I complained to the Independent Police Complaints Commission about that arrest and when they eventually reached their conclusions, they sent the findings to an address I hadn't lived at for a long time. I eventually had to chase the complaint up more than two years later.

And guess what? The IPPC upheld virtually every complaint I made and said it was taking disciplinary action against some of the officers involved.

That broken £30 fitting in the Sheffield hotel? The IPCC inquiry found that the police had obtained a statement signed by the hotel manager – dated before they came and raided and arrested me – saying categorically that I had not done the damage. The manager even identified the culprit for them. Senior officers simply ignored that, because of course it had nothing to do with the trumped up charge and the fishing expedition they were on.

Their warrant didn't allow the police to take away my business paperwork when they raided the house, so officers spent all day physically copying things out. About a £30 door fitting? Really? And as for the Muslim girl on reception – she hadn't complained about anything, to anyone. The police had harassed her, quizzed her about what I'd said, and then they decided my asking where she was from constituted racially aggravated harassment.

What – that sort of stuff only happens in a police state does it? They were only just warming up, folks.

Two months later the doors went in again, this time the Luton police arresting me on suspicion of money laundering and tax evasion.

We'd had the road shut off the first time by armed police with simultaneous raids at my house and my mum's. They even took the neighbour's drains up, putting cameras down them, and used handheld scanners round our house walls looking for cavities where I might be hiding stuff. It took them 10 hours. For what? For nothing, that's what.

I had to go talk to the neighbours because it looked like I was Fred West. I had to tell them they were looking for evidence of unpaid taxes and investigating me for money laundering over the tanning salon. It all came to nothing of course, after years of constant aggravation, but that wasn't much consolation to the people we had to live in the same street as. Forget the terrorists, the authorities were making sure that we were pariahs amongst our neighbours.

We had to move because my wife was embarrassed to take our little girl to school. Then the police came to give us that first Osman warning and placed officers outside the house, who might as well have turned up with a For Sale sign, because the neighbours were understandably going spare. We had to move again.

Later, they would come to arrest my wife when she was six months pregnant over absolutely nothing and force us to get someone to come and look after our little girl. The copper was ashamed on that occasion, and actually said, 'Sorry'. A lot of the ordinary officers knew it was pure horseshit, that we were being persecuted for the sake of it.

They froze my personal bank account and business account. They just walked into the tanning shop and took the computer. I had to close the business for three days.

Mine and my dad's business, T&S Plumbing & Heating, was actually in his name and bank account. Barclays wrote to him out of the blue to say they were shutting his account down. Just like that. No explanation. And not just his business account but his personal account too, which he'd had with them for years. What was he supposed to have done wrong?

Then I got an order saying that I couldn't spend more than £250 a week. I could go into the bank once a week to take out £250 and that was that – to keep and feed and clothe and house my family. No appeals, no hearings, nothing. Just the bastards hitting you on the head over and over again with a police state hammer. Because they can.

At the time I was running a construction job and I was taking home £880 a week, plus I had my plumbing work and the tanning shop. I'd already been to my accountant and gone through absolutely everything to make sure I was squeaky clean, but they spent months, years, trying to build a case. God alone knows how much money and resource they wasted.

I was running jobs for a multi-millionaire, Dave Richman, back in 2006/07 – Hollywood Dave, as we called him. He had hundreds of properties, and I worked for a time on his Spanish portfolio. Dave had no kids and he was great to us, we were like family. I learned a lot from him about property investment, picking up good deals on bank repossessions, things like that. Another pal too, CJ, who we nicknamed 'Businessman of the Year', I learned a lot from.

Suddenly in 2009/10 the police were looking into those properties we'd acquired. Even though I had a mortgage on my own first home, I'd struggled to get finance because of an old dispute dating back to when I was not much more than a kid, about 20. I got a chance to buy a property for £100,000 which I knew I could sell for £150,000. I borrowed £70k from a friend and £30k from my brother – but they paid it direct to purchase the house. However when it was then sold on at a profit, the money came back through my account, at which point I repaid them.

There was nothing wrong with it, except that it wasn't the regular mortgage-style of buying a house. All the police could see though – all they wanted to see – was a bunch of money coming and going. Have you seen how Muslim families help each other buy homes to avoid 'riba' – paying interest which is anti-Islamic? It was no different to that.

Ironically, I was buying all of my plumbing gear for cash – you'll like this, because I was dealing with a Muslim plumbers' merchants in Bury Park and they were giving me a big discount for paying cash. Were they declaring everything to the taxman?

That wasn't my problem, but on the day that I was supposed to go to trial I gave the police piles and piles of receipts and invoices with every single penny accounted for.

I had had a major problem during that case because the police didn't bring charges for three years. The bank only keeps six years of customer records and the police got them when they began the investigation.

By the time I knew the police were intent on charging me and I went to the bank for my records, it was the same six year limit. The police had three years of my records that I didn't.

They added up every penny that came in, declared it all as income whether it was or not, came up with a total of £300,000 'unexplained income' and said I owed £137,000 in tax. Eventually I had to employ a forensic accountant and it was a massive job, proving that a specific item was a loan from a friend or relative – or even winnings from a William Hill betting account! He said he had never, ever seen a stitch up job like the one the police and CPS were pulling.

They even used Noel Lucas QC, one of their very best go-to barristers. They wasted his time though, because the judge took one look at my accountant's report and threw the case out. I'd had to answer bail every six weeks for four years and in the end there was simply no case. All I was guilty of was having messy accounts. After four years, every penny came back as legit.

Meanwhile, during my time at the head of the EDL, I'd run out of cash myself. They had driven me to my knees. Mum had even re-mortgaged their house in order to help us out, keep us afloat and yet at the end of everything, the police, the state, had nothing. But they weren't finished, and this time they were going to play really dirty.

After the M25 arrest I was remanded to Wandsworth and put in solitary over the passport stunt. Not quite robbing the Crown Jewels, or systematically raping dozens of white schoolchildren for 20 years, was it? But still, no money was enough to get me bail. I think I knew that I needed to be in prison, or at least somewhere out of the limelight, and in those first eight weeks inside I sobered up, straightened out, and spent a lot of time thinking about what my life had become, what the people around me – my family, who for some unfathomable reason still loved me – were having to endure because my selfishness.

The Wandsworth governor came straight out and said that I was going to get killed if I was put on a wing, where the prison population was more than 50% foreign nationals, so he sent me straight down the block. I needed the solitude at first and I coped well enough. I wasn't doing the numbers with the child molesters, I was down the block like a chap. Chill out time, if hardly in five-star surroundings.

Did I say five-star? Wandsworth is a Victorian nick. There was no heating and I was wearing four pairs of socks in a dungeon that people were only supposed to spend two or three days in, at most.

Soon enough four weeks had passed and I was ready to be put back into the general prison population, on the wing, and if not at a place like Wandsworth then a suitable nick because I wasn't a Category A lifer. Or so I thought.

The games were only just starting – they transferred me. From Wandsworth I was taken to Bedford, which is trouble with a capital 'T' because while it might not house the very worst Islamic radicals in the country, every local Muslim gangster knew my face like his own mother's.

Abu Hamza's son was on the wing in Bedford for armed robbery, but at least I thought there would be a few local lads I knew, who could watch my back. I thought I'd have a chance in general population there. No such luck. All the Muslims saw who was coming in the joint and they were shouting and screaming like madmen – I was sent straight down the block again. It might have been meant to keep me alive, but I hadn't done anything wrong. The least they could have done was let me have a television, but there was another agenda at work.

From there they really piled it on. November 27th, 2012, was my 30th birthday, so Bedfordshire police chose that day to come down, take me out of my cell and charge me with the mortgage fraud case. For good measure they raised the prospect of pursuing my wife over the tax case I'd just been cleared of. And then they interviewed me about the attack on Sayful Islam on the morning we got nicked on the M25.

On CCTV they had our car pulling up and three of us getting out and chasing him, but there wasn't any coverage of where I actually caught up with him, and he tripped and hurt himself. I never said a word to the arsehole coppers throughout, until they started talking about the Sayful Islam incident, at which point I started laughing. It was the first time I'd been cheered up in weeks.

The officer doing the interview said, deadpan, 'For the record, Mr Lennon is laughing'.

I could still picture this big coward running away in his dress – the man who supposedly loved death more than life itself. I guess he just wasn't ready to meet his virgins yet. How could you not laugh? I didn't get charged over the coward's accidental fall, but they hit me with both barrels over the mortgage and stuff. Happy 30th birthday, Tommy.

I MIGHT HAVE sobered up and got my head back on, but it didn't mean that I was happy with the treatment I was getting from the screws. I wasn't a murderer. I was in the nick for borrowing a mate's passport, however bloody stupid that was. Solitary is a punishment and I hadn't done anything wrong to deserve the punishment.

It got to the point where I thought well, if you want me to be trouble, I can do that. After all I was already on the punishment block so there was nothing to lose. Where was the incentive to behave like a model prisoner? I was being persecuted for a something-and-nothing offence and all the privileges were saved for the blokes plotting to blow us up.

The only human contact outside my cell was when I got a meeting with my solicitor. On one visit I saw all the Muslim prisoners coming back from Friday prayers and the second they saw me they always screamed blue murder, so that time I shouted back, 'Allah, Allah, who the fuck is Allah?' They went berserk. They were calling Catholic priests paedophiles, which seriously angered my old traveller mates – Irish Catholic lads. I sat pissing myself laughing. It was going to be a battlefield when they opened the cell doors the next morning. I should have known better.

I had a rare family visit booked for the following day – so at 6am that morning they pulled me out and put me in a taxi and sent me over to HMP Woodhill in Milton Keynes, another Category A lock-up for mass murderers and major terrorists. They were in such a rush to get me out of Bedford, they shoved me in an ordinary taxi.

No handcuffs and leg chains like a serial killer – even though I was being locked up like one. I obviously wasn't that much of a threat that they couldn't just put me in a cab and send me to another nick. So again, straight away I was thrown into solitary. I wanted to make a phone call but they said I was A-Cat, so I got nothing. No phones, no visits, nothing. It was bullshit.

Once in Woodhill I got a legal visit so they took me up to see my solicitor. You are placed in a glass cubicle, facing your visitor, in a line of similar cubicles. I'd noticed that there were four Muslims in the ones along from me – but then I realised that they were all going off their heads. I saw one bang on the next partition, who started banging on the next one and within seconds they were all eyeballing me and having hysterical fits.

According to the screw, they were the same blokes who had planned to blow up the demo in Dewsbury – the one they were late for because I didn't show up. They were the useless bastards who were planning holy jihad, but had forgotten to set their alarm. It was like a scene out of that comedy film, Four Lions. I was laughing and calling them a set of wankers and poor Brian, my solicitor, went white as a ghost, because he really wasn't used to this sort of stuff.

I was ten weeks into solitary and I spent four days in Woodhill with nothing, just an empty cell, until eventually the Prison Board ruled that I wasn't A-Cat so then at least they let me talk to my wife and arrange a visit.

Boy, what a performance that was, too. I had my own visiting hall, like that infamous prison maniac Charles Bronson. To get me from A to B for the visit they locked down every cell, the whole prison. I felt like Hannibal Lecter. No one could get near me or even see me.

I had a two hour visit with the family, just us and the screws in this big room, but when you're in solitary, all you look forward to is that in two weeks time you'll see your kids again. You count down the days, the minutes.

So they did it again. The Friday before my next visit they hauled me out and booted me back down to Wandsworth. Straight away, back in solitary. This time however, there was some progress – the case went to trial and I was given 10 months for the passport offence.

With time served on remand, I only had a couple of months to serve – but again it was back to Wandsworth and another stretch in solitary. More unjust bullshit. Once a day when I went for a shower I could call Helen Gower. And then they blocked her number, saying she was a security risk which was even more total bollocks.

During one visit I whispered that I had a phone in my cell, just to check if they were listening in on conversations which were supposed to be private. I got back and they spun my cell, turned it upside down and searched me for a phone. There wasn't one of course, because I didn't have a bent screw bringing me drugs and phones and shit in, like the guys in general population, but I knew for sure that I was under constant scrutiny. I wonder if they had someone listening through the night in case I talked in my sleep. They probably checked whether I snored or not, too.

Such as I had entertainment, it was getting on the nerves of the Muslim prisoners down the block with me. If there was one positive to take away from that experience, it was a better understanding of the type of people I was dealing with. I read the Koran during those 22 weeks in solitary and suddenly all of what I suppose people might call Islamic prejudices didn't seem so prejudiced at all.

Most of what I'd heard second and third hand was right there in black and white, absolute encouragement – no, a divine instruction – to act atrociously towards the rest of the world. Obey Allah or burn in hell forever. Page after page of it. Sex slaves, the lot. The thing is horrific.

The Koran was sent to me by a Dawa group – Muslim missionaries who try to turn people to Islam. They probably thought they were having a laugh at my expense, but they ended up doing me a huge favour.

I started writing down key facts, about their hateful attitude towards Jews and Christians, about sexual slavery. I couldn't get my head round it. Here was the holy book the world's Muslims want to rule the planet by – and if you ask my opinion, the thing should be banned for inciting racial and religious hatred on almost every page.

Unbelievable. I read more and more – the Koran professing Muslim superiority over all; that it's permissable to beat wives; that Mohammed is the model for all Muslim men – so it was fine to marry children aged just nine. Hatred towards all non-Muslims was enshrined in their holy book, page after page of it.

I know what argument you're going to use now – that the Bible is just as bad. Well, firstly, no it isn't, but secondly, there aren't any Christian countries wanting to run the world – the entire world – based on the strict teachings of the Old Testament. Christian interpretations have moved on and Christian faith is separate from politics, law and culture. They are all one and the same in Islam, and still rooted in the 7th century. It's a problem folks.

It came in very handy in providing me with a bit of fun, because I would argue with the Muslim prisoners armed with my new-found knowledge. And do you know what? You would be literally amazed how ignorant so many of them are about this religion they all claim to be willing to die for. I was rowing with one bloke, Hobbs, a Jamaican guy, a convert, and I was hammering him because he knew nothing about Islam. I asked him if he agreed that a 56-year-old bloke should have sex with a nine-year-old girl?

He was shouting back, 'What man, what man?' I said, 'It's your Prophet, you wanker. That's who!' I asked Hobbs about his family. He loved his nan. So I asked him if she was burning in hell. He was bouncing off the walls, the sad prick. 'What you say? What you say about my nan?'

'Is she burning in hell Hobbs? Your nan? Is she burning in eternal hell fire?'

'No man, course she isn't, she's my nan, a lovely woman.'

This geezer didn't even know the basics of his own religion. So many of them didn't. One of the screws, a Nigerian guy, opened my cell door one morning laughing, and shook my hand. He said he'd been waiting years to hear something like that. It got to the point that the prison imam came to my door and asked me to stop bothering the Muslims. I said, 'What, stop educating them? Because they know nothing about their religion?'

Every opportunity, I was onto them. How many wives did Mohammed have? They knew jack shit about what they'd converted to and they were giving it all this Allahu Akbar bollocks, going out to showers with their prayer mats over their shoulders. When I got the daily papers in the morning, I'd start drawing on all of the photos of the women. So I'd put a burkha on the page 3 girl in The Sun, and draw clothes on any women not dressed properly, then I'd push it out and have it passed on to the Muslim prisoners, because the fact is, they all liked to look at the naked tits. Of course they did. Being offended and outraged was purely for our benefit. Once the Muslim lad next door was howling laughing at what I'd done. We both were.

I kept on at Hobbs – I told him to bring his bad boys down to meet mine one day outside the prison. The thing is, I knew there was an EDL demo planned for outside Wandsworth. Sure enough, the next day, this chant went up ... 'E-E-EDL!' There were sirens going and these guys thought, 'Fucking hell, he's called an army in!' It put a smile on my face for a while.

Every week in solitary you were taken to see the governor and the mental health officers, for assessment. You might not know this, but in every governor's office there's a photograph of the Queen on the wall. Every one. The same photo. I got to the point where it was a bit like the Mona Lisa thing – as if Her Maj's eyes were watching me. I used to give her a little salute and a nod and say, 'Alright ma'am.' Well, it put a smile on my face, because as far as I'm concerned she's the head of my country, not those wankers in Westminster.

At one demo, Peterborough I think, I went on at length about the Queen, calling on her to listen to her people's concerns. Watching it back, I cringe now at some of the bad language I used. They were early days, but I can see how it didn't impress a lot of people. Either way, Her Maj clearly wasn't listening, because no Royal pardon was forthcoming.

MEANWHILE, AS THE weeks and months were passing with me still locked up in solitary confinement, my family were doing all they possibly could to get someone to take my case seriously.

From about eight weeks in, with no end to the isolation in sight, they started getting in touch with human rights lawyers. They'd explain this prisoner's circumstances, the lawyer would express outrage, and then they'd explain that it was the leader of the English Defence League – and the spineless arseholes would drop it like a red hot brick. Not one of them would touch my case.

One said that most of their clients were Muslims and representing me would be bad for business. My family even went to the lawyer who represented Jon Venables, the lad who murdered the Liverpool toddler, Jamie Bulger. He could argue the case of someone who battered a two-year-old to death, but he wouldn't touch me with a barge pole. It seems that human rights only apply to a select group of people.

During the first spell in Wandsworth I had a weekly review with the governor, a mental health specialist and the prison chaplain or whichever faith representative was on duty. Sometimes it was the imam. They knew I shouldn't be there, but they couldn't put me on the wing, and the governor said they couldn't find another prison that was happy to take me.

At one point a priest visited me and spoke about specialist units at Woodhill and the Isle of Wight nicks where they kept 'Queens Evidence Unit' prisoners. In short, these were havens for snitches, criminals who'd grassed on their mates. I wasn't volunteering for that. No way.

When they finally returned me to Wandsworth for a second stretch there, I was in a pretty bad way. There was a screw, a former Royal Marine who I knew from my first spell. He sat me down and said he was worried.

I'd lost two stones, I was coming out in sores and he said that I needed to get out of solitary. That period inside might have dried me out, but now it was pushing me to the edge. I talked to the chaplaincy and decided to go on hunger strike, because all I could see was that they were deliberately trying to drive me insane. There was no end to it. So I went on a seven day hunger strike, taking just liquid. There were times I got locked up when I just did the time, but there were occasions that were complete stitch ups, totally unjust.

What I was now being subjected to was state-sponsored torture to my mind. I was nearing the end of my tether when the governor called me in and told me that I was finally being transferred to Wayland Prison in Norfolk – a Category C nick, complete with a gym, proper facilities, a civilised prison for people with my actual level of so-called offence. I couldn't wait for Monday to come.

You know what happens next, don't you? They took me to Wayland and put me straight down the block again. Solitary. I lost it. This was inhuman.

I had my family coming for a two-hour visit and the screws normally come down at 11.30am to get you – except they told me they had Muslim prisoners on visits before me. They just left my family sitting there and didn't come for me until 1pm, by which time I had just 45 minutes left and by then I was so boiled up, the visit was ruined.

The Muslims were down the block for fighting and I hadn't done a thing to deserve to be there, but they got preferential treatment, again. The bastards were trying to break me, whatever it took.

At Wayland your daily shower lasted seven minutes, exactly, so I'd go have my shower – then they'd leave me standing there, bollock naked, for 45 minutes. When they opened up for one certain Muslim prisoner to go take his daily shower, as he walked past my cell he'd pull the flap in the door open and spit through it at me. He did it every day.

In the end I put paper over the opening. That way I knew that I'd have enough time to react when he next did it. That was my entertainment, sitting 23-and-a-half hours a day, planning what I could do about this bastard. I put

225

the paper over the opening so that when he pulled back the flap, he had to push it off – which gave me just enough time. I'd pissed in a cup and he got it right in his face. I laughed my bollocks off. That was a rare highlight in and amongst some very dark days.

I got shit for that too – not for the cup of piss in his face, but for covering my flap with paper. That was against the rules, so I got a 'loss of privileges' penalty. Loss of privileges? Absolutely hilarious. What privileges? I was the one man in the entire prison who didn't have any.

My tag date came and went – I should have been home, but I was still in solitary confinement after more than five months, let alone 72 hours. Eventually my family managed to find a great lawyer, a woman from a firm called the Stokoe Partnership in Manchester. It was only when she threatened them with a Judicial Review, citing multiple human rights violations that they gave me the tag and sent me home the next day. The governor of the nick could be found personally liable for maltreatment of a prisoner. It took that threat to get me a semblance of justice.

At that point however, the state was cranking the pressure up from all angles. My passport offence had been turned into a nightmare of solitary confinement, but other things were now coming to a head. Not only hadn't the police not finished with me, they'd barely started.

WE OWNED SEVEN properties at the time the EDL started. One was in my name and six were in my wife's. Those old credit problems of mine made it easier just to do the paperwork through her name. When her brother wanted to buy a house eventually, to get on the property ladder, it was an £80k property and I lent Little Stevie the £20k for his deposit. He's like a younger brother to me. I also introduced him to my mortgage adviser, who'd arranged our legitimate loans. That was in 2006.

He bought the house, sold it six months later and made about £30k profit, the problem being that he'd overstated his earnings on the application. He sold it to a bloke who also bought it on a self certification mortgage that he shouldn't have had, strictly speaking. But like I said, everyone was doing it at the time and it didn't seem a big deal. This was before the financial markets went tits up a couple of years later. But that wasn't any of my business.

I got my £20k back, that was all.

No one lost any money at any stage, but what made me feel really bad was that the mortgage adviser got 18 months jail as well. She wasn't in great health either, but in order to nail me – the main point of the exercise – the police had to crack down on her too for facilitating it.

The police must have spent hundreds of thousands trying to build the tax case against me, then seen their 30 or so charges all whittled away one by one, until finally they played their trump card. They were going to nail my wife over the taxes, a woman who knew nothing about our finances – unless I took the blame on everyone's behalf.

They were going to get Tommy Robinson once and for all, through a blameless woman. Put her face and name in the public domain, destroy any hope my family had of living a normal life. They'd poured all those resources into trying to nail me, and they had to have something to show for it. My wife and kids? Collateral damage, nothing more.

Initially, I was potentially looking at three-to-five years in jail. Although I'd only lent her brother that 20 grand, as part of the overall case involving that mortgage adviser, my cousin was being prosecuted and the sum involved in her self-cert mortgage was £375,000. The police wanted to tie me into that, which was bullshit. But that would have raised the combined value of the properties involved in the case over a nominal £500,000 threshhold, which made it more serious, hence the possible 3-5 years.

My wife insisted that I wasn't pleading guilty to that, whatever it meant to her, to the family.

It was 2013, I had finished the passport sentence and I was pretty much convinced in my own mind that I was quitting the EDL, but I was still messed up. My mum was having serious health issues with an aggressive form of cancer and on her first day of chemotherapy I was on the piss. I was supposed to take her to chemo at 9 o'clock in the morning and I got home at 8.30am still drunk.

Dad took a day off work to take her instead and I felt shit. A complete scumbag. With good reason – because I was being one. I knew what they were doing, using my family to get to me, but I just wasn't coping. I also knew deep down they were going to offer me some kind of a deal and that I'd have to take it. The deal originally was that I took responsibility for the lot, and in return everyone else would walk – the brother-in-law, cousin, and a mate of mine Gooders who, like me, had just lent some money.

He lived in Thailand and they kept having him fly all the way back to answer bail, about half-a-dozen times. He was pissed off and rightly so. Poor Gooders even got refused service by a Muslim member of staff when he went to Selfridges with me (although the management gave us a free meal by way of apology!)

But if I pleaded guilty, they all walked. The bottom line was that I was going back to jail and all I could think was that my mum was going to die. All she would say was that she wanted to know her grandchildren were alright, that everyone was going to be okay. And I so, so didn't want to be in jail when she was dying.

I was a mess. So I went to see Kev and told him that was it, I'd had enough. I'd already met the guys from the counter-extremism group the Quilliam Foundation during the filming of the documentary, 'When Tommy Met Mo' and Maajid Nawaz had told me to get in touch if ever I was considering leaving the EDL. Maajid saw the publicity opportunity for Quilliam if they could take the credit for Tommy Robinson quitting. We met and talked things through. In return for me throwing my hat in with them they agreed to pay the family bills if I got sent down. I'll come to my final days in the EDL shortly, but it was October 2013, I was at my wits end, and the trial was looming in January. I had to go.

That was the first time in five years I'd put my family before the EDL, but I thought that if mum died while I was inside, she would at least have seen that I was leaving the EDL, that I was finally ticking the right boxes, getting my priorities right. As things were playing out, I still intended pleading not guilty to the bigger charge and the jury was actually sworn in before we did the deal.

It was interesting that in St Albans, a town with a 2% Muslim population, they managed to select a jury with 25% Muslims – plus a community police officer for good measure. Nothing like stacking the odds!

I was relying on the fact that if I got off, the authorities would be left looking completely stupid, because they'd spent five years on this witch hunt. The chance of me being found not guilty wasn't a realistic option for them.

Just before the trial started, they offered to reduce the case against me to my brother-in-law's initial property deal. At that level, my solicitor said the sentencing guidelines indicated a suspended sentence – not that that was necessarily what Tommy Robinson would get.

I said I'd take it if they agreed to me having no financial benefit, meaning if they admitted that I hadn't gained anything from the transaction, so they couldn't come after me on a criminal proceedings case. They said they had no intention of doing that, so I agreed, for my wife's sake.

In court when I pleaded guilty the judge received a letter from the Archbishop of Canterbury's office asking for leniency, while Usama Hasan from Quilliam came to court in person and pleaded on my behalf.

And so the judge whacked me with an 18-month prison sentence anyway. Smells a little fishy to me, your honour! I've since checked other similar cases, and many a lot worse. No one gets 18 months for that stuff. But I did.

While I was in jail, mum had a 12-hour operation. We didn't know if she was going to survive, or be able to walk again if she did pull through, which was only 50-50. I was sitting in Winchester jail waiting for the chaplain to come and tell me whether mum had made it or not.

I had so many regrets for how I'd been as a son, what I'd put her through. Not just what I'd done but the way I'd been – a complete arsehole. Even then I was selfishly thinking of myself I suppose, feeling sorry for myself, but I couldn't face it all. The hours passed, evening came and I guess the chaplain went home without receiving word and I was crying, for my mum, for myself. I didn't sleep a wink. The next morning the little cell window opened up and the chaplain said, 'Your mum's alright'.

I still didn't see her throughout the whole sentence because she was so ill, but she was still with us. That was all that mattered. I still had some way to go before I was out of the woods with the law, but I was clean of the booze, the lifestyle, the EDL and most importantly of all my mum was still with us. And then, when I came out of HMP Winchester on licence and got home to my family, the police 'changed their mind' over our plea agreement and said they were pursuing me for £315,000 proceeds of crime as well. That's what they estimated our total assets were worth.

Because I'd lent my brother-in-law that £20,000 the police said every penny we'd ever earned, saved or accumulated was a proceed of crime – and they wanted it.

Why? Because the vindictive bastards could, that's why.

What an absolute piss-take.

16: THE END OF THE LINE

IF THERE WAS a moment when it seemed that the EDL might become something meaningful on a national scale it was after Lee Rigby's death in May 2013, when the whole country was outraged. Outraged, but only briefly.

At that time I'd straightened out while inside for the passport offence, the mortgage stuff was pending and I was having second thoughts about leading the EDL. Things were getting worse at home, with Ibrahim Anderson, Sayful Islam and their crew chasing my cousin home and the ensuing ruck outside my uncle's house.

There was another incident too, just before that, when I took the kids to a birthday party over in Marsh Farm. It was mostly women with their kids at one of those big, council-run indoor play gyms.

However when I arrived, Ibrahim was in the play area with his children and some women in burkhas. But he didn't look at me, so I thought that's okay, he's with his kids, I'm with my kids, just ignore each other.

The next thing, a bloke said I needed to look outside and there must have been 40 Muslims, bearded mullahs, all sorts, led by Sayful Islam. I got straight on the phone to Kev and a bunch of mates, then took my kids to some of the mums and asked them to look after them.

Six of these pricks came in and told me to come outside. Everyone was watching. I went into the kitchen looking for something to defend myself with, which naturally had the chef panicking but thankfully someone had rung 999 and the police came with the sirens going full blast.

I walked outside – and the police were there for me, shouting 'get down, get down'! All these Muslim extremists had come to kill me – 40 against one – and the police were telling me to get on the floor. It was barely believable.

There was a mob wanting to tear me to bits, and the police were making me the villain. Again.

At that point Kev came tearing up, some of my uncles arrived, my brother-in-law – the reinforcements were just in time. That was the time they identified my cousin, who they would later chase back to his house.

There were still only four police officers and it could have turned nasty, but then more officers started arriving. It was a children's party, all the parents were watching what was going on, and I thought, 'wonderful'. I couldn't even take my kids to a birthday party in peace.

I explained what had happened and for once the police didn't nick me. We even got a police escort home, but all I could think was that no one would invite my kids to a birthday party again. In fact when my little boy started school, that happened for a while – he wasn't getting invites from his pals. That was one of the most difficult things I have ever had to come to terms with.

I realised that I couldn't keep putting my family through all of this, although it wasn't like just turning off a switch. Whether by fate, bad luck or worse decisions, I had created a Tommy Robinson figure which had gotten right out of hand. Short of living in a cave, or having major plastic surgery and wearing platform shoes, it had become impossible to switch off from being 'me'.

I was wanting to buy myself some time, to consider what the future might hold. Some elements of the EDL had given Kev grief while I was inside and my family would have had it really tough but for help from people like Pamela Geller.

During my 22 weeks in solitary some EDL members had rallied round and donated a total of about £1,800. A big thank-you to each and every one of those people by the way, but that wasn't going to keep my family afloat for long. And I couldn't – wouldn't – have them going to the state cap in hand, asking for benefits.

Friends helped out. An old pal, Cash, who came to Luton from Jamaica when he was 11, would regularly come round and shove an envelope with £100 in it through the door. It's funny, we have all these immigrant issues now and Cash, as integrated and hard working a bloke as you will find, couldn't get a passport to go on holiday with me, because of the circumstances of his mum and her big family moving here all those years ago. The system's worse than useless.

But back on the outside, I was feeling both sorry for myself and pissed off with life. Some people had turned on me, some on Kev, and not one of those people would last a day walking in that bloke's shoes. Or mine for that matter (although in fairness, my shoes might be a bit tight for them). I told EDL people that I needed some time with my family and that I wouldn't be attending demos.

It was March 2013 when I got out and I was asking myself why I continued putting up with all the aggravation. I wondered how I could make a clean break. Regional organisers should have been keeping the extremists out, but while I was inside they'd opened the doors again to any idiot who wanted to create strife. In Manchester and Liverpool the regional leadership had basically welcomed the North West Infidels with open arms. I just wanted to sort my life out, try to find 'normal'.

Kev and I were talking about how to handle things when, on May 22nd, while at my little boy's birthday party, I got a call telling me to switch the television on. All the family were there, but I stood and watched what was happening in London, in Woolwich, with the attack on Drummer Lee Rigby. And I just told the wife, 'I'm off'.

You can imagine how that went down with the family. Not good. There I was trying to get my head round how I could leave the EDL, and boom, suddenly I was being dragged right back onto the front line. I had calls coming in saying Muslims were celebrating in the streets, shouting

'Allahu Akbar' at the news of the young soldier's murder. All I could think was that I had to go to Woolwich.

We didn't know at that time but it transpired that six months before he was killed, Lee Rigby was at a wedding in Luton with Kev. We jumped in the car, drove down to London and met a lot of lads down there.

There was real anger in the air and groups of blokes were charging about in the streets, but I wouldn't say it was anything that looked like getting out of hand. It was mostly a lot of shouting and chanting, people expressing their anger that one of our own troops could be killed in cold blood on the streets of our own capital.

Predictably enough the newspapers were quick to hammer us over the noise and fury on the streets. No one made the point that at least the EDL had never tried to saw anyone's head off their shoulders. No one ever felt the need to mention that.

I posted a video talking about the Lee Rigby incident and it got 600,000 views in a few days. I went up 50,000 Twitter followers overnight and spoke to Kev about what we were going to do. There wasn't a choice, we were straight back in. We would go round again.

ALWAYS AT THAT time, hanging over my head, was the mortgage case, but with that atrocity there was suddenly renewed momentum within the group.

On the Saturday immediately after Lee Rigby was murdered we organised a 'Walk For Lee' in Luton, about 80 or 90 of us. People began spontaneously organising similar events across the country. There was a new impetus. One of the first things I did was get rid of the North West regional leadership. It was zero tolerance where right-wing idiots were concerned, if I was going to be back involved.

That movement, to 'Walk for Lee' was picked up everywhere, with rallies announced in 68 towns and cities, of EDL members and ordinary members of the public, eager to pay their respects to this young hero.

I thought the government missed a massive trick there, if they were sincere about wanting to tackle Islamic extremism. We all saw what happened in France after the Charlie Hebdo massacre – the French people came together, people and politicians alike, they renewed and they strengthened their national resolve. Their whole country effectively went into mourning.

I thought that Britain should have had a national rally for Lee Rigby, a formal, state-led response so that people from all communities could go and pay their respects, and more than that, feel that they'd got the anger out of their system.

Imagine what a positive signal it would have sent if ordinary Muslim people came out in support of that young man? But that's not the British government, is it? They spent more time mobilising the PR machine, insisting that his killers Michael Adebolajo and Michael Adebowale were lone wolves, Muslim outsiders – as if they'd been dropped here from outer space, as opposed to being radicalised by the BBC's darling hate preacher, Anjem Choudary.

The entire political and police effort was concentrated instead on protecting Muslim communities from the possibility of outraged people being pissed off and threatening some form of recrimination.

Someone swearing at a woman wearing the full burkha gear? Lock him up, throw the book at him! Can't tolerate such 'race hate'! Tick another box on the police's 'We're monitoring Muslim race-hate' agenda.

It was an attitude that drew only an embarrassed silence when leeches belonging to another government-funded group exaggerated the number of hate crimes after Lee Rigby's murder. Fiyaz Mughal and former Labour MP for Dewsbury Shahid Malik ran a scheme called Tell Mama (which stands for Measuring Anti-Muslim Attacks) and which milked fortunes from the soft-headed authorities.

When Lee Rigby was almost beheaded, these jokers produced all kinds of statistics suggesting that bigoted Britons weren't stopping far short of burning Muslims in the street. Except, oops, it turned out they were made-up figures.

These people were exaggerating problems in order to justify their existence. They weren't a part of solving anyone's problem – they were all about creating division while furthering their own interests, in my opinion. They used Lee Rigby's murder to bolster their divisive racket – not that a big song and dance was made about it. It never is. And as for all of those fake statistics they produced about anti-Muslim offences? I'll bet that in the same period I had more legitimate death threats made against me personally, than all of the ones against Muslims in the UK combined. Islamophobia? What a joke.

And Lee Rigby? He was a soldier, that was all. An upright lad whose mates died for our country's freedom, and effectively to protect the creatures who slaughtered him. When modern Britain's history is written, Lee Rigby will be remembered as a lovely young family man and loyal servant, but whose murder was basically an inconvenience for the government's attempts to pretend that all was hunky-dory in multi-cultural Britain.

I watched those walks, every one of them, as EDL groups across the country paid their respects, filmed them and uploaded them online, all incredibly moving tributes to this young man.

There was aggravation in two locations because the UAF troublemakers came out and blocked the lads getting to the war memorials, but everywhere else, ordinary people paraded and walked and left flowers in tribute. There's video of them ripping up the flowers. Absolute scum. As sad a day as it was, the outpouring of love and respect for that young man was huge and it was heartfelt.

And here's the thing that again the media conveniently overlooks – those walks, parades, for Lee Rigby, they were absolutely, entirely peaceful. This wasn't a rampaging mob demanding revenge on the people who did it, using it as an excuse to declare war on Muslim communities.

The EDL could have marched to east London and descended on Tower Hamlets; we could have picked a city with a large Muslim community like Birmingham or Bradford and provoked confrontation. Instead we chose Newcastle and London – we went to Downing Street.

At Newcastle we must have had a crowd of up to 10,000, the biggest demonstration we'd ever staged and it was brilliant. I stood up and said that we should recognise there are hundreds of Muslims in the UK's armed forces.

I said that it is honourable to oppose sharia law and paedophile gangs, but that you are a coward and a scumbag if you abuse a Muslim woman walking down the street, purely because of her faith or how she dresses.

Not that you see that reported of course. It doesn't fit the stereotype. If you don't believe me, just Google the speech.

We'd been having trouble as I've said with the North East Infidels, a group of about 30 people on that wild, mad right fringe. I saw those outsiders there, that day in Newcastle, and not one of them said a word to me.

The numbers really were overwhelming. It's worth mentioning that when there was trouble at an EDL demo the police liked to big-up the arrests and the trouble, to remind the world how difficult a job they have – in order to justify the overtime payments and the budgets, mostly.

But when everything went calmly, to order, went as we planned it in short, they tried to make it sound like no one could be arsed turning up. I've been to rallies with 2,000 people where the police said there were 300-400. It's what they do. Looking at the images, the video from that day in Newcastle, I'd say there were as many as 10,000 people present and I clearly remember a woman of about 60 who came after watching a video from the Sheffield parade for Lee. She told me that she 'had to come', to support us, to pay her respects with us.

This was a different feeling from before. This time I was healthy, feeling switched on and clear-headed about things, as opposed to being a frazzled mess.

And despite all of the thousands of people who turned out in Newcastle, it was a peaceful rally. When we went to Downing Street next there was trouble, but again I have to wonder how much that suited a part of the police agenda.

One of the frustrating things about trying to lead such a loosely organised thing as the EDL was the work that went into trying to ensure conflict was avoided. We always asked the police to keep us well apart from the UAF headbangers, who followed us around like fleas on a dog's arse, but it was sometimes as if the police wanted trouble. It went force by force. Some were a lot better than others.

At the walk the week after Lee's death in Sheffield, the police had the nerve to prevent people paying their respects – so we went back again. Whatever it took, we were going to make sure the people of Sheffield could peacefully pay their respects at their war memorial.

The UAF were there howling their abuse every step of the way, but I read the riot act to our lot. We would walk in total silence. There would be no reaction to the provocation, no shouting back, no nothing. Bricks and bottles thrown at us? Ignore it.

An angry reaction – that was exactly what the press wanted from us, all waiting with their cameras, and today was our day, not theirs. We would get to the war memorial, stage our silent two minutes, and just raise our arms giving the sign of peace.

So I said, 'When we walk in, don't start chanting 'EDL'. We walk in showing a two-fingered sign of peace, that's all.' We walked round that corner, in complete silence – into a wall of UAF fanatics screaming their hate.

It was a vision, because there were about 1,000 of us, making not a noise, everyone with their two fingers of peace in the air, accompanied only by shouts and boos from the Lefties and all the Muslims going off their heads – but everyone amongst us stayed completely silent.

And so you know what the press reported, don't you? That the EDL walked in giving Hitler salutes! You can't win. You just cannot win.

A senior female Sheffield police officer, who liaised with us on the event, rang me up that night and said she was absolutely disgusted at what she was reading.

She said we had done everything by the book, that we'd been completely respectful and that our behaviour was absolutely impeccable. I even recorded our conversation because I doubted that anyone would ever believe us, about how hard we tried to do things right.

We laid our flowers, we walked off, and it was only when we got back up to the pub and the UAF mob turned up looking to instigate trouble that actually, yes, there was some aggro. Here were the so-called peace-lovers, starting trouble with blokes who'd simply had enough of their country turning its back like cowards.

But at that Sheffield war memorial? Everyone showed complete respect. No one bit at the taunting. A young man was murdered on his own soil, serving Queen and country, and his so-called countrymen – Socialists and Muslims – were celebrating it. If you disagree with how we tried to pay our respects, I'd love you tell me what we did wrong.

IT WAS A SIMILAR scene when we then went to Downing Street. We preached restraint to everyone who attended, we really wanted to give the right impression, but when we arrived there were bottles raining down on everyone.

You have to ask yourself, exactly how much of this do the police want to happen, to suit their own agenda?

They could have kept the UAF and Muslim protestors at a decent distance if they'd wanted, when we walked down Whitehall. But how much did it suit their political, their financial, their actually divisive agenda, for the cameras to be able to capture shit going down – shit which they always, inevitably, blamed directly on us.

On that occasion I caught most of the trouble on film myself. It just happened that on that particular day there was a group of Sikhs, also protesting at the end of Downing Street, about a cause personal to them involving someone overseas. I'd actually spoken to the organiser of the Sikh demo the night before and assured him they would have absolutely no trouble from us.

So what the Metropolitan Police did was place the UAF and Muslim protestors directly behind the Sikh group – down Whitehall towards the Houses of Parliament – and then they escorted us in from the top of Whitehall, from Trafalgar Square. I don't know what the police were hoping for or expecting, but when we saw the Sikh group, the whole EDL support, without any prompting, started clapping and applauding them.

I remember so clearly looking at the faces of the Sikh protestors and seeing how surprised they seemed. This didn't match the image and expectations they'd been fed.

Before this however the police had already played their trump card. They blockaded our PA system about a mile away and wouldn't let it through. Very clever. It's a bit difficult to give speeches in the middle of some of the baying mobs we attract, without a PA system.

Me and a Wolves football lad, Gilly, plus Jason Mariner from the Chelsea lot, went and got the entire system and carried it back. The police said we'd be arrested if we tried, but we called their bluff and got it through.

Finally, we had our rally and I began my speech, referencing what Winston Churchill had to say about Sikhs and how Britain would be forever indebted to them.

The UAF started throwing bottles into our crowd and although our lads started to surge towards them, there was this wall of Sikh protestors in the middle. So everyone stopped. That was that. The gent who was leading the Sikh protest came up to me afterwards and said – on camera – that the police had set us up, and I said that I knew. They set us up to fail every time. They always do.

You won't have read about the time we were contacted by a Sikh community group whose summer school was being harassed by gangs off the nearby estate, calling them terrorists and extremists. We went along, met those kids, talked about the contributions Sikhs have made to our country, how they were showing their ignorance with their aggro. The trouble stopped. Maybe we should have been better at PR with stuff like that – not that I think anyone would have printed it.

We would talk to the police about arrangements for demos so that everything could pass off peacefully, but then they'd orchestrate it to get just enough disruption that they could look heroes, whack in their overtime bills and complain about being overstretched and under-resourced – but never enough that they couldn't quite cope.

Even that day in London, when we were organising a meet near Downing Street and we got a pub sorted, they rang me at 8am, just as lads were turning up, to change everything, to just mess us about, to try to create a problem where none needed to exist. A complete set of bastards.

If you ask me, Britain's Chief Constables are playing the government for fools every bit as much as they did us.

IT STILL SHOCKS and surprises me that there wasn't a greater public reaction to Lee Rigby's murder than we saw. I couldn't believe that Britain could effectively just glance out of a car window at a passing accident, and drive on, a moment's curiosity and no more.

No big deal. Just another meaningless death, something for the tabloid newspapers to have a wetty about for a few days and show how clever they are with their headlines, weep a few crocodile tears and then move right along, find a new something-or-nothing to get worked up about.

Armchair revolutionaries, the British. If they could get something done by pressing a button on their Sky tv remote, then maybe there would be a chance. Beyond that? Can't be arsed, for the most part.

We tried to keep the momentum going and Kev and I decided we'd do a charity walk in Lee's memory. This was about five weeks after his murder and we decided we'd walk from the Houses of Parliament to the spot where he was killed in Woolwich. Now, me and Kev didn't map out the streets of London – he'd have probably done a much better, more thorough job of it – but however you look at it, that walk takes you through the borough of Tower Hamlets.

We just wanted to lay a wreath where Lee Rigby had been killed and we raised £6,000 on our Just Giving page, for Help for Heroes – and then they refused our money. They said they didn't accept political donations. That's complete bullshit anyway, because whatever the EDL was, it wasn't a political party.

This was a simple charity walk, that's all. Fund-raising from two blokes. It was just more PC bollocks. I got a phone call from one of their organisers apologising and we also got support from the actress who plays Sonia Fowler in Eastenders, saying she was outraged by it.

A serving soldier contacted us saying that he'd do my walk instead – and sure enough the shit came pouring down on his shoulders from the army top brass, threatening his career and his pension. It got better though – or worse, depending how you look at it. We decided to donate the money to a charity for a little girl aged two, Amelia Mae Davis, who needed £250,000 for life saving treatment overseas and who had only 6-12 months to live.

Guess what? The charity refused the money. Seriously.

The country can spend £8m on Maggie Thatcher's funeral, £2m protecting that scumbag extremist Abu Qatada and not only can we put a price like that on a child's life, but refuse charity to try to save her. Amelia Mae's family were happy to accept the money, but the charity it was going through, National Children's Cancer Association UK, said they wouldn't accept anything from the EDL.

I went to that little girl's funeral when she died and since then I've been to her auntie and uncle's wedding. I'm not sure if anyone from the charity showed their face.

We were walking anyway, and then Scotland Yard officers came to see us in Luton and said they didn't want us to go there. They might as well have told me to cut off my own arm, because I was not having that bullshit. Is this a free country or not? You know the actual answer.

Our intention was to set off from Westminster and on the way to Woolwich stop at the 7/7 memorial and then the Churchill memorial. I had a Union Jack made out of flowers to lay at the spot where Lee Rigby was killed. I said to the police, that for me to walk from A to B I have to go through that area. Why wouldn't I do that? Because of 'community sensitivities'? Because there are Muslims and mosques there, means that I'm not allowed to walk where I want? It still burns me up, I tell you. The number of times I've felt like holding a protest on my own outside the East London Mosque, on a Friday afternoon...

If there are more than three people the police can ban the assembly or the procession. However with there being only me and Kev they couldn't officially act. A leading local imam then warned the police not to let us into Tower Hamlets and I asked the officer, who did he work for? This geezer or the British public?

On the day we had an escort of police officers, but there was also a rag-arsed collection of UAF pricks too, trying to start an argument. They are like flies round shit that lot – and they're about as much use to mankind. The police actually, deliberately, physically, allowed one of them to walk up and punch Kevin Carroll. It's all there, online – just search for Tommy Robinson Charity Walk on Youtube and see it for yourself.

The police probably calculated that we would fight back and as a result they could dive in and lock us up – but we'd already discussed all the possibilities and made a conscious decision that whatever happened, we would not react. It wouldn't be the first time or the last time that we would willingly take a punch just to highlight a problem.

I was raging at the police to arrest this guy who'd just assaulted Kev. Did they? Don't be silly. Do you know what they did? They stopped the pair of us, and the senior officer, a woman, told us that we were being arrested for obstructing the police in the course of their duty.

When we demanded to know exactly how we were obstructing them, she refused to reply. We kept asking and asking, and she eventually said she just couldn't explain. She had an earpiece in and was obviously taking instructions from someone. We hadn't reacted to the attack, their plan hadn't worked, so they just arrested us anyway.

I don't think we'd put a single foot in Tower Hamlets, but I said to her, fine, we would go wherever she directed us. If that meant a detour, we'd take the detour. Whatever you say officer, yes ma'am, no ma'am, three bags full ma'am.

We would follow instructions – but they banged on the handcuffs anyway, because this woman clearly wasn't empowered to do something so daring as to actually think for herself, and we were thrown in the cells. Again. At the police station I was given bail conditions not to enter the Borough of Tower Hamlets, but of course in order to be bailed, you have to agree to be bound by the conditions of it. So I refused the bail conditions. I challenged them to remand me.

That wasn't what they expected and it also put them in a bit of a difficult position, because they weren't particularly used to such an objectionable little so-and-so as me. In the event they transferred me to an emergency court hearing for a judge to rule on the bail conditions. I was charged with obstructing a police officer in the course of his duty and in what I consider – from some experience – to be one of the British judiciary's finest moments, the judge threw a wobbler. She was raging, completely furious with the police and what they were playing at.

'I'm not limiting this man's freedoms,' she said. And I was free to go. I always believed the CPS was supposed to be independent of the police, but they weren't in that case. I was out on bail but would be brought before a court three times over that before it was thrown out. And I still fancy visiting the East London Mosque after Friday prayers, just for the hell of it. Maybe one of these days.

NEXT UP CAME AN occasion when the media took things to new heights – The Day Tommy Robinson Kidnapped Tulisa. That's as in the singer and X Factor judge, Tulisa Contostavlos. You really couldn't make this rubbish up.

With the judge saying I couldn't be banned from Tower Hamlets we decided we were going back there in force to protest. Of course, it's never quite that easy because the Home Secretary got involved and imposed a new ban – they wouldn't let us in and kept us near the Aldgate East tube station, close to Tower Bridge.

We went to the High Court the night before the march to contest the order, which also limited us to 30 minutes of speeches. The reasons for it were that the police could not control the reaction of the local community, and our argument was that under European law the British state could not infringe on one person's rights because of the reactions of others.

The Metropolitan Police commissioner turned up and admitted it – they had no worries about policing the EDL, the worry was about the reaction from Tower Hamlet's Muslim population. We said that if they can't enforce British law they were effectively capitulating to sharia law. Who was running Tower Hamlets – the Met or the imam of the East London Mosque? We all know that answer.

It cost us eight grand to get a solicitor and barrister and still the judge sided with the police and Home Secretary. I'd found someone to put the money up for the appeal and then the judge made an order for the EDL to pay the police's costs – except the police said no, they didn't want the order making against the EDL. They wanted it making against me personally, Tommy Robinson. The judge agreed and I had 28 days to pay the police costs of around £7,000.

The demo itself started as one of the highest points I ever experienced in the EDL. We were escorted across Tower Bridge, over 2,000 of us and we absolutely filled the length of it. It was a great sight, a great moment, and I was one very proud Englishman, with the iconic Tower of London off to one side, tourists all looking on in awe.

When we got to the demo point the police asked me to move our supporters, so being keen to do the right thing, I did. You can guess what they were doing – they'd already started the 30 minute clock. Me and Kev gave our speeches and were about to introduce a member of the Armed Forces when a police officer came over and said, 'You're getting close to your time'. I invited the police to pull the plug on the PA system and make mugs of themselves, but our soldier was going to speak – and he did. The whole thing went just six minutes over, mostly down to the police messing us about. I finished by telling the crowd, 'Everyone expected us to cause trouble and you've done yourselves proud. Please leave the same way.'

Officers then came up and asked for my help calming some supporters who were playing up. I walked round the corner and about 10 coppers jumped on me, knocked me to the ground, handcuffed me and threw me in the back of a police van. Meanwhile there was a black-clad UAF crew battling with the police and throwing at least one petrol bomb that I saw – but we'd run a few minutes over our time thanks expressly to a police stunt, and I was getting shit-kicked into a black maria.

Back in the cells, back in front of a bail officer and more conditions, surprise, surprise, not to enter Tower Hamlets. So I said fine – I'm going to do a sponsored walk round the entire 28 miles of Tower Hamlets instead. Up yours.

And eventually we did, me and Kev having a 28-mile pub crawl, going from boozer to boozer round Tower Hamlets, with a dozen coppers following our every step – the fat, unfit slobs having to take turns, an hour on, an hour off – and police cars lining every side street that we passed. At one boozer, Kev popped his head in the door and went, 'Pssst, don't look now, but are we being followed by the police...?' all the while with these mugs wheezing along behind us. It was hilarious.

Meanwhile, after being bailed and on the way home from the Aldgate demo, I stopped in a layby with Mike, the tv producer who was compiling footage for a documentary. We wanted to get some stuff posted online, to let people know what had happened after the police ambushed me.

I was looking into the camera, standing in front of a big house, talking away, when someone came running out. He was a scrawny little bloke, looked like a junkie, and he was all over the place, wanting to know what we were doing.

Before you knew it, there were cop cars appearing from everywhere. I thought, is it just me? What now? I explained to the cops, we were just making a video – did they want to watch it? They aren't the most imaginative individuals, British police officers, so they decided they were going to search the car on suspicion of going equipped for burglary. I was with a television producer, for crying out loud. And still the cop cars kept coming.

I said, 'Lads, do you not get any crime round here? Have you got fuck all to do? Get yourselves down to Luton, help them out, because people are getting shot there on a daily basis.' This one police tosser was giving it 'The Big I Am' and I said to him, 'Oy mate, you know they named a box of chocolates after you, don't you? Miniature fucking Heroes.'

He said he was doing me for some bullshit or other to do with leaving the keys in the ignition with the car unattended. Seriously. That was the best he could dream up. So we went with the camera up to all of the patrol cars – and guess what, all the keys were in the ignitions!

'Are you doing this lot then?' I asked him.

Flash forward two weeks later and I was out in Liverpool with some of the lads. Suddenly my phone was going nuts with everyone telling me to grab one of the daily papers, so I nipped out to get one. Right there in black and white – 'EDL Boss in Tulisa Kidnap Probe'. Yep, that's why the little hyped-up bloke came panicking out of the posh house we'd pulled up in front of – it was Tulisa's gaff and this was when she was going through a high profile drugs case. The drama queen was her Personal Assistant.

We were walking through Liverpool and this Scouser was at a bus stop, looking at his paper, then looking at me. I pointed at the story and winked. 'We've got her mate,' I said. His face was a pure delight.

I then tweeted Bedfordshire police a photo of me pointing at my car boot, saying to come and get her...

THE END OF THE line with the EDL was a mixture of factors. It wasn't just what was happening to me and what I'd been going through in prison, but the attitude of a small section of the EDL both to me and Kev. As great as the vast majority were, we'd been having more and more problems with the regional organisers, doing their own things.

It's important to realise there wasn't a constitution or anything formal about the EDL. It had grown based upon our wider message and our demonstrations, but more and more, it was becoming a magnet for right wing elements.

It was more than that though. Both me and Kev were struggling to get by, and every time we challenged the authorities with our marches, shoving our noses where we weren't welcome and getting locked up for it, there was a price to pay. Literally a price to pay. I barely had a pot to piss in with the taxman and the law seizing and freezing everything I had. We had appeals for money to help pay the legal bills but they weren't getting us anywhere fast.

We were both pretty much unemployable anyway, and there was a real pressure on our families. And then, when I got banged up for my American jaunt, the pressure outside got cranked up on Kev.

I won't say the EDL turned on him as such, it wasn't quite like that – but as the whole thing fractured and the regional organisers started going in their own directions, me being sent down gave people the chance to make their own mark. The bottom line was that Kev was getting shit that he didn't deserve and certainly hadn't signed up for.

He was the bloke whose life was in danger, getting chased by some geezer with a shotgun, having his van torched, and now a bunch of faceless characters wanted to call the shots. They were okay to walk the streets, their wives weren't on Valium because they were terrified in their own house.

This bloke had been by my side, every step of the way and now he was getting a ration of shit from people who hadn't a clue what it was like to even try to run something like the EDL. Seeing what Kev was having to contend with just helped me towards the decision to walk away.

I had messed my family up, no end. But I had also gone through all of this thinking that if I got killed, then at least my family would be looked after. I thought this movement, these people, the EDL, would be there for my wife and kids if anything happened to me.

Talk about daydreams and fairytales. It was anything but that. During that spell in solitary I realised that if I got killed, my family would have nothing. Our assets were all still frozen and we didn't even have the money to pay the rent. Things were not only not getting any better, they were getting massively worse.

I phoned my wife from prison once during the passport case and she was crying her eyes out. We'd had problems at the three previous places we'd lived and she was understandably at her wits end, she was close to breaking.

When armed police come and lock down your road, the neighbours tend to notice. When they come and raid your house looking for non-existent shit, just to mess with you and your family, it creates a bit of an atmosphere up and down the street. We'd moved again, got the kids settled again, in a different school, and were trying, hoping, to live some semblance of a normal life. And there I was back in jail and my wife was flat broke.

At that point I was sitting in a cell thinking that if she couldn't find it, she'd have to go cap in hand to the council – and knowing them they'd stick them in a bedsit, probably in a Muslim area. What, you think they wouldn't do that? You obviously don't know these vindictive bastards.

I was in a bad place all round, and I felt betrayed. I also felt a complete arsehole myself. I'd got so into everything, been so wrapped up in it all, and I'd been so selfish. I suppose in a way I'd hit the wall.

My four weeks in solitary had turned into more than five months. I'd lost two stones, I had abscesses on my face. I was a mess. There had then followed this spike of fire and fury around the Lee Rigby murder, but when that died down, really nothing had changed, nothing was changing.

I started catching up with what was going on with the EDL around the country and I saw these White Pride clowns getting involved. I'd tried so hard to keep them out. I saw they'd been involved in a Manchester demo, saw them flying their flag. I thought, what am I up against?

At that point I realised that to carry on with the EDL I would have to take on a whole different battle – against people who were supposed to be on our side. But the fact was that I simply didn't have it in me any longer, to fight battles on all fronts, hardly knowing who was a friend, who was an enemy, and who were the traitors.

Even when I was successful in removing these people, they only went off and formed their own splinter groups. If you saw the Channel 4 documentary 'Angry, White and Proud' in January 2015, you saw some of the people I got rid of. And suddenly, for many of them, I was the enemy!

I'd already confronted the North East, North West and Yorkshire Infidels, the South East Alliance, kicked that lot out. I couldn't see where the end of it was. It was a continual power struggle and I'd reached the end of my tether. That's when I decided I was going. One thing on top of another, and a big red cherry on top.

Before that 22 weeks in solitary I'd been completely caught up in this ridiculous imaginary life. I was drinking, taking drugs, I was this little bloke who saw himself as a big-time Charlie and the truth of it is that I was a loser. A complete loser. A shit husband and a worse dad and when I look back at how I was then, early in 2013, I can't see the person I had been a few years before, when the EDL started. I was a horrible person. No kind of a man.

I don't know if it sneaked up on me, if being followed by cheering crowds of hundreds and thousands sent it all to my head. If the whole 'Tommy Robinson' persona had taken over my real life – or even what real life was any longer. I didn't realise how far I'd gone until I went away and when I came out of jail, I'd had five months of no alcohol, no drugs, no nothing.

I still had the worry and the pressure over the mortgage case, but before that long spell in solitary I had been a ticking time bomb. Did I have a death wish? I thought a lot about that. I'd say it was like living with a terminal illness. If you're told you're going to die then you're going to go one way or another, and I went nuts.

In my own mind someone was going to kill me at some point, make good on the repeated threats, and I was determined to go out with a bang. I remember walking into the snooker club in Luton where a lot of the Muslim gangs hung out. I'd purposely go in there for a beer, just to put it in everyone's faces, to give them a big, 'What-the-fuck-are-you-going-to-do-about-it?' look. I was off my head.

And here's the stupid thing. I imagined that if the Muslims killed me, it would spark a revolution. That the British people would get off their lazy backsides and realise what was happening, that they needed to make a stand. Well, the way the country reacted to Lee Rigby's murder gave the lie to that idea.

There would be a lot more celebrating than crying if Tommy Robinson took a blade or a bullet. That was the cold and brutal truth of it. I had good friends, long time friends like Tom Stoker and John English, properly worried about me, but I'm not sure I was a great friend back, at that point.

Neither could I get my mind off my mum's condition. I was convinced she wasn't going to make it and if she didn't, it would be while she was still worrying about all of the chaotic stuff messing up my life. I couldn't do that to her.

Kev was hurting with what he'd been through while I was inside. Because of how high profile we'd become, he'd lost most of his work. Nobody wanted him on a job, not because he wasn't quality at what he did, or wasn't a good bloke that they all liked. It was just too much trouble for people. Too hot to handle.

Was there a formal blacklist affecting him, me, maybe even people we were close to? Probably. Every which way he, we, could be squeezed, we were squeezed.

I told Kev, 'I'm leaving mate, I need to concentrate on my family'. And he said, 'I'm right by your side bruv'.

And it wasn't just Kev and me. Other people were getting disillusioned with things within the EDL. After we stepped down a group of them left and formed a 'Team Tommy' to keep me up to date with what was going on, even when I was in prison.

People like Ivan Humble, Tim Ablitt, Kieran Hallett, Glen Saffer, Stewart Austin and Tony Lancs – and of course the ever dependable Helen Gower – they always had my back. They were allies, people I counted as good friends.

17: QUILLIAM

USAMA HASAN IS a senior researcher in Islamic studies, affiliated to the Quilliam Foundation. When I quit the EDL in October 2013 you might have seen a lot about Quilliam taking the credit for effectively 'converting' me to the right side of the battle against extremism. I smiled to myself a lot about that. But I liked Usama. I still do.

My involvement with the so-called counter-extremism think-tank originated from an invitation to take part in the Channel 4 documentary When Tommy Met Mo, after I got out of prison from the passport offence in 2013. A Scottish girl contacted me from a production company, Mentorn, and I told her I was leaving the EDL. Then Lee Rigby was murdered and everything was back on, so I rang her back.

Mohammed Ansar was one of the left-wing media's pet go-to Muslims and clearly someone thought it would be fun to watch the two of us wind each other up. He seemed to be on the fringes of Quilliam at that time.

The producers wanted me to take him around problem areas in Luton and vice versa. I was supposed to introduce Mo to groomed girls and their mums and aunties, for him to hear first hand what Muslim men were doing to our young people. He refused to come and visit at night, because he said he had to be home during Ramadan to break his fast.

Another date was set up for him to meet EDL members and he said he wouldn't walk into the pub. He wasn't being asked to have a drink, just come in and meet these people. But no. The world had to revolve around Mo and his big bag of religious bullshit.

It was interesting that after the Breivik slaughter in Norway, Mo Ansar wrote to the then Parliamentary Under-Secretary for Crime and Security, James Brokenshire MP, calling for him to outlaw the EDL. Brokenshire replied, 'We can't proscribe them but we are working with a wide range of agencies to address the driver of the EDL.'

I should have taken a bit more notice of that, given what they subsequently put me through. It seems my persecution went right to the top of government – literally an enemy of the state.

Mo was very much a cartoon character, a muppet Muslim – and he got into character for when the camera was running. He wears normal clothes, day to day – a business suit – but then gets into character, pulling on the robes, the old Muslim cap, playing the pious man of religious reason. He's not, not in my book at least.

All that programme managed was to reassert my view that none of this game-playing is going to work. Everything else had to fit around Mo, like the world has to change to fit around Islam. All take, no give. That doesn't have any happy endings I can see. Not in a world I want to live in.

Through it however I met Usama from Quilliam and Tom Holland, a renowned historian. I was involved in an argument with Mohammed Shafiq, who basically 'is' the entire Ramadhan Foundation, another one of these pop-up organisations. I was saying they don't even know their own book – that Muslims don't know the Koran as well as they pretend. I brought up the subject of sexual slavery and Shafiq was busy denying it, but then Usama backed me up. Afterwards he shook my hand and said, 'Keep doing what you're doing'. He went so far as to say that I had an undercurrent of support from within the Muslim community – but just not to attack their Prophet.

His view was that there were a lot of things about ultra-right Wahhabi and Salafi Islam that many mainstream Muslims agree aren't the way forward. So I looked into Usama and found interestingly that four imams in London had come out and pronounced that he should be killed. I knew something about Quilliam, and at this point I was ready to leave the EDL. By the end of filming the documentary, I'd decided that I was going.

When I met Maajid Nawaz, the senior director of Quilliam, during filming, he was standing for Parliament as a Liberal Democrat in Hampstead and Kilburn and said he couldn't be seen physically sitting with me – which was kind of rude, but nothing I hadn't been through before. He said that if ever I did quit the EDL to let him know whether I'd be interested in working with them.

It all started from that one chat. I dare say my motives were a bit muddled, although I honestly wanted to discover Quilliam had something legitimate to offer but I'm not sure it has. Quilliam wanted to be seen facilitating my exit from the EDL and taking the credit for it. That was okay, I know how the world of public funding works. They have to show results from somewhere and I ticked a box of sorts.

At the same time there was mum's health and I was due back in court with the mortgage case which still looked like earning me three-to-five years. All of that was in my head and somehow I still had to find a way to keep my family with food on the table and a roof over their heads.

My mentor Dev came to the meeting in a hotel near Quilliam's office in London to chat. I'd rung Kev Carroll and put it all out there, that I was going back inside for who knew how long, the EDL didn't have the resources to help, and I needed some. Quilliam might be the answer. Kev thought it – they – were bullshit, but he made the decision to quit the EDL and sit down with them alongside me.

Our agreement was simple. While I was inside Quilliam would pay my wife's rent and help with the basic bills. In return, Tommy Robinson would be their poster boy. On the day of the expected trial, when I changed to a guilty plea, the judge adjourned sentencing for eight weeks, a break I wasn't expecting but during which time I was able to get involved with a few Quilliam-oriented projects.

I organised a meeting in Luton with regional organisers of the EDL and a group of Muslims, trying to get a better understanding of their opposing viewpoints. It was chaos. Everyone argued amongst themselves, but what was interesting was that most of the things they were pissed off with weren't anything to do with each other.

There aren't any easy answers, that's for sure.

The Quilliam agreement didn't work out quite so straightforwardly, because the monthly allowance got cut in half after just two months of me being inside – because of funding cuts, they said. What a liberty. Dev was livid, but it wasn't as disastrous as it might have been. I'd imagined being inside for two or three years before I could get out on licence and in the end I only did six months.

OUT OF THE whole Quilliam thing, I was left with admiration for some individuals, but despair at the overall reality. I was using them, they were using me, but the bottom line from what I witnessed was that nothing truly productive was going to come out of it. And here's why.

Usama Hasan is such a genuine guy, a model for what we'd all like to characterise as a moderate British Muslim. That's why there are death threats hanging over his head. But that's the reality of the Muslim issue which not just Britain but the world has to come to terms with – not the isolated good guys like Usama, but the fundamentalists, the hardliners. You cannot reason with these people. Full stop. End of. You can bribe them maybe, definitely even, but don't ever think you can win over hearts and minds.

It may prove convenient for them within their longer term agenda to achieve the caliphate, to apparently come onside, to buy into whatever bullshit 'the man' is selling, but more fool you if you take that response at face value. You will have your pocket picked and your loyalty thrown back in your face, as and when it suits.

I'll probably get called racist for saying that. Except it isn't. There is a massive cultural divide which is the elephant lurking in this room. We are dealing with a culture that has a particularly creative idea of what 'the truth' constitutes. For instance, what was yesterday's truth might bear no relevance to today's truth. Tomorrow? That could be a completely different 'truth' again.

Whatever works best for the circumstances. And we simply cannot get our heads round this different way of looking at things. At least our politicians and all the funding bodies throwing money at these communities and groups can't understand it, not from what I see.

I can imagine people saying, 'But the ones on the make are the minority!' Sure, just one or two chancers here and there. Just like the one or two extremists who are on the fringes, not representative of the mainstream.

I certainly hear David Cameron and Theresa May and the head of every law enforcement agency and local authority say it week in, week out. They say it so often that they start to believe it. They're daydreaming. Daydreaming their way into a nightmare.

Kev and I were in a presentation at the Quilliam offices on one occasion, and Usama was outlining the problem that specifically Quilliam has, but also the country.

He drew this simple chart on the whiteboard which was a line, marked by 90 per cent and 10 per cent, representing British Muslims. His message was that we've convinced ourselves this 10 per cent here is the minority, whether vocal or silent, that sympathises with the introduction of a sharia state in the UK, that believes in fundamentalism, and supports what ISIS is trying to achieve in Iraq and Syria – even if they don't support the means they use.

That doesn't make them either extremists or terrorists, but it means they're not of a mind to condemn fellow Muslims who are. It's silent support for the global caliphate

– but 'only' 10 per cent. That's what people at large accept and appear to be comfortable with.

Meanwhile the hefty 90 per cent are willing to buy the idea of a secular British state while quietly following their faith in closed communities like Bury Park, Tower Hamlets, Rochdale, Dewsbury and large swathes of Bradford, Birmingham and Manchester. We've convinced ourselves that this 90 per cent is the key to integration. That's who we need to keep preaching 'community cohesion' to.

However it's happened, it's now accepted almost without question that the 90 per cent is on 'our' side – but we've got there without any evidence whatsoever, except for a few Muslim community leaders telling us it's so. Well they would, wouldn't they? The reality – said Usama that day – was that the positions are in reverse. It's a 90 per cent proportion supporting right wing, conservative Islam and a sharia state, and only 10 per cent with a moderate and modernist British viewpoint.

I'll probably get called a racist troublemaker for saying that, like some kind of Holocaust denier. Except that it wasn't me saying it. That's the entire point.

You can see why that constituted a problem for Quilliam, given what they were trying to achieve, what they were all about. But they're just a fringe pressure group so who cares? What that 90:10 split represents is a much bigger problem for the UK and, I would say, anywhere that Islam has taken root and has established a fundamentalist base – which is pretty much to say, everywhere Islam exists.

When we hear reformist Muslims like Maajid Nawaz, politicians like Sayeeda Warsi and others, we all buy into the idea that things are going to change, and more than that, they are the geniuses with all the answers to how we effect the change.

But the reality is that it won't and they aren't. The only thing throwing money, power and influence at those individuals claiming to have all the answers achieves, is enriching and empowering them.

If you listen to Warsi long enough, who has never won an election but been made a Baroness based simply on being Muslim and female, you find yourself going round in circles. One minute she's slagging off her own community – or she used to be, when it suited what her boss David Cameron wanted to hear. Then, when she lost political favour and was trying to boost her credibility within 'the community', she was getting all over the government's case. Everything is all our fault, we don't love and understand (and spend) enough buying Muslim loyalty, blah, blah, predictable blah.

You cannot buy loyalty. You can buy a measure of allegiance for a while. That's all Cameron did with Warsi.

Usama came to see me when I was first out on licence from the mortgage sentence, concerned at some of the things he'd seen me tweeting, wondering what I was going to do when I was finally 'free'. I'm pretty sure he thought I'd be going back to the EDL but I assured him that I wasn't.

But when I saw some of the things going on in the name of Islam, more and more cover ups of child sex exploitation across the country, ISIS beheading innocent people and massacring others just going about their daily business, then I'm sorry if it upsets some people, but I found it impossible to just sit on my hands and say nothing.

While I was in prison I watched the rise of Islamic State, the publication of the Rotherham report. I saw Lutfur Rahman, the corrupt caliph of Tower Hamlets finally being exposed and rooted out at long last. I was sitting in a prison cell watching everything I'd said over the past five years being vindicated. And yet I'd been persecuted for saying it, more than the guilty culprits themselves. Wouldn't you be pissed off? And I know for sure that every week, every day, in British prisons, young men are being converted to the violent, radical forms of that ideology.

All across the country, the Wahhabis and Salafis are converting moderate Muslims and 'lost' Christians to extremism, whether in prison or on their Dawa stalls, in town centres and shopping centres like Luton's Arndale. They are not going moderate, they are going hardcore. Not only are we not winning that war, we're not even fighting it. I might not have been able to fight it while on licence, but it didn't mean that I couldn't talk about what I was seeing.

If I had known that I'd get realistic financial support for my family from the EDL when I was facing prison then no, I might not have turned to Quilliam. I can't say for sure. But I was in a desperate place and here was a deal with a group of people who could help. But I also honestly thought that they were saying the right things. They were calling out the extremists and I was willing to listen, to be convinced. Sadly, the reality I found was just a handful of well meaning people unfortunately with little influence.

If you think about it, the EDL had grassroots support. Sure, Britain's establishment and liberal middle class looks down its noses at angry people who march and protest, who shout and swear and chant and say enough's enough. But at least it's real, it's the voice of men and women who are patriots, who believe in their country.

Quilliam didn't have anything like that, no bedrock or backbone of people in any number, able to create any kind of impression, to make a difference. They had the support of London's wine bar liberals, that was all.

I'm not saying that it's a purely cynical exercise for Maajid and Usama and the guys. They mean what they say, they would love to make a difference. But the evidence of my eyes was that they were an organisation that was useful for the government to throw money at. It helped the politicians and establishment feel good about themselves and it fed the idea, the illusion, that they were making some kind of difference. I didn't see it, if they are.

When Usama came to see me in Luton, concerned about some of the tweets I was putting out, he brought chocolates for the kids and we had a heart to heart. I didn't have cross words with him because you can't, really. He doesn't do angry. But I asked him, in the past week how many people had converted to his way of thinking, to Quilliam's way of thinking, of becoming more moderate, of publicly taking their reformist position? You already know his answer. And I find that sad because I know how well he means.

Everything I see tells me that more and more people in this country are converting – whether that be in prisons, schools, mosques, whether it be men, women or children, and they are all converting to a radical form of Islam. I ask you – have you ever heard of anyone who converted to 'moderate' Islam? No. And why? Because for the most part, apart from a few people trying like Usama, or ignoring the worst excesses like a lot of ordinary people, there is no such thing as 'moderate' Islam. There is Islam. The Koran. The Prophet. Non-negotiable. And the people doing the converting aren't interested in the watered down version such as it exists. They are hard-liners. I meet so few people willing to accept that truth.

I told Usama I was struggling because while I wanted to find an answer through a group like Quilliam, I couldn't see one. He asked outright if I was going back to the EDL and I assured him, no, that I wasn't, but that the EDL shouldn't be isolated from the conversation about what's happening in the country.

The Quilliam experience convinced me that we have to bring all communities together in order to isolate the extremists, but the reality is of a Muslim mainstream at best refusing to condemn, and at worst defending, all of these extremist acts.

Usama said the people at Quilliam seemed to respect and like me, but that they wondered what direction I would take. And in fairness, he told me to always follow my heart. Like I said, a nice guy. After that visit, Maajid got back in touch and asked me to go to lunch with his friend Iqbal Wahhab, who owns the Roast Restaurant in London.

Iqbal mixes with Boris Johnson and people like that. He's a big hitter with an OBE. Very establishment. Their idea was to link me up with Terry Waite and something called the Forgiveness project. The cheeky bastards.

I told them that I didn't need forgiveness and I didn't want forgiveness so they could talk to Terry Waite until they went blue in the face, but I wasn't taking part in anything called the Forgiveness project. It was all part of their little pet Tommy Robinson project.

Maajid, if you don't already know anything about him, is a former extremist member of Hizb-ut Tahrir, who saw the light while he was in prison in Egypt for five years. When he came out he renounced extremism and co-founded Quilliam along with other reformed Islamic extremists like Ed Husain. Very noble, even if someone like me would naturally have doubts about the convenience of it all.

Unfortunately for Maajid, and indeed for all concerned, the bottom line is that Quilliam has zero credibility in the Muslim community. Worse than that, while in their circles I discovered that most of their leaders were more despised by Muslims than I was. Maajid himself is seen as an apostate and a government stooge by some Muslim clerics.

He might have seen the light from his terrorist days, but he isn't even Muslim any more, except possibly in name. He's married to a white woman and in 2015 he was photographed by the tabloid papers giving it large in a lap dancing club. I haven't a problem with that, far from it, but the people Maajid and Quilliam are trying to have a conversation with certainly do.

I find Maajid a good guy who sounds sincere in wanting the right changes. But me saying they are all good guys with the right message is not going to change Islam in Britain. And if they're not going to make a difference, then what's the point? Making the government feel it's at least trying to back the good guys? I'd say so.

I told Maajid and Iqbal that I might not be needing forgiveness, but I was happy to meet Terry Waite, or anyone, to discuss any options that could do some good – and then they moved the subject onto my Twitter feed, saying that a lot of people had problems with it. It had taken a while, but we'd finally got to the point.

I asked them to highlight specific tweets or incidents that were causing such offence, but again they couldn't. No one ever can. It's just uncomfortable for them, for someone to be highlighting what's going on around us all. In Quilliam's case they needed to be seen to have some form of control over me, to have influence over the 'reformed' Tommy Robinson. That was the real agenda. I got another email soon afterwards asking me to be more 'nuanced' on my Twitter feed. I replied, 'Mate, I tweet what I see'.

And it is what it is. My Twitter timeline is full of people messaging me stories, so it isn't as if I go looking for them. And when I read something, if I think it's outrageous, then I retweet it. What's the problem? If someone messaged me a story about white paedophiles getting away with raping hundreds of children for a decade, and the police and Social Services and elected councillors had deliberately ignored it, don't you think I'd do exactly the same? But they're not.

The problem this country has isn't just the amount of crime or the depravity of it, but the religious, ethnic and cultural identity of who's behind so much of it. That common thread in the vast majority of these disturbing cases is what makes the authorities squirm, no matter how much they protest or try to pretend otherwise.

Even after Rochdale and Rotherham and Oxford, and now Aylesbury and God-knows how many other instances just waiting to be uncovered, there's still an institutional unwillingness to confront who is doing this and why. Shutting me up isn't going to make a damned difference to that painful truth. But it would make Quilliam's life a little bit easier if I didn't contribute to the exposing of it.

I told Maajid and Iqbal that I would make a decision by the time I got off licence about what my future was, but that I still didn't see people facing up to the big issues, not even after the Charlie Hebdo massacre. And that was before the Dewsbury kid Talha Asmal blew himself up in Iraq fighting for ISIS, before a maniac went on the rampage with an AK47 on a Tunisian tourist beach, before Paris. Nothing we're currently doing seems to be working, does it?

The only person I see regularly speaking the truth directly to middle England is the social commentator Douglas Murray. I think he's speaking for the vast majority of people, but he doesn't get accused of being a racist or a right wing thug like me. Then again, he's not a working class white lad from Luton, with an accent like mine.

It makes a world of difference, it really does. Lads like me march and we're thugs. Middle class tweedies march and the nation is speaking. I think it might be too late by the time the British people get off their complacent arses. Too busy catching up on the latest Sky Atlantic box set.

Every day mainstream media commentators debate the best way to de-radicalise the would-be murderers coming back from ISIS, while I'm sat knowing that these trained killers are going to come back from Syria with orders to find me! Meanwhile the suits and Guardian sweethearts talk about welcoming them home and 'curing' them as if they'd caught the flu. Brilliant. Absolutely brilliant.

EVER SINCE I LEFT the EDL and started a dialogue with Quilliam they've kept trying to get me to distance myself from people like Pamela Geller and Robert Spencer. Why?

Probably because the truth they speak and the credibility they have in the USA is a bit too uncomfortable for the message that Quilliam are trying to peddle on this side of the Atlantic.

When he heard that I was working on this book Maajid arranged for me to see his agent and publishers. He'd written a book himself about his 'journey' called Radical. Anyway, I went along, but again, this was a bunch of left-wing luvvies who wanted to turn my life into a fairy story. They didn't trust me to have my own voice – they wanted one of their hand-picked writers to turn out something that suited their agenda. My experiences, but their agenda. Thanks, but no thanks.

I did feel a little bit under pressure, if only because of my initial financial agreement with Quilliam. What did that make me, if I suddenly walked away, or otherwise let them down? You'll have your own views, but from being as low as I'd sunk, it made me mostly a survivor. I honestly wanted Quilliam to have some answers, even if it couldn't be the complete solution, but there was one basic problem. They simply couldn't answer my questions.

I don't believe I'd sold my soul to them. I'd said I was going to try to be a part of the solution with them, as opposed to part of the problem. Not everything works out the way you wished, even with the best of intentions.

I would challenge them about what Pamela Geller was saying, I'd ask what was wrong about making a certain statement? What's extreme about this or that? What is factually incorrect here? And I can't recall that they ever had an answer worth calling one. They said Robert Spencer had claimed there's no such thing as moderate Muslims, so I messaged Robert and asked him about that. Guess what his reply was? 'Who's told you that, your Quilliam friends?'

The more I saw at Quilliam, the more disheartened I was. Because as righteous and sincere as some of the people like Usama undoubtedly are, for some it's just a well-meaning way to attract significant amounts of public money to fund what, behind all the gloss, is a business.

There was a young bloke in the office, Jonathan Russell, Quilliam's Political Liaison Officer, whatever that means when it's at home. He was about 23 or 24 then, just a kid.

We were in London just after we'd left the EDL, Kev and I, at the Quilliam offices, and we were talking about extremist groups, about whatever Anjem Choudary's latest made-up name for his jihadists was. Jonathan's thinking was that we couldn't and shouldn't ban these extremists. He believed we should be debating their theology and ideology and trying to combat them that way. That was his answer to getting everyone in the world to live happy-ever-after. If only we'd all known it was that easy!

I can understand how that theory was well received at his university and in his debating society, but he'd never stood in Luton town centre on a Saturday, listening to them spewing their hatred. This kid, so wet behind the ears, was full of this ridiculous idea that you can negotiate with people who delight in seeing innocent people getting their heads sawn off with a knife.

Doesn't he watch the television? See ISIS murdering other Muslims by the thousands because they're a slightly different strain of Islam, let alone full blown kuffars like us? Beheading children, throwing homosexuals off buildings? There's not a lot of debating going on there.

He once said, 'I've studied Islam all my life.' He was 23. Some life. I said I'd forgotten more than he knows and told him to shut up.

I'm not sure there would be much point in debating the different solution to Islam that Kev Carroll and I had, after a lifetime of witnessing what the street reality is – to ban them, shut them up, get tough on them, and try to make it impossible for radical Muslims to exist in British society.

We couldn't see any other answer. What we saw wasn't a forgiving faith that understood the concept of moderation or dialogue. It understood, it understands, and it only respects strength. Yet all the British state gives it is capitulation and appeasement. Every day on every street.

And when we do have to confront the guilt of what these people are doing, then we're even fabulous at displacing that. It was Rotherham Council's fault, the police's fault, for all of those thousands of children being raped and abused. Well, those people might have been complicit in letting it all happen, but let's not lose sight of who committed the physical crimes.

Either British Muslims buy entirely into our democracy and our liberal values or they paint themselves the wrong side of the line. That's the only future that I can see, although everything I've experienced in recent years tells me that our political classes are lagging a million miles or so behind that realisation.

They're still busy being impressed by kids like young Jonathan, with all of his degrees in Islamic studies and his expertise in Arab politics and his magic wand for solving all our problems. Good luck, because that's the problem.

Quilliam Political Liaison Officer Jonathan and his pals are the ones getting rolled out to speak with authority on something which, frankly, I don't think they have a clue about. He and another young bloke in the office can both speak a bit of Arabic, which is one big whoopy-do deal, because they don't know a thing about my world.

The only Muslims they meet are Maajid and Usama and mostly well educated careerists whose aim is to climb up the establishment ladder, people like Sayeeda Warsi and Shahid Malik and others. It should say, right at the top of their CVs: Qualifications – Muslim.

Young Jonathan needed to come and spend a weekend in Luton town centre with me and big Kev and get a first hand introduction to the heroin-selling scumbags and the holy men recruiting kids to go blow themselves up. When Kev and I left the EDL, Jonathan put a Tweet out saying 'Quilliam have just facilitated the decapitation' – the decapitation – 'of the EDL'.

The cheeky little bastard. When we pulled him on it he reverted into all this swallowed-a-dictionary bullshit and started saying 'that's the terminology used in conflict and terrorism'. Because he'd know of course. He'd studied it all. Got a degree in it.

I told the squealing moron that 'decapitate' was what had just happened to Lee Rigby. And he'd just tweeted that he'd decapitated the EDL? Didn't he see where that might be just a little bit misguided, unwise, in some way?

Maajid came in and bollocked him, for what it's worth, but I'm afraid that's what we're dealing with. Kids like him are the front line in tackling the Islamic plot to take over the country, then the world. God help us. Literally.

QUILLIAM MIGHT BE a well-meaning organisation, but it is living something of a lie in terms of having any influence whatsoever within the Muslim community, mostly because of the people who are involved in it.

When Maajid Nawaz went on a particularly explosive episode of Newsnight with Jeremy Paxman, he was face to face with Anjem Choudary. Time after time Maajid interrupted, challenging Anjem about his view of him, Maajid, as an apostate – someone who had turned their back on Allah – and insisting that if it was up to Anjem and his colleagues, Maajid would be put to death.

It almost became comical, because Paxman was trying to separate two cats fighting in a tied bag, but eventually Anjem shut him up by saying, 'You know the answer to that'. So yes, Anjem would gladly see Maajid Nawaz put to death as an apostate. Brought to you by the BBC.

If I came out and said something like that my feet wouldn't touch the floor on the way to the nearest police cell, but for some unknown reason Anjem Choudary gets free rein to come out with that. Either way, you'd have to say that Maajid pushing Choudary into the admission hardly strengthens the case of the Quilliam chairman being in an influential position when it comes to talking to extremist Muslims. They all want him dead!

Having said that, from my experience half of the groups set up to tackle extremism, as part of the government's so-called Prevent strategy, end up throwing money at exactly the people who are the problem.

I met someone who went on a race awareness course only to find that the bloke delivering the training was Abdul Qadeer Baksh. He was supposedly teaching the police about Muslim ideology. Here was someone who wants to kill apostates and execute homosexuals and yet we had him teaching the police, and council execs from local authorities. A Jewish woman remarked that anti-semitism is on the rise amongst Muslims and Qadeer flatly denied it. And then Qadeer told the woman she didn't know Muslims, she hadn't a clue about Muslims.

The guy is an absolute, rock solid radical in my book, and the government was paying him to peddle his bullshit back to us in the name of community relations. That's the reality that I see time and again.

In 2012 Luton's political morons decided to open a 'Discover Islam' centre in town with someone called Yusuf Bonner, an Islamic convert, as manager. All the usual suspects were there – Labour council leader Hazel Simmons, my useful-idiot probation officer Sue Beaumont – although not the new manager Bonner.

I'd already uncovered him as an extremist because I had been using a fake Facebook profile (as a Muslim) and was 'communicating' with another extremist convert from

London, Abdur Raheem Green, who specialises in Dawa – in converting non-believers. He acknowledged that was what Luton's centre was an effective front for, and Bonner actually resigned before the centre opened. According to his own blog, Islam was Bonner's 6th religion. He said that Christians are wearing a suicide belt of wrongful belief which must be deactivated. He would not rest until Islam was brought into every home in Luton. And the moronic, idiot council and all of its do-gooders, had this bloke pegged as one of the good guys?

So, you'll imagine that the centre closed down after the EDL protests and revelations? Don't be soft-headed. It's still there, a PR machine for the caliphate to come.

The fact is we're sponsoring this effective fifth-column infiltration everywhere you look. Haras Fariq, who's also in Quilliam, is someone I found to be another really good guy. I think Haras is from Rochdale – anyway, he went to a meeting of a government task force and when he returned he told us that 70% of the people there were exactly the people who were the problem to start with.

Baroness Warsi, when David Cameron brought her into the cabinet as the acceptable face of modern Islam, put together a task force and Haras reported back that it was full of Salafists and radicals, and all they were talking about was foreign policy and getting their agenda across. Those were the people being given the government's ears on so many of these huge issues. Haras resigned. He said he couldn't have anything to do with it, that they had all the wrong people there.

So I don't know what the future is for Quilliam. I expect they'll keep going until someone gets fed up of pouring money down a black hole for no visible results. Maajid didn't expect to get in as an MP at the general election, but he said that he had some kind of four year plan and that he wanted me involved in it.

Honestly? I think Quilliam have had no results to speak of and taking credit for Tommy Robinson leaving the EDL is probably as close as they've come to one. They needed me as their poster boy I guess, and for a while it suited our mutual needs, but that's not how I go about things. I don't do bullshit. Some things don't change. We've not spoken for a while.

Meanwhile, whether you're working with a right-on group like Quilliam or not, it doesn't make the rest of the rubbish in your life go away. When you walk away from something like the EDL, you don't suddenly get to close the door on the people who want your head on a plate.

I'd left the EDL in October and my court case over the brother-in-law's mortgage was coming up in January 2014. The police had finally hit a brick wall over the taxes, but then they immediately announced that they were preparing charges against my wife and set a date for two weeks ahead – unless I swallowed the deal to plead guilty. She had been left hanging on bail from early 2010.

When I told her she broke down in tears. She didn't know a single thing about what she was supposed to have done wrong. But that was just it – she hadn't done anything. I think it was the very next night that the police came banging on the door at 3am, causing merry hell with the Al-Shabaab death threat.

The pressure was being cranked up at every turn.

18: THE METROPOLITAN INTELLIGENCE BUREAU

I DON'T EXPECT that you've heard of MIB – and no, not Men in Black, the Hollywood sci-fi blockbuster with Will Smith and Tommy Lee Jones. This lot are the Metropolitan Intelligence Bureau, or at least that's how they described themselves to me. I think I was supposed to assume that they were a division of the Metropolitan Police, but that never became clear.

They might have been police, they might have been MI5 – or the FBI/CIA/KGB for all I could tell. But they certainly had long arms, long tentacles. They knew what was happening to me before I did, most of the time.

I've explained previously about the police tactics of arrest and detain, harass and intimidate and inconvenience and generally piss you off, just because they can. You would like to think that once the authorities have finally got you on your knees, sorted you out to the point of you admitting defeat, of submitting, of throwing your hands up and saying 'I give in, I'm walking away', that they would have the good grace to go away, to finally leave you alone. Think again.

The beginning of this sequence of events started when two characters approached me in Winchester Prison. When I did the deal over the mortgage case and got 18 months I was sent straight to HMP Woodhill, an A-Cat nick despite the white collar nature of my offence.

Early in that stay there was an incident where a big white bearded convert started screaming his head off over being in the same room as me. I think it was the next day that I went up for a legal visit with my solicitor Rhiannon. People were already concerned that I was in A-Cat Woodhill and had emailed the governor about it.

After the visit I was taken to a holding room with large windows and I could see there were a few prisoners in there, but three of them were bearded Muslims including the big white guy. The screw put me inside – they knew what they were doing – locked the door and calmly walked away. The room had bench seating all round but I never sat down because I knew what was coming next. I kept my chin down but my eyes up, and my back to the corner.

The big white bearded bloke charged and laid into me immediately the screw had disappeared. I got hold of him with one hand because I couldn't afford to go down on the floor, and I was lashing away with the other, as the other two Muslims came wading in.

The other prisoners just sat and watched, but that was okay. If they'd tried to help, their lives wouldn't have been worth living in that place. By the time the screws came and broke it up my teeth were gone, my skull was gashed open and my eye swollen shut. I was lucky I guess in that it wasn't fatal. There was a camera up in the corner warning prisoners that they were being watched. The prison told my lawyers that unfortunately it wasn't working that day.

I was put in my cell – no hospital visit – and from there I was shifted to Winchester, a decent nick where I could do 'normal' time. I was on the mend when these blokes came calling, unannounced.

I had never heard of anything called the Metropolitan Intelligence Bureau, MIB. I was told that I had a legal visit and waiting for me were two young blokes, probably my age or even younger. They were all suited up, smart. The first thing they said was that no one knew they were visiting me, except the governor. No one knew what the purpose of their visit was, and I could tell other prisoners, my family, anyone, exactly what I wanted. Cloak and dagger, or what?

Later, when I went back to my cell, I could think of a dozen things I wished I'd asked them. I inquired of people on the outside about this so-called MIB, including my solicitor, but no one ever came back with anything. What do

I think now? Who they were? I don't know. Possibly exactly what they said, but possibly MI5 too.

The man doing the talking said his name was Olly, and that the MIB was a secret unit within Scotland Yard that deals with high-end, organised crime. I've still got the phone numbers he gave me – and for good measure, a minute ago, I've just tried calling them. One number was dead and one on a strange divert set-up. There was no answer by then though. I was one that got away.

Olly said, 'We're here first of all to understand you. You've left the EDL, so explain to us, talk to us, why, how, what's going on'. So I did. I started chatting. I told them the truth, which I tend to do – and which I have to say hasn't always served me well. There you go.

They said I was very different to what they thought they'd find and were surprised that no one had been in touch before – whatever that was supposed to mean.

And then they told me they needed my help and started talking about what was happening not just in the EDL but the far right generally, especially Paul Golding and Britain First. They were talking about fragmented groups, no control or leadership and then they came right out and said they needed my help in rooting certain people out.

They wanted help dealing with Golding. They thought I could command the respect of the entire far right – which I took issue with, as I always have done – and when they asked me what I was going to do when I got out of jail, I told them I was going to work, to get on with my life.

Not the right answer, Tommy. They wanted me to help with what they called 'troublesome people', at which I said no, what you want is for me to become a police informant.

Can you believe it? These bastards had spent five years persecuting me, turning me and my family's lives upside down, and now I was supposed to change sides, to sign up and help them? The complete and utter dickheads. The meeting lasted two hours and the bottom line was that they said it would be financially beneficial to me to play ball. I actually laughed because, as I told them, I was sitting in jail for something they knew was complete bollocks, and here they were, asking for my help.

As best I can remember, I sent them packing with a speech, something like, 'They've sent you in here looking like a pair of wankers. I've done a lot of things wrong, but what I'm in here for, I haven't done. This is bullshit, what you've managed to pin on me – and it's all because you couldn't get me on anything else.'

I told them that after the time I'd done, the things I'd been through, my only intentions were getting out of prison, walking away from the EDL and spending time with my family. Full stop. I was going to clear my debts and get back on my feet.

I didn't want favours from anyone and I didn't want to be under the control of anyone. I had no interest in the EDL, and at that point I didn't particularly want to talk about Islam again. It was back to work for Tommy.

At that first meeting they didn't give me any contact details, they just said they'd get back to me when I got out, when I'd had some time to think. And they were persistent, devious bastards, Olly and his friends.

I'D BEEN OUT on licence from Winchester for about five or six weeks and I was driving up the M1 in south Yorkshire, when three police patrol cars pulled me over and boxed me in. Not one, not two, but three squad cars. That doesn't happen by accident. That's not what you get for doing 75mph on the motorway.

I was on my way to see a company in Doncaster that I'd sold the sunbeds from the tanning salon to. I was out on licence so there was no reason whatsoever for me to be up to no good, but suddenly boom, nicked, right out of nowhere.

The three police cars swooped on the M1 just past Sheffield, at 2 o'clock in the afternoon and I found myself arrested and in a police cell yet again. Why? I'd no idea.

I was driving a blue Audi. It was registered to a motor dealer mate of mine in Daventry. I hadn't told probation where I was going, but the police clearly knew anyway and they said the car was suspected of being involved in a burglary about 70 miles away. In fact the bloke who bought the sunbeds rang me up later to say the police had been all over him. They've done that with anyone and everyone I've spoken to over the last few years.

I swear that if I went to buy a pack of bog-roll, within 20 minutes the police would know whether it was luxury Andrex or the sort of cheap stuff your finger goes through. There's probably an entire file on Tommy Robinson's toilet habits.

The police told me they were arresting me on suspicion of burglary, at which I started laughing. I'd been asked to speak to the Oxford Union – which was coming up – and my main theme was going to be about this sort of shit, this perversion of what people think British justice is about.

I got pulled in at 2pm and taken off to some nick or other. They eventually got me to interview at 6 or 7 o'clock and said they had a witness to this burglary, which happened to be way across the other side of Yorkshire, in Hull. Really. Hull was a place I think I might have been to once in my life, with the football. That's all. And you'll really like this – their witness said the villains were a black bloke, and a 6ft 1ins blond-haired bloke. I was laughing my arse off because you couldn't make this kind of shit up if you tried. Not and keep a straight face anyway.

This female copper, she asked me, 'What colour would you say your hair is? Browny blond?' I couldn't stop laughing. I thought, oh my God, they're trying to say I was the 6ft 1ins blond bloke, because I obviously couldn't be the black bloke! Then she said, 'How tall are you, 5ft 10?' The cheeky cow was even trying to big up my height! I'm a 5ft 6ins short arse and the law was trying to grow me an extra leg!

All of this is on interview tape, I swear, it is ridiculous. Talk about trying to make Cinderella's shoe fit one of the Ugly Sisters! I gave them some shit over the entire farce, because it was completely unbelievable.

A lot is made about there being a shortage of Muslim police officers in the British police force. Well, they must scour the county looking for one when they've got me in the cells, because sure as anything the arresting officer was a Muslim again. I wonder if this is to big up their street cred, so these geezers can go down the mosque and brag, 'I had that Tommy Robinson geezer cuffed in my cells today' like a London cabbie who's had George Clooney in the back. Maybe that's their latest counter-terrorism strategy. It's probably an improvement on whatever else they've got going.

I'd done my interview at about 6 or 7 o'clock in the evening, and my solicitor said it was an absolute joke and that I was going to be released without charge. But I wasn't released without charge.

At 3am, after 13 hours in custody, they put me in a police van and took me to Humberside. When I got there I was drugs tested – even though I had been arrested for a burglary offence – and I thought maybe that's what it was all about; because I was on licence, if I failed a drugs test, they could throw me back in prison.

They stripped me naked again, body searched me, made me squat. They were going through everything. They were completely intent on humiliating me as far as they could within the law. Well, I say the law. I think those pricks were following someone's orders and that the whole pantomime had nothing to do with a burglary in Hull, not by a black bloke, a blond bloke or even the flaming Jolly Green Giant.

They bailed me in the morning after I agreed to do an identity parade. That would have been something wouldn't it? Little fat Tommy Robinson next to a bunch of extras from Central Casting? I don't doubt they'd have found someone or some way to finger me though, if they'd been that way inclined.

For some unexplained reason they then decided that they didn't want to do the ID parade and let me go. They kept my clothes, everything, and threw me out into Hull in the middle of the day wearing a prisoner's jumpsuit and a pair of plimsolls, with my car impounded over in Doncaster.

I'll be honest, given everything that I'd been through, I was petrified. I was doing everything I could not to put a foot wrong, but all I could think was that if I was charged for burglary, I'd get a recall to prison anyway.

The headline would do all the damage required, and I'd seen this so many times, with different charges, different incidents. Accused of this, suspected of that, arrested on this and that ... and then the charges are dropped, but all the damage is already done. This will sound ridiculous, but I was embarrassed that the headline was going to be about burglary. I mean, if it had been for whacking some bloke trying to put a knife in me, okay. But burglary? That's the most cheap, scumbag offence. You can't walk round Luton with your head up if you've been nicked for burglary.

This is where it gets interesting though. When I got home later that day my wife said that Winchester Prison had been on the phone. Apparently they still had some of my stuff from when I was released. Except when I looked at the number that had been left it was an 0207 code which is central London. I rang the number and sure enough it was this prick Olly again. Straight out, he said, 'We can help you out of your current predicament'. He said, 'Imagine the

279

newspapers, the headlines, Tommy Robinson on burglary charge, you'll be recalled to serve out your sentence for certain, we can help...'.

I told him, 'You dirty, fucking bastards.'

The first thing I did when I got out of the cells in Humberside was have a conversation with probation because they had to know, and they told me that if I got charged I was looking at a full licence recall until July 2015. I was panicking.

My solicitor thought that because it was such clear bullshit, that I would be released without charge – but they didn't, they bailed me. He said there was no evidence, they couldn't bring charges. I replied, Oh really? You think that will stop them?' It hadn't before.

Olly said, 'Come and see us, we can help.'

They were behind that arrest, I'm convinced. I told him I didn't need their help, that I'd never even left the motorway, let alone gone anywhere remotely near Hull, Humberside or wherever. I told him to fuck off, again.

The police said I'd be required to go back for an ID parade, then that I'd have to take part in a video ID parade, but nothing came through. The day before I had to answer bail, they dropped it. The lot. It was all totally fabricated shit, they were messing with my head, trying to wear me down. My solicitor just couldn't comprehend what was going on. He said that none of it made any sense, none at all. But it did to me.

So was that it, finally? Were they done? Get serious.

Next came another bullshit inquiry over something and nothing from way back – which went nowhere again – but which gave the MIB characters another opportunity to come back on the phone, saying they could help me, get a letter to the judge if I got charged – they could smooth things over. They got another earful of abuse for their trouble. I put the phone down and explained things to my wife and I swear I just felt like I was trapped. I didn't want to get recalled to prison because of my kids but at the same time I would never work with the police. Never, ever. How and where I was brought up, there was nothing worse than a grass. That was and is the lowest of the low.

So that was it?

Not quite. There was a different approach next. With perfect timing after the M1 episode, we had another panic incident at home. I was out with a pal in Hitchin when my wife rang and said two strangers had turned up at the house, so I raced back home.

There was a man and a woman and they were standing outside, which was strange because they didn't have a car with them. We don't get buses stopping on the road where we live. They handed me a business card which said they were from a company based in London and explained that they were some kind of intermediaries for people who didn't want to co-operate with the police.

We went through the whole pantomime again, how they work with people in difficult circumstances who don't want to turn against their bosses, their gangs, to snitch on this gangster or that one. They said that when there are gang killings in London, they intervene on behalf of the police to 'mediate' with people, whatever that meant.

Now, I don't know about you, but if that story is true and not the fairytale that I took it for, I reckon those people deserve to step up in public and get a medal, not hide in the shadows. As you may have worked out, I wasn't in the most trusting of moods given what I was being put through. This was just one more attempt to turn the screw.

I asked who was paying them to come see me. Who had sent them to sit in my house and try to get me to turn traitor on my former colleagues? If they weren't working for the police, the Home Office, the Government, who was paying them to try to recruit me?

They said they couldn't reveal that, that they had many different donors, but that they were absolutely not from the police. They got quite shirty too, saying they were there to offer their services as mediators between me and the police.

I can't get my head round why they thought I would have more trust in them than every other snake who had stitched me up. So, true to form, I told them to fuck off too. They were wasting their time and mine.

The following week I received the letter saying the police were hitting me for £315,000 under a Proceeds of Crime claim, despite our agreement that there would be a 'no benefit' clause in my guilty plea. I'd thought that we would still have our property, or most of it, and that I could still get back on my feet once the deal was done, but now the police were trying to rob us of every last penny. It was one thing after another after another.

At that point I sat down with Sue Beaumont from probation and told her everything. I was still on reasonable terms with her at that stage. I was being straight and I thought she was. I thought that probation was meant to help you rehabilitate, re-integrate into society, get back on your feet. What a fool I was.

She said she couldn't comprehend what the police seemed to be doing to me, though I wonder now if she knew all along. My hope of living a normal life was disappearing in front of me, one attack after another. It was non-stop. I don't expect you to feel sorry for me. I can tell you I was feeling sorry for myself by this point though. They were just like a bulldog at my throat. Apparently what my solicitor missed when we made the original plea deal was the police statement that ... 'At this time we do not believe it constitutes a lifestyle case'. You've got it. 'At this time'.

I'd done my sentence and now, bang, they were changing the rules. I would never have done a deal to plead guilty if I'd known they would or even could do that. I'd always thought I was the bloke who could take anything they threw at me, then this came through – they weren't going to stop until they ruined me, until they ground me and my family into the dust. I'd lent a lad £20,000 and everything I'd made in 15 years was being taken away.

So once again, right on cue came the next contact from Olly and MIB, sticking like dogshit to the sole of your shoe.

He said, 'I understand that you've got confiscation proceedings. See that figure? We can make that go away.'

Olly said that although the confiscation order would be made, they could ensure I would only have to pay something like £25 a month, just a token contribution. That would be the limit of my financial burden – but of course in return these characters would have control of what they considered the far right.

They'd be able to steer the EDL through the strings they had attached to their puppet – me. That £25 a month was supposed to be a temptation, although I'm sure the pricks would remove it as soon as it suited them. The fact is, I would be completely owned.

Part of me, the old streetwise Tommy Robinson, was thinking that I'd agree to it, then I'd just ignore them afterwards. But as Sue Beaumont said, truthfully for once, they'd have me back in court and I'd have to pay it one way or another. If nothing else, I had learned that these people don't let go.

So once again, I told them politely where to go.

That wasn't foremost on my mind though. I went to court to fight the £315,000 and the judge at least ruled against that – but I did get hit for £125,000, which was the value of that property I lent the £20k on, when it last sold. The judge actually said that he was 'extremely uncomfortable' with what the police were doing. He referred to the agreement and the fact that I'd pleaded guilty based on it, plus the police now saying that legally it wasn't worth the paper it was written on. The judge replied that whatever the legality, morally it was wrong.

So guess what happened next? Go to the front of the class! MIB rang the moment I came out of court and said they knew I was in a fix, that I was going to have to sell my properties, but that I didn't have to, because they could make the problem go away. Their problem was that once the figure got down to £125k, as much as it was going to hurt and as unjust as it was, I knew that I could find a way to handle it, even if it did take everything I had.

'I don't need your help,' I told them once and for all. 'I will pay the £125,000 then you lot can fuck right off.'

THIS ALL HAPPENED on the Friday before I was first due to talk to the Oxford Union, the following Thursday.

One of my main issues about being on a white collar charge was that my licence terms dictated that I could have no contact with the EDL. What was that about?

I'd already told Sue Beaumont that I was going to let those students at Oxford know exactly what goes on in the name of both law and democracy in this country. They'd get the full lowdown on MIB, the M1/Hull stunt, the financial persecution, everything. I suppose in hindsight it was a mistake telling my probation officer all about this anyway, let alone that I was going to expose it to the Oxford Union – although one part of me was still worried about what these people were going to do next.

They hadn't shown any sign of letting up so far, and I thought I had to share it with someone. I stupidly thought I could trust my probation officer.

I'm not quite sure how much of what I told her she believed. I suppose that being 'inside' the system she has blind faith in how it all works, even though she admitted that what I was experiencing was blatant disruption tactics. It was quite funny in one way. She asked me to stop slagging the police off and to draw a line under things – as if I was persecuting them, for crying out loud!

Sue said she'd talk to the Bedfordshire police about starting with a clean slate and asking them to leave me alone, as though this was just some PC Plod with a grudge.

They went after my old schoolfriend down in London because we'd done some business, and they put the squeeze on the bloke who bought my sunbeds. Then there was my motor sales friend in Daventry who'd been lending me vehicles while I was struggling.

Sure enough, they went in and raided him for tax and VAT, even though the bloke is as clean as a whistle. But you'll like this. A copper up that way was bigging himself up, going on about this garage they had under surveillance, saying it was involved with really dangerous people. He couldn't keep his fat mouth shut. I got a call and at least was able to give my pal the nod, to let him know what was coming his way. He had all his books neat and tidy and ready to inspect when the donkeys came lumbering in.

But Sue Beaumont had this blind faith that everything is done by the book. I suppose I should have known, given her left-wing background. When she came on probation visits to the house, we wouldn't go anywhere near the mortgage case, which you'd think was be the point of my 'rehabilitation'. She would always want to talk about my views on Islam, and she'd get all worked up because I'd said that Mohammed was a paedophile.

I said I didn't know what else you call a 56-year-old man marrying a six-year-old and having sex with her at nine. Not me saying it, Sue, that's Islam saying it. And it counts as paedophilia in most people's eyes. She'd end up in a sulk saying that young Muslim girls are being groomed as well. And I'd look at her and say no, they are not. And certainly not by gangs of white men, whatever their own fathers, uncles and friends might do to them at home.

I should have known better than to trust her. Following the Friday mortgage claim hearing, the next morning, Saturday, I went swimming with my kids. When we got home the police were waiting for me with news that I'd apparently breached my licence.

Not only wasn't I going to be talking at the Oxford Union, I was going back to jail.

AT THE BEGINNING of this book I talked about spending far too much time on Twitter. I still do. Part of it is just nagging away at the system, me being pissed off at the world. And part of it was having too much time on my hands, what with the state having frozen my assets and prevented me from getting out there and making a living.

Indulging yourself on social media can have major drawbacks, though. It taught me a lot about the ridiculous notion of free speech.

I'd first been invited to speak to the Oxford Union in 2013, but that was called off after the news went public and the university was inundated with threats from people like UAF. A similar thing happened with Trinity University in Dublin.

At that point I guess some of the Oxford students heard my comments about them pandering to people threatening the concept of free speech, and that ultimately led to me being asked back in 2014. The Oxford Union officers for that term stood up to the race bullies and good for them. Many bigger organisations have bottled it.

I've had BBC Newsnight and ITV Daybreak invite me on only to suddenly back out. I worked out that when I tweeted my appearance they were inundated with shit from both outside and upstairs. To me it was blatantly clear – someone higher up the food chain decided they could do without the aggravation. Cancel the booking. Robinson is too much like trouble. These days I try to be a little bit smarter when I get media invitations. I don't put it out on Twitter until it's actually happening.

The next invitation from Oxford didn't work out quite so well for me. The new President of the Union, Mayank Banerjee, decided that he wasn't going to be browbeaten by the UAF or anyone else, and that he would uphold the Union's historic traditions. Top man Mayank. And when I did eventually appear, it went down as a huge highlight of my eventful career. I'd warned Mayank that they'd get threats and protests again, and I didn't want to waste both of our time, but he was a pretty staunch kid. Good for him.

A few days before the police came to recall me to prison I'd been on the receiving end of some vile Twitter threats from a Nazi with the tag 1488Hitler. He was going to rape my mum, find out where I lived and kill me.

And then some clown in Birmingham called Barry Butler tweeted out my mum's address. I got onto the Hitler character and told him, if he wanted to see me that badly, I'd be outside Bedford probation office the next morning at 11. I didn't want him finding my mum.

Meanwhile we tracked down an address and within an hour I was banging on the bloke's door, giving him grief. He said he hadn't a clue what I was on about. I must have raved for 10 minutes before it dawned. Wrong Barry Butler. I made my apologies and left, and this time we found the right Barry Butler – only five miles away.

It was the right place, because his wife opened the door and immediately slammed it. He wouldn't come out, so I was shouting at the top of my voice. That brought the neighbours out and before long the police sirens were sounding. When he came out Barry Butler was an old bloke, a thalidomide.

I asked him what he thought he was doing, tweeting my mum's address? Did he want her raping and killing – because this was real life, not a computer game. Did he want me to put his name and address on my website? The police asked what I was doing. I said I was there because they wouldn't do their job. The bloke took the tweet down.

Long before I'd been told by Bedfordshire police that if I re-tweeted threats aimed against me, I could be arrested. Nothing would be done about the offensive tweet, but my re-tweeting it was illegal. Got that? Me neither.

You don't need sitcoms when you have rubbish like this going on around you. So, with me being a paid up member of the Awkward Squad, I would always put the threats straight back out on Twitter anyway, asking why the cops were going to nick me when they weren't going to nick the people threatening to kill me?

I'd had that phone call from Sue Beaumont a couple of weeks before asking me what I intended talking about at Oxford and when it would be. It was a strange call. Something didn't feel right. I had a sense even then that other people were listening to the conversation. But it was part of my licence conditions that I had to tell her everything – and I told her in no uncertain terms.

This was free speech in action. I was going to tell the Oxford Union all about it and why wouldn't I? I'd rejected the MIB deals, taken my punishment, done my time. My turn now. And how stupid was I? That outburst would cost me a month in jail and another state-sponsored attempt on my life. What an idiot.

The morning after the 1488Hitler rant and the Barry Butler episode, I went for my appointment at 11am. He wouldn't be there, I knew that. These weirdos never follow through with their rubbish.

I remember afterwards thinking it strange that this time Sue never raised the subject of what I intended saying at the Oxford Union a few days ahead. She just wanted to know the date. I think I know why she never asked about my speech – the bitch knew I'd never be getting there.

After I'd seen her I spoke to one of her junior colleagues Helen Bean, a probation officer who's always been really nice with me. Helen asked why I'd told someone on Twitter that I was going to be at the probation offices today.

I explained all about this bloke's threats. It was pretty straightforward. I didn't want anyone trying to find my house or my mum's and this was the Probation Service, linked to the police, so what better place to tell someone where I'd be? Of course he wouldn't come, because these clowns never do. But it would be nice to be on the doorstep of the forces of law and order if he did.

And then it occurred to me, so I asked Helen – how did she know about this? She admitted that the police had been in touch.

So I said fine, if the police saw this bloke threaten to rape my mum and he turned up, they would arrest him. Job solved – and if not, then why aren't the police arresting these people? What possible explanation could there be?

Helen said that I was meant to call the police if I got a threat, even though she knew that I'd called them hundreds of times over such threats without a single thing being done. It would just be wasting everyone's time.

I reminded her I'd been into Bedford police station with print-outs of 300 threats against me and my family. I'd even videoed myself going into the station, reading out all these death threats, raping my mum, killing my kids, burning the house down, pictures of knives, with people saying they were going to stick them in my head.

The first time I went to the police they sent a Muslim constable out, and I sat down with him and explained that I cared less when people threaten to kill me, but when they talked about chopping up my children, it wasn't right.

He replied that unless there was something religious or racial about the threat, they wouldn't act on it. They took all of that evidence away and it was a full year before there was an answer message left on my wife's mobile, from a DC Mohammed Hussain saying that they would be taking no further action.

I took the tape of that message into probation and played it to them. What was I supposed to do, if the police were saying it was open season on me and my family for every lunatic in the land?

It's almost comical. The celebrity columnist Katie Hopkins likes to upset the apple cart, but when she used the expression 'Sweaty Sock' as rhyming slang for a Scottish 'Jock' on Twitter, the police were all over the poor lass, investigating it as a race hate crime! But people by the dozen, by the hundred, can threaten rape, murder and dismemberment on her and me, and it's fine and dandy?

It seems so. That's the brave new world our Politically Correct police live in. No wonder crime rates are supposed to be falling when they ignore any so-called offence which doesn't fit neatly into their quotas or agendas.

I'm not sure what either the police or probation thought I was intending doing that morning – starting a riot outside the probation offices? I thought I was being reasonably responsible, given the fact that they all knew the very last thing I wanted was to find myself in another cell.

Anyway, Helen Bean asked me not to do it again and I agreed. However I continued getting threats from this character through the week. I didn't respond, I didn't re-tweet him, I just ignored him. I even wondered later if that was Olly and his MIB mates playing games, trying to provoke me. Too far-fetched? Isn't it all?

Then on the Saturday morning we got home and there were two blokes sitting in a car outside the house. I didn't know who they were. I ran inside and grabbed a knife because this could have been that character on Twitter for all that I knew. There was a knock at the door and after they passed their warrant cards through the letterbox I let them in. The two officers were nice blokes. They said they were sorry, they didn't want to be doing this. I sent my kids upstairs and asked what it was about, and one copper said something to do with Twitter. I was going back to jail, over that tweet saying that I was going to be outside probation.

Catch this though. I read their warrant and it was to arrest me at St Albans Crown Court, which is where they knew I'd been the day before, for my house confiscation hearing. So why didn't they arrest me there?

I can tell you why – because I had a film crew with me, Mike and the guys getting footage for the documentary. They didn't want to look complete dicks on camera, so they waited until the next day – and did it in front of my wife and kids instead. The copper told me they'd been told to raid me at 4am. Being reasonable blokes they didn't do that at least.

I rang Sue Beaumont and the cold-faced cow might as well have been wearing a judge's black cap. All I got from her was that probation would come and see me in prison. I wanted reassurances that I wouldn't be sent to Bedford, where I might as well have been on the scaffold talking to the hangman.

'Stephen, we will come and visit you,' she said. Bitch.

I asked the officers to take me to Winchester nick, where I'd finished my time safely the last time and they said they were happy to do that. They rang Sue Beaumont back. She said, 'No, you're not going to Winchester. You're going to Bedford'.

I was pretty emotional when the police took me away. My kids were there and I had promised them daddy wasn't 'working away' again. I felt such a let down to them all. Afterwards I couldn't stop crying.

Later, in prison, I read that someone had called a Northampton footballer a black something-or-other on social media and – whoosh, nicked! Mo Ansar tweets some provocative stuff with no comeback, but other people respond and like a ton of bricks the law is all over them. Double standards doesn't even come close to describing law and order in this country.

I said to one officer that all they had to do was nick one of these Twitter trolls and it would put a halt to the rest. Instead what they were doing was giving the world a free pass to say whatever they wanted about me, my wife, my children and my mother.

One Scottish geezer said that he was going to chop my head off, which I reported to the police. He saw that I'd passed it on and he laughed. He replied that nothing would be done because, 'The police fucking hate you'.

I found it difficult to disagree.

BEING A WEEKEND, those two officers took me Kempston Police HQ and kept me in a cell there until Monday when they came to take me to Bedford. I said to them, 'You know what's going to happen. Why are you doing this?' They couldn't look me in the eye.

I could see it all as it would go down. They were going to put me in the middle of a war zone, it would all kick off – which was what they wanted – and I'd end up on another charge. A total fit up. Back to jail for the duration of my sentence. No more licence, nine more long months inside.

Since I'd left the EDL I'd been trying to change my approach, to avoid trouble if at all possible. In the old days, it had been a straightforward mindset. If you run once, you run every time. And I didn't run, whatever the outcome. But I was trying my best to change all of that – and now shit was coming down anyway.

When I got to Bedford I recognised the main screw on reception – I knew his brother from knocking about years before. He said he was going to help me as much as he could. He knew that I was going to get badly hurt in there.

There were lads, blokes that I knew in Bedford nick, who if I was going to have to do time, I needed to be close to. This screw said there were a few lads on B Wing who would cover my back. He was actually checking out the percentage of Muslims on the wings and what tariff they were doing, because if someone is doing six months they're not going to want to kill you. If they are doing 15 or 20 years they'll reason that they have nothing to lose. I would be fair game.

He was going through this list, saying, 'There's a lifer here, a lifer there...' and I thought, 'Jesus, I'm in on a 28 day recall' – that bitch Sue had told me that much.

I would happily sit down the block in solitary confinement for 28 days, but they were insisting on putting me in general population among half the blokes in the country wanting to see me dead. I told the screw he was wasting his time because there was nowhere really safe for me in that building. The prison offered to put me on the numbers with the pervs, but I still wasn't having that. I hadn't sunk that low.

I asked to go on B Wing where at least I would know some lads, and my request ended up being sent upstairs to the governor. I asked for a pen and paper and wrote a long note to him, explaining that I was on a 28 day recall. I named all of the different local Muslim gangs, explained that they all knew me and that every one of them wanted to kill me, that there was money on my head. I laid out all of the Osman warnings I'd had, and detailed how I'd been violently attacked in nearly every prison I'd been in.

I went on about the duty of care the prison had to me, and that I didn't want to be in a position of confrontation where I had to defend myself. I don't know what more I could have done to spell the situation out.

So what happened? The governor turned around and declared that I was being sent to A Wing. We'd just checked the system and guess where the most radical and violent

Muslims were? Correct, you've won a star prize – A wing! The screw on reception apologised, and said it had come from upstairs, there was nothing he could do. I asked him if he knew what was going to happen. I told him I wanted a signature to show that the governor had seen my note.

I have been in a hostile prison environment before but this was like, 'Fucking hell man'. It was over the top. It was 11.50am and as they walked me onto the wing a roar went up. Everyone was shouting once they saw who was coming in. I was put in my cell and I thought, here we go.

I listened to what was coming from the other cells and they were all shouting. 'He's there, we're going to do him!' I heard someone apparently from Sierra Leone shouting, 'I'm going to chop his head off, he's going to get shanked.'

I'd had that before, but this time they were putting me right in the middle of it. How do you deal with that? How do you think you would deal with it? Fold up into a ball and hide in the corner of your cell? Wait for it to happen? Cry and scream and make a fool of yourself? I had to put myself into the exact mindset that I was trying to leave behind, because in that situation I was out of options.

I had no other choice but to come out of that cell fighting. Lunchtime was up pretty soon, so I went for some food and I walked into the canteen on my toes, ready to go – although a problem more and more these days is that you just don't know who the Muslims are. Everyone's dressed the same, and it isn't just Asians who are Muslims, especially in prison. It's a gangland world of its own and criminals like to belong to the biggest, most dangerous gang. So blacks, whites, mixed race ... anyone and everyone can be a Muslim in the prison system. You just can't tell.

After I'd got battered in Woodhill I got it into my mind, straight off, to establish where I stood amongst anyone I was standing or sitting close to. I walked up to the servery and asked who was Muslim. Dion turned round, Dion Ellis, a Luton kid whose brother and sister I used to knock around with. He was in there for being involved in a big mess of tit-for-tat shootings. And Dion looked at me and said 'I'm Muslim, brother'. That's what happens, the gang thing, but I knew Dion so I wasn't too worried about him.

And then a moment later this white geezer, McDonald, said 'I'm fucking Muslim bruv'. And the way he said it, well that was it. We ended up fighting across the servery and I battered him.

I had literally just walked in there from my cell, but I knew this was going to have to happen. I wasn't going back up until I'd had a kick-off with this lot, because I'd heard them all shouting that they were going to do me – and I might as well be in some kind of control over where and when it happened, how it all went down.

It was blatant that the prison service was going to let them have a free shot. If I walked out to get my dinner and they put me back up in my cell, this lot were going to get me there. Probably 10 or 15 of them and I was going to get stabbed up, my head kicked in, hit with boiling water – I was going to get badly hurt, or quite likely killed.

There wasn't much of a happy ending either way, but certainly not if I waited for the confrontation on their terms. So this McDonald mouthed off and away we went. Dion didn't get involved. At that point the screws came piling in and dragged me out, kicking and screaming. I was going mad. I said, 'What the fuck do you lot expect?'

They dragged me back to my cell, locked the door and I went to the window and started arguing for 10 or 15 minutes with the Muslims. I called them cowards, fucking cowards. They gave it back, they were going to have me.

And I shouted back, 'Yeah, but every time a non-Muslim walks past the cell door they give me the thumbs up, it's just that everyone's too scared to tell you bullying fucks what a set of cowardly mugs you are.'

I was shouting at all the converts, asking them questions about Islam, asking them to tell me about Mohammed's wives, to talk me through each one of his wives' stories. They couldn't of course, because they know jack shit about what they've signed up for. Ignorant pricks.

By that time the whole prison was erupting. I heard one of my mates, Walshy, and a few other white lads shouting support. I was raving and laughing in equal part. They were all going to batter me and I was shouting, 'Yeah, yeah, yeah, I've just battered their brother and I'm sitting without a mark or scratch on me. Fuck you!'

From my point of view it was all a safety mechanism, because once that much shit kicked off the prison had to do something about it. The last thing they needed or wanted was a full scale riot. They were doing effectively the same as they did to me in Woodhill – they let the Muslims have one shot and if I hadn't acted as I did, if I hadn't taken control, I would have gone to the shower and when the door opened I would have got it. A knife, a blade, a sharpened screwdriver, whatever.

Before and after I kicked off and they were dragging me back up to my cell, I'd noticed the governor standing at the end of the landing taking it all in. He stood there while I went down to get my dinner, watching. I have no doubt in my mind that it was the probation services and whoever was pulling their strings that put me on that wing. Someone wanted to teach me a lesson, that's for certain.

And ask yourself – why wouldn't I think that? Where, in the entire system, had I come across someone who wanted to achieve anything except grind me into the dirt?

Dev, yes, a top bloke. He came into a police station with me once for some reason or other and I told him that despite there being a well publicised shortage of Muslim officers, they would certainly find one for me. He thought I was paranoid, told me to leave it out. And he was right, I was wrong – there wasn't just one, but two Muslim police officers who came out to see me! It was quite funny, I was howling laughing. He couldn't believe it.

Anyway, the fight had the desired effect from my point of view. They came and took me to see the governor who said that he was putting me down the block – in solitary – for my own safety.

I asked him, 'Why now? What's changed? Why didn't you put me down there three hours ago for my own safety?' I knew exactly why – because they wanted to get me killed. I didn't get punished for it in terms of further charges because when I was in the dinner queue, it was the Muslims who came up to me. I might have thrown the first punch, but they came at me, started the confrontation.

I spent two days down the block in Bedford, where again, it was quite funny. One of the blokes down the block was a complete nutter, Johnny, who was as close as you can get to a career villain. He was in solitary because he'd smashed up a cell that morning after being in court.

He was in the next cell to me and next to him was another lad, Ryan O'Leary, who I used to knock about with a bit. He was mad as well. But then they brought down this McDonald, the white Muslim I had been fighting with – and when he was put in the cell the other side of me I realised that I recognised him too.

He was worried and wanted to know if everything was squared away, if the argument was finished. Seems he was from Stopsley and then it clocked, he and his brother were a couple of years younger than me.

So I started arguing through the doors, asking him why he needed to go on like that, saying he was a Muslim. It went on like that for a while, me giving him shit, and his pals. And then, finally, they took me to Winchester, where the governor was a top bloke. I got to see out my 28-day recall period in relative safety, in peace and quiet.

Ten years before, when I'd been sent down for that late night fight with an off duty policeman, I'd emerged a different person, but one who thought he could handle being inside. And to an extent, I knew how to cope. But what I went through as a result of my EDL activities changed the nature of what prison time is. A few days in a police cell because they're messing with your mind and your life is easy. By the time you come to terms with the fact that people not only want you dead, but that the people supposedly trusted with keeping you safe don't care either way, the entire experience takes on a different nature.

WHEN I FINISHED my 28 day prison recall in autumn 2014, the Oxford Union got back in touch and said they still wanted to go ahead. I thought that would be a problem, at least until my licence period was over, but each Union president only has a limited time in office and it was a now-or-never deal, while Mayank Banerjee was still in the chair.

The first attempt had been called off under pressure from left-wing activists and the second was thwarted by the law hauling me back to jail. It was third time lucky in that I got to appear, finally, but it was hardly a golden day for freedom of speech.

When she heard that I was persevering in going, Sue Beaumont came to the house and said she strongly advised me not to, because of my licence. I told her I didn't care, this was one of the most prestigious institutions in the world and it was an honour for someone like me to be invited there. She knew where she could shove her objections.

She insisted again that I had to tell them what I was going to say, so I went through the list of subjects, mosques, Muslims, Mohammed the pervert and she was saying, 'Whoa, whoa, whoa... you can't say that!'

I thought she'd shit her pants in panic. So I asked her, 'Is that in your job description Sue? High Priestess of free speech?' I told her straight up, 'If you'd worked in Rotherham Council you'd have been the person covering it all up – that's exactly who you are. And now you're telling me that I don't have freedom of speech – very Magna Carta of you!'

And she was absolutely solid on it – no I couldn't. I could not mention anything that caused offence to anyone, no Islam, no Koran and no Mohammed. And nothing about the police and my licence conditions either. She didn't give me any of those warnings the first time though. Probably because she knew I was going to get recalled to prison.

What she did next was send an email to Nicola Perry, one of the directors of Luton Borough Council, saying they'd tried everything to stop me talking and been unsuccessful and for the council to have their solicitors ready.

How did I know? I use a hotel in the middle of Luton for most of my meetings and somebody left an envelope with my name on it. A print-out of the email was inside. I took it into probation and confronted Helen Bean, asking if this was professional – spying and passing on information. Where was the supposed guidance and rehabilitation?

Sue Beaumont nearly shit herself again. All she could fret about was how on earth I'd gotten hold of the email. 'That's classified, that's classified!' she bleated. Oh, and she said that if I made it public I'd be recalled to jail again.

That was pretty much the end of me and Beaumont. She knew I couldn't trust her. After that she took a step back – for a while at least. She had one more attempt at getting to me, and not very long ago, towards the end of my licence.

On that last occasion we had an 11am appointment booked and Helen Bean called to ask if we could make it 3.30pm because they wanted to see my wife. The thing is, she didn't want to see them. And she wasn't the one on licence. My solicitor wrote to them, stating exactly that. I said it was 11am or nothing because I was going to be in

London, but they never replied. And then sure enough at 3.30pm there was a knock on the door – which I answered, much to their surprise. I wasn't in London at all. I was raging. My wife just shut herself in the kitchen because she couldn't face them.

What happened next was that my little girl, the youngest, came into the room and in a flash, Beaumont pointed out some bruises on her leg, saying they were really bad and asking how she'd got them. It's a wonder I kept my hands off the ... well, you know. Helen Bean stopped her in her tracks, saying she has a five-year-old as well, and they were always getting bruises. Kids did.

So that was it – all else had failed, let's see if we can get Social Services in on the action. And don't say it can't happen. We had a female EDL member who was threatened with having her newborn baby taken away from her because Social Services worried about the child being radicalised. That woman ran away to Ireland.

Tell me something – have you ever heard of Anjem Choudary being threatened with his kids being taken into care? Sayful Islam? The children of the hundreds and thousands of Muslim radicals around the country being taken into care? We all know the answer to that.

I'd been subject to a MAPPA programme – Multi-Agency Personal Protection Arrangement – because of the threats on my life. They are usually reserved for murderers and paedophiles the authorities are trying to re-settle after finishing their sentences. Representatives from the Home Office, Police, Social Services all meet and discuss your case and I came under pressure to move again into a safe house.

I said no, our address wasn't public, the kids were settled in school. We were going nowhere – and then I heard from inside one of their meetings that one police officer said they could get to me through Social Services because by refusing to move I was putting the kids in harm's way. That's the way the system operates folks. Believe me, I know. I stewed on things after that 'bruises' conversation and eventually went in to see Helen Bean to make a formal complaint.

At what stage had it become their job to question a four-year-old child? Beaumont left a panicky voicemail saying my fears were unfounded and it wasn't meant that way. I kept the voicemail though, just in case.

BACK TO OXFORD and I was ploughing on regardless, completely committed to appearing. These people, my audience, were the elite, they had very wealthy parents, they had mostly lived a sheltered life and they hadn't seen the impact that mass immigration and Islamification has on a community like mine.

I got my best suit out, went and had a haircut. I was thinking, this working class lad from Luton doesn't scrub up too badly – although I got a bit of banter about my shit haircut. I don't mind admitting, I was nervous, but excited too. These people wouldn't understand anything about my life so I prepared a video presentation and I worked hard on it. I'm glad I did, because as nervous as I was, afterwards I thought the evening went really well.

We had to be sneaked in through a back entrance to the Union because the usual UAF arseholes were out front doing their baboon act. There weren't many of them though and one of the security people came in and reported that they were all outsiders. Oxford students weren't involved.

There was quite a mix of people in the audience, a student with an Iranian dad who had an Ayatollah in the family and a young Pakistani girl. She was quite reserved and unsure, but has since sent me a few emails, saying how the talk really opened her eyes.

She's back in Pakistan now, doing a research paper and she is trying to address some of the problems the cultural differences are creating in the UK. She told me that when she came to England, to Manchester, she felt intimated because she wasn't covering her hair – more intimidated than she does back home in Pakistan.

The theme of my speech was to ask these mostly young people, 'What would you have done in my position?'

Because I think that when my story was told, not many of them would have done things much differently, or at least felt different emotions to what I did. Maybe they wouldn't have reacted the same, but it was about the human reaction to situations.

The Oxford Union itself is fascinating, very impressive. There was a good crowd and I think they were quite reserved, a bit dubious to begin with, but they were very respectful and their questions were well informed.

But of course before I got started, I had to tell them that when we got to the questions and answers part of the evening, there were subjects that I simply couldn't go near; that I faced spending the next eight months in prison if I even referred to them. I'd already decided that I didn't need to go near the whole MIB affair either.

I was made up to get a round of applause when we finished, because I think a lot of them went into the room not liking me, with this preconception of a bigot, a racist or an extremist who doesn't like Muslims. The reality is very different to that, which is what I wanted to show them.

I told them that I'd love to come back one day and fill in the gaps, to tell them the full extent of what was happening, what I'd been forbidden from talking about, but whether that will happen or not, I don't know.

Still, little Tommy Robinson, Luton bad boy, talking to the world renowned Oxford Union. Who would ever have thought? And I didn't jump up and down shouting Mohammed is a paedo or whatever, so they couldn't drag me back to jail even if they wanted to.

It was all plain sailing from now on...

19: ONE LAST SHOT

AS YOU MIGHT have come to expect however, that wasn't quite the end. There's always an outside chance of one last shot at the target. The order to pay up the £125,000 had been haggled over and reduced to £117,000 because of various incidentals. Going into July 2015, with the days ticking down to my licence period expiring, I'd managed to pay £99,000 of it, with £18,000 left to find. A judge had given me until October to cough that up. So far so good.

On the 10th of July the police turned up at the house to recall me, but I wasn't home. Apparently I'd been in breach of my licence conditions again, been somewhere or said something that I shouldn't. On Monday the 13th the police came back, arrested me and took me to Luton cells, at which point they sent someone in from 'intelligence' which didn't quite work for me. He was a 25-stone mess of a fat bloke who said he'd done 30 years working on radicalisation and that they could do with some help.

I don't know if he wanted a round of applause, a bouquet of flowers or for me to get down and kiss his fat arse, but he was in the wrong cell. All I could think was that it was the MIB mob again in a different guise, or maybe the dopey mediation sorts from London. Did I want to chat, to help? I said, 'What exactly can you do for me?' He said, 'We can make things easy for you.'

I was a week or so from being clear of these people and still they were trying.

So by way of farewell I said, 'Fuck off and tell your boss to fuck off as well.' They might have the last word in terms of keeping me in a cell until the very last minute, but they were not going to break me, not so close.

But prison it was. Woodhill wouldn't have me near the place and Bedford refused to take me as well. HMPs refusing to take Tommy Robinson? I reckon I can wear that as a badge of honour given that I'm not holding my breath on David Cameron naming me Lord Lennon of Luton.

They took me to HMP Peterborough and I told them at admission that I was there for just eight days, and to put me down the block, for everybody's sake. They knew what was going to happen if they didn't.

Anyone got a sense of deja vu? Pardon me if this is getting a bit repetitive, but you know what happens next. Same again, the screws told me they were putting me on the wing. I know I should have been used to it, but it was unbelievable given what every other prison had seen.

I told them to go see the governor, tell him or her that it was going to get violent, that I'd get hurt, someone else would get hurt ... I'd got eight days, that was all. Lock the door for eight days for all I cared. Wake me up and let me out when it was all over. So they put me on the wing.

I told five different prison officers what was going to happen, that it would not end well. The next morning they took me down to the office and I said this is going to go to shit. My first instinct, as previously at Bedford, was to find the first Muslim I could, start a ruck and hope they got me out of there to solitary before any real damage was done.

Except all that I could think, was that that was precisely what they wanted – I was at the end of my licence period, but if I got in deep shit, there could be a whole new charge sheet for them to go at.

So I tried to keep calm and stay out of trouble for that eight days, even when they threw me on a wing, in a cell two doors away from Fahim Khan. Khan was doing 28 years for the murder in Bedford of a teenage black rapper Isaac Stone, an attack during which he also sliced off another kid's nose and ear with a meat cleaver.

My new neighbour. Happy days. One time I saw him sitting on top of the stairs of the wing and I thought I should just up and volley him, but I didn't. I really was trying. He didn't make eye contact with me and nothing happened, so I just tried to keep calm.

We went on prison induction and by now I'd been in HMP Peterborough for 16 hours without incident, which might have been a record. But then a lad from another wing came over to me saying word was out, trouble was coming. Most prisoners have got mobile phones, despite whatever shit the politicians talk. Word gets around very fast.

And then later another bloke came over, whispering behind his hand as though he wasn't talking to me at all. I'd been taken in on the 14th and got through until the 17th. Suddenly it was D-Day. I was told this gangster Fahim Khan had put up a mobile phone, a half ounce of 'spice' – a legal high, similar to skunk cannabis and gold dust in prison – plus £500 in cash. All of that, in return for Tommy Robinson being done with boiling water.

A favourite trick is to put sugar in the boiling water. Apparently it ensures your skin and scalp comes off in your hands. I don't know first hand and I didn't fancy getting to know, either. What's more I was wearing flip-flops, which isn't your best commando-style fighting gear.

They had just called exercise, it was 10am and there were just two female screws left on the wing. The thing is this, for a price like that, it might not even be a Muslim who did me. The bloke whispering thought it was going to be a Somalian kid that I'd noticed loitering about.

I so much did not want to be in that place, either geographically in terms of being in nick, or physically in terms of what was about to happen.

I've written about these scenarios so much now that it must sound like a cheap repeat of a bad gangster script. As if it's routine, so-so. It is not. You are physically shaking with the adrenaline and your nerves are bouncing. That never goes away. I'd just been given notice of an imminent attack, I was wearing a pair of flip-flops, and the prison wing had two – sorry ladies – pissy women screws on duty, who would struggle to put up an umbrella in a strong breeze. I was up shit street. So much for Plan A and a quiet eight days seeing out my time.

I looked up and actually saw this Somalian guy, the one who'd been fingered by the lad who'd spoken to me, talking to Fahim Khan through his cell door. Game on, I thought.

So I just walked over because quite literally I couldn't wait for what might come next, I couldn't take a chance. I just waded right into him, to force the issue. What would you do, with that or a face full of scalding water as the two choices? The women screws didn't even jump in to try to stop it – not that they could have, even if they'd wanted to.

The other prick, Khan, hid behind his door, the coward. Maybe he'd have grown a pair if someone had given him a meat cleaver and three friends for company, like when he killed that poor kid in Bedford. All he could do was shout through the door, 'You're fucked, you're fucked.'

And I shouted back, 'Do I look fucked? Because your Somalian mate does.' I turned and screamed, 'Do any other Muslims in here want to serve me up?'

That probably counts as a tut-tut racist comment. Well, if you want to swap places, you're entitled to have a view. If not, you know what you can do with your opinion.

I was raging, because in a life or death situation like that you are raging, you need to be, in order to survive. It's an on-off switch, it's not a volume control.

The girlies had obviously sounded the alarm, because in no time at all there were 10 or 15 male warders flooding the wing. There was actually quite a funny moment at that point, with this Somalian geezer Jabir hiding and bleeding while the screws were telling me to get behind my cell door, now. I said I wasn't going anywhere until I got my missing flip-flop back, which had come off in the ruck – well, they were Gucci flip-flops, the real thing too, not cheap imitations! I got it back. And the situation was mostly good news all round, firstly because I was still in one piece and secondly being that as a result of the fight I was destined for the block – and safety. The turning of the lock in that cell door would be sweet music to my ears.

There was a bit of 'mission accomplished' in that, but then I got the news that the Somali wanted to press charges against me for assault. Was that what they were hoping for all along?

When I got down the block there were three white lads already locked up for their own protection because they'd argued with one of the Muslim prisoners. Peterborough as a city doesn't have a massive Muslim population that I'm aware of, but their problems as a nick were no different from anywhere else.

When the governor finally came to see me it was a woman and I straight out told her that it was all a stitch-up, that I should have been in the block all along.

She said that in order for the prison to take action I needed to have been up before a governor inside 48 hours and that, lucky for me, it had already been 50 hours. I could have kissed her. If she was a bloke I'd still have kissed her.

That wasn't quite it though, because I then heard the Somali geezer wanted to press charges via the police. Are you getting as exhausted with this yet as I was? Days left, hours left, of my licence period. Where was it going to end? I was ready to drop on my knees and crawl home. And very shortly, I would be staring down the barrel of another two-and-a-half years in prison. From right out of the blue.

RIGHT BEFORE THIS, I'd paid £99,000 of the final £117,000 ordered against me, and been given until October to settle the final £18k. As soon as I was recalled to prison and sent away to Peterborough, the police went back to court and said that I was in breach of that order. We had been selling up, trying to get ourselves straight, but the authorities were monitoring our accounts day to day. They spotted that for a while there was enough money in my wife's bank account to settle the bill in full – even though the order was against me, not her.

As soon as I was recalled the police went before a judge and said that I was in breach of the order and applied for the extension on payment to be overturned. The judge agreed and ordered that unless the full sum, the other £18k was paid up by 4pm on July 16th, I would be given another 30 months inside for being in breach of the order.

I swear, there was no end. We were liquidating everything, trying to organise a new house of our own, to get back on our feet after years with everything frozen and suddenly we were being ambushed again.

And of course because I was banged up in Peterborough, I couldn't pay the money anyway. I still didn't even know why I'd been recalled. All my solicitor got back from probation was that I'd been in breach of my licence conditions. That was it, and I would be released as per the original sentence schedule on July 22nd. Meanwhile at home everyone was panicking because the bastards were stitching me up and time was running out.

My mum was back in hospital, but she discharged herself, came home, arranged another loan against her house, and paid the money until I could get out and square things up.

Finally, finally, you must be thinking ... like I was.

Not quite. On the outside there was a ton of speculation on social media as to why I'd been recalled in the first place. Even the Peterborough screws were mystified. More than one told me, 'No one ever gets dragged back with a week to go, unless they've robbed a frigging bank'. I certainly hadn't done anything like that.

One left-wing website, old-time Tommy haters, reckoned that it was all a government conspiracy to stop me taking part in a stunt to pin cartoons of the Prophet Mohammed up around the country and – in their fantasy world – 'start a civil war'.

You can't fault these clowns for imagination, that's for certain. It probably was known however that I was due to appear at the House of the Lords on July 23rd and as usual someone was putting two and two together and coming up with 99.

But there was still one last roll of the dice, as ever. With the money paid off, it was just a case of twiddling my thumbs and waiting for the 22nd. The day I was a free man.

And then July 22nd, 2015, came and went, with me still inside HMP Peterborough, locked in a concrete cell. Down the block. I got a visit from the police who, on the face of things, were bringing good news, which was that I would not be 'gate arrested' over the fight on the wing when I was released. Gate arrested means that you finish one imprisonment, do a Strictly Come Dancing 180-degree twirl at the door and get banged up for something else.

The copper sat down and looked every which shade of nervous, out of his comfort zone. He asked me what I was doing when I got off licence, what my plans were. So I asked him what business was it of his? I was going home, back to my family. He came back, 'Yeah, but what are your plans? You going back to the EDL or what?' And that's what it was all about. They were shitting themselves over my plans.

I said, 'I'm going home mate, I'm not doing anything.'

Lastly, I got another one of the governors through the door. I sensed he was the big boss, he was Scottish and pleasant enough. He asked me, 'How many have you got meeting you, when you get out?'

I told him. My dad. They clearly thought I would have an entire EDL army waiting outside, bearing me home in triumph like Napoleon or Julius Caesar. I said, 'I'm going home, mate. Just going home on the 22nd. With my dad.'

EXCEPT THAT I wasn't and I didn't. I still don't know why, and you'll all tell me that I must know, but I promise, I've not had the explanation in person. They simply kept me in beyond my licence date. I know they can't, but they did. Different rules apply where I'm concerned, clearly. There's no way I can't have been told why I was recalled? I'm telling you, I wasn't.

And I wasn't allowed out of prison until July 24th, the day after I was supposed to be meeting a high profile member of the House of Lords, to talk about what I might do next, once I was finally a free man.

I'd like to say that having my liberty at last involved stopping looking over my shoulder, but I certainly don't feel that free yet. I suspect that it might take quite some time.

I came out, dad was there – and for once there were no sarcastic, vindictive coppers saying 'Surprise surprise!'

We went home to the wife and kids. Finally.

20: RADICALISED

IF MY TIME IN various of Her Majesty's penal institutions has done anything, it's given me a very clear insight into one of the major problems facing the penal system – Islamic radicalisation.

I guess it's something that varies and depends to some extent where you are in the country – Winchester prison being a prime example, down near the south coast, as opposed to serving time in London, Birmingham, Luton, Bradford or Manchester. The criminal populations they draw on are bound to have some impact.

HMP Woodhill in Milton Keynes was the worst that I experienced. It's generally worse at the lifer jails, the Category As. The Muslim gang who travelled to Dewsbury to bomb the EDL rally in the summer of 2012 were working in the servery at Woodhill and the main radical in the general population was Kamel Bourgass, the terrorist who stabbed and killed PC Stephen Oake in Manchester in 2004.

It's the wings where most of the religious conversions, the radicalisations take place, by the hardline prisoners, not the prison mosques and the imams. On a daily basis the cells are used for de facto mosques. You'll come out of your cell and see a parade of shoes outside one of the cells and they'll all be in there several times a day. When I was in Wandsworth they were all out praying on the wing itself. They only went to mosque on Friday.

While I was at Woodhill I met one white lad who hated the Muslims with every bone in his body. He hadn't when he came into nick, mind you. He said that he had never given a damn about anyone or anything until he got sent there, where he discovered that they practised sharia law on the wing.

He had some music playing in his cell one time and the Muslims came up and told him to turn the music off, because it was prayer time. He wouldn't have stood a chance if he'd tried to resist, although obviously some guys do, at which point it gets messy and people end up down the block or in hospital. When they confronted this young lad there was a 'beard' at the top of each flight of stairs to his landing, and another beard to let him know how things were going to be in future. No screws to be found.

And as much as religion is the theme, our good, clean-living Muslim brothers also control the drugs, mobile phones, whatever it is that you want from the outside. The screws bring a lot of it in, while some of it simply comes over the wall inside tennis balls that are thrown to inmates at a pre-arranged time and place.

I remember in Winchester seeing this big white lad with a massive beard and a Muslim hat on, who had transferred from another nick. Once he'd settled in and worked out the lie of the land he shaved the beard off. He said he did it for protection while he was locked up in Bullingdon.

Is it right that Bedford and Woodhill prisons are entirely halal food for the prison population, no matter what your preferences? I know what I think. In Winchester, you at least had a choice between halal and non-halal.

One kid in Winchester, a young white lad, had converted in a previous prison but knew absolutely nothing about Islam. I got talking to him – a nice kid who'd been close to his grandparents, who had passed away. I asked him one time, 'Are they burning in hell, your nan and granddad?'

He hadn't a clue what I was talking about, until I reminded him that that's what he believed in; that every non-Muslim burns in hellfire. It was like the Hobbs thing. It didn't matter that they were his lovely nan and granddad, if he believed in Islam he believed they were evil and burning in hell. No halfway house in that religion, kid.

Before you knew it he was back getting pork pies on his menu.

There were incidents everywhere you went, some bad, some worse. When I was in Wayland there was a massive kick-off when a bunch of Muslims rushed a Scottish geezer and they brought six of them down the block.

And you would be amazed at how many of the converts are white or black previously 'Christian' prisoners, who are turned so easily. And they end up being the worst, the most violently radical – without having a clue what it is they're talking about.

AT WOODHILL THE main man amongst the Muslim gang was that big white lad the screws locked me in a room with when I got my front teeth knocked out. I was told that he'd been a 'normal' prisoner, had gone away to another nick and returned a complete radical.

I always wonder if anyone in authority really knows what is happening inside, how it works, how the state is actually running its very own breeding ground, a recruiting school for extremists.

Because of my reputation with the EDL a lot of the screws used to talk to me about the problem with Muslim radicalisation and the recruiting. A few of them pinpointed a time about 10 years before, when they were suddenly inundated with a large contingent of new prisoners from Feltham Young Offenders Institute.

They said they had 60 kids convert to Islam in a week. It happened all the time, the physical pressure, the threats and intimidation, were massive, and people decided it might be time, it might be wise, to change sides. And then once they're 'in' they get all these messages of hate which, let's face it, they're already susceptible to.

A lot of prisoners think that society has let them down, they might be friend or family-less on the outside, and

313

suddenly here's this new family that has their back both inside and out. So you've got hardened criminals, often men of violence to begin with, suddenly coming out of prison as religious extremists. It doesn't exactly fit the bill for rehabilitation within the penal system, does it?

Let me give you an example – Barry Chin, a mixed race bloke from 'Tintown' in Luton, one of the lads. He was a bit of a hard case Barry, a couple of years younger than me and he got sent down for four-and-a-half years, following a massive gang fight with Muslims, ironically.

When Barry came out of prison he claimed to be a Muslim – but he still hung around with us, rolled with the football boys, drank alcohol, used drugs.

Then, on the day of the soldiers' homecoming parade, Barry was there and came straight out with, 'Brit soldiers are raping, murdering bastards!' Gilheaney told him to watch his mouth. I walked off, I couldn't believe what he'd said. But flash forward a while to the UPL demos and the start of the EDL and suddenly we were having all of these attacks on properties round Bury Park – the ones that we were suspected of and particularly me. I found out that Barry Chin was giving the Muslims information about me and my mate Keir.

The Muslim community was on the prowl and this prick was giving people our addresses. I confronted Barry about it, told him that if anything happened to me or mine, that he was in the frame – and his reply? He said, 'I'd kill my own dad for my mosque.'

What had they done to him? I've not spoken to Barry since that day, but that's what you're dealing with.

But can we do anything about it? About radicalisation within the prison system? Probably not, firstly because we won't even accept that it's a problem, and secondly, I doubt that you could physically segregate the entire prison populations. They're overcrowded as it is and to tackle this issue you'd have to create an entirely new, custom-built and segregated prison system specifically for Muslims, to keep them apart from everyone else.

Terrorists, radicals, anyone showing signs of extremism needs to be put in isolation – and before you mention it, allow me to say what you're thinking. The left wing lobby won't wear anything as radical as that because it will stigmatise these poor lambs, infringe their human rights and before you know it they'll not only get their own way, but they'll all be pocketing fat big compensation payouts thanks to either our Supreme Court or the European Court of Human Rights, ruling that they've been victimised.

If you think I'm saying that we can't win, then you're not far off. So we will carry on as we are doing, leaving the weak and vulnerable from our own culture to be preyed upon by the one that is hell-bent on destroying ours.

The prison system is breeding an Islamic army and I read recently that MI5 said they're having to monitor an extra 500 radicals a year coming out of prison. Is that all?

Just as I'm finishing this book a report on the prison service has come out highlighting that 'jizya' – a Muslim tax, what we'd call a protection racket – is rife in our category A jails. They are being run by Muslim criminals and extremists, with sharia law running the wings. People pay up or convert. Their families are having to pay the bribes on the outside.

No one's offering any solutions though.

21: WHAT TOMMY DOES NEXT

IT IS A BIG question, one that I'm not sure I have the answer to – what does Tommy do next? Go back to work running plumbing contracting jobs? There will probably be some of that. Another house move is in the pipeline, as we try to physically rebuild after what we've been through. We're renting still. Not that the police were quite finished with their little surprises, even with the mortgage conviction now history.

I've had some interesting approaches from a variety of people who think an association with the 'Tommy Robinson' persona provides an opportunity for them. They'll have to be patient because I'm not sure that I automatically trust everyone who turns up, and take them into my confidence, quite so easily as I have in the past.

Obviously my link with Quilliam is well known, and I'm not sure where that will lead, if anywhere. I expect they'll be disappointed by what's in this book, understandably so. There might not be a future there.

Some people seem to think I could have a role in helping to highlight some of the continued problems and issues that separate most British Muslim communities from the rest of us. Because here's the thing – the problems the UPL and the EDL highlighted back in 2009 haven't gone away. They aren't going away. With every passing week and month the problems and the divisions get bigger and wider. I would like to think I can contribute in some way to that debate. How and where, I'm less sure.

On Remembrance Sunday 2015 – literally days from finishing this book – staff at a town centre bar in Luton told a bunch of blokes having a drink to either remove their poppies or leave. The owner's a republican Irishman apparently. I hope we're not related, but I went down with a few of the boys to give him some grief, a bit of banter. He deserved it. And so within hours there was a police meat wagon at my house wanting a word. They're not going to miss a single chance.

Back when we started the UPL, then EDL, there was a generally settled Iraq and Syria and Libya. There was no ISIS beheading people in their hundreds, burning captives to death and threatening death and destruction worldwide.

We didn't have hundreds of radicalised young Muslims flocking overseas from the UK to join that mayhem. Our political leadership is still in denial about how and where their heads were turned. Everyone likes to pin all of the blame on the internet, but I'm not so sure.

I used to say in interviews with radical Muslims that they seemed to want everyone to turn against them and that if they weren't careful, everyone would, there would be an uprising. But today I have to question, would there? Could it happen? Would Islamic terrorists have to kill the Queen to force our hands? Would we react even then? And what would we do? What could we do? I'm not sure.

Meanwhile we are sleepwalking our way towards a Muslim takeover of the country. The demographic profile is changing radically in England year after year. The birth rate in the Muslim community is going through the roof, double, treble that of non-Muslim families. We're getting fewer and older while the Muslim community is not only younger and growing, but it's staying tied fast to the apron strings of the mosques. That's what I see. I see men with Muslim wives who are also spawning second, third families, that the state funds. No? You disagree? I'm only describing what I see. Where's your evidence otherwise?

I'm not a sociologist, but I know migrants over the centuries have blended in with time, adopted the language, customs and as well as sharing or at least respecting our Christian traditions, obeyed our laws. I don't see any such common ground with the Muslim population. The mosques control the parents who – mostly – keep their children under strict control. There is limited integration into the wider community. Instead there is concentration then creep, street after street, estate after estate, town after town being turned into essentially a self-governing entity. A caliphate, some people might say.

And with the massive imbalance in population numbers, you don't have to be Einstein to work out which direction we're heading. Compare some of the census figures from 2001 and 2011 and do the maths. That's a trend that is not going to be reversed any time soon.

Meanwhile the EU has thrown open the doors to a million or more impoverished Muslims, with ten times that number waiting for the starting pistol next spring. Those nations are committing cultural suicide.

I'd like to think we'll see a more secular, accepting side to ordinary Muslims, but again I don't see evidence – just the opposite. Everything I see cements the idea that the Koran is at the centre of everything about Islamic society.

People who try to apply modern interpretations to it, good men like Usama Hasan, are declared apostates and there is only one punishment for that – death. How do you talk to or negotiate with people who live their entire lives bound by that hateful, unforgiving script?

Is it possible to turn back the radical tide at the heart of Muslim communities like Luton's? Again, I don't see a willingness to even try. Unless we outlaw sharia, ban the veil and start somehow trying to de-Islamify these places, we'll continue breeding trouble for our children's futures.

If we can't change this dangerous ideology, and we can't, then we should at least make clear our own values and put a flag in the sand that shouts loud who we are and what we stand for. Flag in the sand? We can't even draw a line in the sand. Our political leadership, whatever the party, is more interested in making sandcastles with the bad guys, still hoping to make friends of them.

I mentioned Kev standing as the Bedfordshire Police and Crime Commissioner. He campaigned well, but lost to a Labour arse-wipe called Olly Martins. Kev forked out for a roadside billboard but that got vandalised. There were supposedly public meetings that he was never told about. In his acceptance speech Martins couldn't resist telling EDL supporters they could crawl back under their rocks. That was over 10% of the voters he was calling low-lives. Very righteous – and he's our Crime Commissioner?

Just a few weeks ago I bumped into our MP, Gavin Shuker, in a takeaway in Luton. He's about my age and boy has he given me some shit over the years – without ever meeting me, naturally. So I asked to have a word. I'd seen him front and centre of a 'Celebrate Mohammed' day. So I asked him what he knew about Mohammed.

'I know's he's respected by four million British Muslims.' That was his best effort. I said, 'No, what do YOU know about him? You call me ignorant, you mock me, so you tell me about Mohammed.' He couldn't. He knew nothing. So I told him a few things, like, 'Do you know he was reputed to have cut off 600 men's head in one day? Raped one of his soldier's women? Tortured a man for his gold?'

The useless waste of Parliamentary space hadn't an answer. He knew nothing. Yet, typical of the nationwide problem we have, he was out there 'celebrating Mohammed' when he should be challenging the third world, medieval rubbish being preached behind most mosque walls. Idiots like Gavin Shuker MP are Britain's problem, just as much as the vast majority of Muslims who only respect strength, but never face any.

And that's a major problem, right there, the Shuker problem. Whatever else my last six years have been, they've been an education. The British establishment, the people preaching PC rubbish about Islam and the Koran, don't know the first thing about it. Here's a thought – put David Cameron, Theresa May and friends in an HMP solitary confinement cell for 22 weeks and I'll provide the reading list. Maybe a few lights will come on in a few dumb skulls.

SUCH AS I SEE there being a tipping point I think it will probably come in Europe, where a lot of their nationalist parties are far stronger than here in the UK, and where they draw on much broader support. If a politician like Geert Wilders in Holland or Marine Le Pen in France gets in power you might see a popular movement big and strong enough to take on Islamification, to start what seems to me an inevitable battle, in Europe before here.

As I near the end of this book, it comes after speaking at a rally in Utrecht in Holland, then another with the Pegida leaders in Dresden before a crowd of 40,000 people. That was quite an experience, really humbling, and I was very impressed how calm, measured and mature the protest group was. Far more mainstream, middle class than here. It was how we need to make a stand in Britain.

I've just got back from another rally along with Pegida leaders in Prague, which was calling for the closing of Czechoslovakia's borders to the flood of Muslim migrants. Czech President Milos Zeman was a speaker and he said people who stand up to radical Islam should not be demonised as racists or extremists. Hallelujah.

I've been to speak to students at Harrow School, to add to my Oxford Union experience. The feedback I got from that was really encouraging. It's an audience I could never have dreamed of while I was in the EDL.

It's reassuring that there are people interested in the journey I've been on, my mad ride of the past six years, and who think I might have something to offer to the debate. Those were very different experiences to my invite to

Swansea University, to speak with a moderate Ahmadiyya cleric – they are peace-loving, moderate Muslims. Instead I got there and got lumbered with a hardline Sunni imam. Sunnis consider the Ahmadiyyans to be apostates.

Those were relationships I was clueless about once, but while recent years might have left me battered and scarred, I'm far better placed to debate these issues. The imam tried some bullshit about Islam being the Arabic word for peace and I said no mate, it means submit, surrender – and he said, 'You're right Tommy', before skulking off. They've got away with that lie for years and no one ever challenges them on it. As you can see, many things in my life have changed since the day those Royal Anglian Regiment soldiers were so unfairly abused.

I also got a visit from Nick Lowles, who runs the far left 'Hope not Hate' anti-racism and anti-fascism group. They've never missed a single opportunity to give it to me and the EDL. However Lowles was full of surprises. He came and apologised, said that they had underestimated the threat to us of radical Islam.

Basically, he said that we had a point, that grooming, ISIS, everything we are seeing, is a huge problem. Wonders never cease. I asked him out of interest about the area he lives in, its ethnic make-up and how he'd feel sending his kids to a school that was 80% Muslim.

I think he got it. He still hates the far right – but so do I!

It's not all good news though. As well as Harrow went, long-planned appearances at Durham and Edinburgh Universities were cancelled. Durham weren't happy with me appearing at the Pegida rally while Edinburgh hid behind the excuse that they couldn't handle the security.

ONE SMALL BUT important thing I think we need to beware of, is what seems to have become a fashionable styling of 'Islamists' and 'Islamism' as being separate from

Islam. It's an invention to make us feel better about things. I doubt that playing word games is going to get us anywhere and I really don't think it makes a difference to Muslim communities. But it goes back to that Quilliam delusion – the 90/10 perception. We're pretending that someone who is an 'Islamist' is a separate variety of Muslim that we can neatly blame for all the wider woes the ideology brings. We're deluding ourselves.

Watching the progress of Germany's Pegida – which stands for Patriotic Europeans Against the Islamisation of the West – I hoped it signalled the opportunity here in the UK to create something more mainstream. Pegida rapidly gathered a lot of support from ordinary Germans without suffering the EDL's problem with all of the extremist hangers-on. That's what we need.

At Dresden, that 40,000 crowd was largely middle class, civilised, concerned but respectful. I was part of the football hooligan-identity that drove the EDL and you could say got it off on the wrong footing, but it was never going to be thousands of female schoolteachers on Britain's streets confronting the Muslim mobs, was it? For a meaningful change in attitude here, if ever our politicians are going to take any notice, it's going to require ordinary, middle class Englishmen and women to say enough's enough.

It won't be easy and Pegida have already had their share of problems. The political classes have turned on them and there's still no sign that their leaders, just like ours, are minded to listen, or to recognise the scale of the problem the people on the streets are seeing.

The conservative commentator Douglas Murray made an interesting speech to a conference in Europe when he referred to what the British state had done to me. You've just read it warts and all, but he made the critical point that it's a knee-jerk reaction of western democracies. When you get a street protest movement like the EDL, the political elite's only focus is on silencing it, crushing it, instead of taking a minute to actually consider if the people inside it actually have a point.

Ordinary folk don't take to the streets for nothing as a rule. Murray said that he didn't like me or the EDL which is fair enough, but that my experience was typical of the bigger problem politicians have.

That speech reminded me of an early EDL demo at Blackburn. The night before I stayed with a local family whose 12-year-old daughter had been groomed by Muslim men. When they told the police she was missing, they'd go see the usual suspects and try to get her back – but they never tackled the problem, made arrests. That girl's 18-year-old brother was in a right state over it all.

The next day at the rally things were kicking off with the police and I went down front to try to calm matters – and saw the young girl's brother in a rage. And I stopped and thought, 'Who am I to put a lid on this kid's fury?' If it was my sister, I'd want to raise hell, scream at the gods too. The lawmakers and politicians never see that – that behind these people on the streets can be awful, agonising stories, all because they don't do their jobs, don't listen to us.

So yes, I really do think we need to start objecting to the silent Islamification of our island. Take halal meat for instance – why the hell are we putting up with our schoolchildren, like I had to as a prisoner, being made to adhere to a brutal, medieval practice that most of us find abhorrent? Who voted for that in Parliament?

But the liberal elites that run schools, hospitals, local authorities and prisons, are imposing this behind our backs and without any kind of legislation. Why is it happening and why are we allowing it? Because we certainly are.

But it's no good just me saying it. Ordinary people have to start waking up to what is happening, but instead everyone is sleepwalking into it. The public needs to target businesses and companies that are effectively selling-out – like supermarkets that sell exclusively halal meat. Maybe there's a role for me in helping to highlight these problems, because someone needs to. Around the world, in Australia and America especially, people are waking up to the threats to their ways of life. It's not before time.

Something as simple as introducing halal to mixed-community schools, or allowing sharia courts to set up in heavily Muslim areas, might seem a million miles away from beheading innocent people in Syria and Iraq, but is it? Is it really? How does someone go from a normal everyday life, to screaming support of medieval butchery? Germany watched Hitler do it and it's happening today in Iraq.

I've watched all of those horrific videos posted by ISIS.

I think it's important to, because when people talk enough about such barbaric acts, they become de-sensitised to it. They know it's there, but it drops off the front pages and suddenly it's just someone else's problem. No big deal.

You'd think it was a big deal if you were the wife or child of David Haines or Alan Henning, good, honest men who had their heads hacked off by Jihadi John. So yes, I think it is important to watch, to have it brought home, to ask yourself, what possesses these creatures? We have to keep asking – what has created these monstrous people?

Because whatever made it happen, it wasn't watching a bird in a mini skirt come tottering out of a Luton nightclub, I can tell you that much.

When I watched the video of the Jordanian pilot being burned to death in a cage, I felt sick for hours. I thought, 'His mum and family are going to see this'.

Turn the page if you must, but it was how slowly he burned, how long he was alive while burning. It was horrific, absolutely inhuman and in the end he just folded down onto his knees, on fire and still alive, with his skin just dripping off him, melting off him.

It's not easy to read, is it? It's not easy to watch either, but I thought the sacrifice that man made deserved being acknowledged. If it steels people about the challenge facing us, about the depravity of the people who have declared war on our way of life, then I reckon everyone should have a responsibility to see it. With that captured pilot, there was a little boy on the video who was shouting that he'd burn the man himself if he could. A kid, already poisoned. And we can negotiate with these people? Seriously?

Let's see Gavin Shuker MP go celebrate that.

Then you turn on the television or radio, open the newspapers, and all that I see are the usual responses, mostly led by non-Muslim politicians, upper class toffs like David Cameron, saying this is nothing to do with 'our' Islam, blaming instead these fictitious new 'Islamists' that we've conveniently created to help us sleep at nights.

After November 13 in Paris some British Muslim leaders took out full page adverts condemning the atrocities. Good. Now follow through with it gents, preach that there is no Paradise, no 72 virgins for suicide vest-wearing murderers. No, we're not quite there yet? We're not, are we?

But some of those clerics also declared of that Jordanian pilot, 'It says in the Koran you cannot burn...' Sorry, we are such suckers for wanting to fall for these deceits – like that imam in Swansea saying that Islam is Arabic for peace.

I read a biography of Mohammed describing an occasion where Muslims who didn't want to go into battle were locked in a mosque and he set fire to it – burned them all. On the video of that pilot being burnt alive, music played and on-screen verses from the Koran justified it.

So yes, I'll buy the argument that some moderate Muslims contest the interpretations of the Koran, but don't tell me that one of our biggest problems isn't that book, constantly held up in many quarters as an instruction manual to inflict the horrors of hell on anyone it objects to.

325

I'll listen to explanations otherwise, but from everything that I've read and learned, and from its very own words, that means everyone who isn't Muslim.

I watched an ISIS execution where the killers used a bayonet to stab a man in his head and chest, and as he lay dying they kept moving him, finding new places to stab him without killing him – maybe 200 times. And he was still alive, which was the point. These aren't men, they are monsters. But in the west we still won't open our eyes and accept their declaration of war – although it seems Paris has edged us closer. It can only be a matter of time.

Would I send our troops into Iraq again, and Syria? I think the responsibility should initially be on every Muslim country that claims to be 'against' ISIS and al Qaeda to show willing.

Why aren't those so-called 'friendly' Muslim states forming an armed coalition to destroy ISIS? That would be a huge first step in signalling to the non-Islamic world that they even care. I'm not sure sure they do, at all.

Refugee babies drowning in the Med? Chaos, starvation and murder? If you can show me one Muslim state that 'cares' as much as any bleeding-heart European nation, I'll buy the drinks. So no, I certainly don't think our troops should be on the ground in Iraq and Syria. I don't think we should be sacrificing more British lives.

I also think the British and increasingly European public is aware that the Muslim world won't take responsibility for this humanitarian crisis. They won't crush ISIS, just like they won't house the fleeing millions soon to be heading for bed and breakfast accommodation near you.

We get tough talk from Saudi Arabia, Jordan and Qatar, even token gestures of military action, hence that Jordanian pilot being captured and burned alive, despite being a fellow Sunni. But it's also the case that the Saudis are financing some Sunni terror groups, playing both sides of the bloody mess in some cases. Better minds than mine can't work all of that out.

The Saudis are also financing the west's new generation of mega-mosques. Is someone on the payroll, in our own country, in Europe? I can't think of a better explanation.

So if you're asking whether I think the Saudis, the Muslim middle eastern countries, can be trusted, you haven't been paying attention. I used to trust British justice, let me remind you.

What I am saying is that we should, at the very least, be asking why Britain and Europe should open its doors to a mass of so-called refugees, when their own Muslim cousins won't have anything to do with them, or, at very best, provide only token gestures of assistance. They don't seem keen to find a permanent solution.

In Britain we appear to take for granted that care and compassion is a Christian quality, as if we shouldn't even expect it of less developed Muslim countries. Jesus. And I mean that literally. Are you surprised that they all take the piss out of us? I'm only trying to say things, to ask questions, that our political leaders seem terrified of even raising. Could the mass migration we're seeing right now from the middle east be an invasion by any other name?

I'm only asking. Not many other people seem to be.

CLOSER TO HOME, we show no sign of understanding the size of the domestic problem, let alone finding a realistic way of dealing with it.

Take the grooming scandals that just keep emerging up and down the country. Every time it happens there's a day or two of public outrage, while the establishment holds its breath until the fuss blows over. What I see is ideologically motivated rape, specifically targeting non-Muslim girls and it needs to be made a national issue of. Upsetting the locals? It's time someone did.

I don't think there's been a fraction of the money thrown at squaring away the investigation into the rape and abuse of 1,400 children in Rotherham, that there was on finding a few journalists who hacked celebrity phones.

That's a crime anyway, because it's not just the groomers to blame. The people who knew and looked away, who allowed it to happen, should all face justice. Police officers, council managers, social workers, they should all pay. They should lose their pensions – in fact their pensions should go to the victims of the crimes they've nodded through.

So many people have now accepted and admitted that they knew this was going on. What's their punishment been? A tut-tut and a slap on the wrist mostly. That's what I call perverting the course of justice. So there has to be accountability, but there also has to be the courage to confront the communities doing the offending. Stop hiding.

Education is actually going on among the Sikh and Hindu communities. Authorities are going to their temples, getting all their mothers together, talking about modern issues in society. I've seen it myself, first hand.

We need to be doing it in our schools, talking about the dangers and actually saying which community tends to be the problem. Children need telling what the grooming process leads to and who is doing it. But will we? Not a prayer. There's still too much fear of causing offence.

I've asked virtually every imam I've spoken to in recent years what the legal age of sex should be – and without exception they've said when a girl starts her period. So that could be as young as 10 or 11, quite easily.

Are you comfortable with that? Because our legal system seems to be. Sharia law is effectively nodded through in this country and I have a massive problem with that. So should you. I do not apologise for having a problem with an alien ideology, an alien way of living and thinking that is being given a free reign to infect the country of mine and my children's birth. No one consulted me on it. Did they consult you? They certainly didn't ask our children.

Those imams have not been challenged because the people who have a voice are afraid of the answers they'd get. They would be put in the position of having to act if they acknowledged the uncomfortable truth and they're petrified by the fear of giving offence. So they pretend the problem doesn't exist. They don't ask, they don't challenge. So many imams have admitted in debates with me that they are never challenged by authority.

Take Anjem Choudary, currently on bail as I write this, charged with supporting a terrorist organisation. We were on a radio interview once and I asked him straight out – you have a daughter, would you let her marry someone 30-years-old when she was just nine or ten? He said yes, no problem.

He didn't hide from it and that community's leaders don't either – but we do, because when Choudary says it live on tv or radio, all I hear from the authorities is an uncomfortable silence.

And we wonder why there's a problem?

MEANWHILE, JUST being 'me' continues to be a problem. I went out for a drink with a friend in Hitchin. In minutes it was on Twitter, someone telling people to find Tommy Robinson and give him a kicking. A group of students did.

I've had an operation for a blood clot on my head. Scarred for life. So I went to the house of the ringleader to give him a chance to apologise, to not have his life ruined like mine at his age.

But they're posh and I'm Tommy Robinson. Mummy slammed the door. I'd already reported it to the police – so I ended up being the one interviewed under caution again, despite them having the CCTV of the attack and having seen the tweets leading up to it.

I asked the officer how many people were in their gang. She said, 'Nine'. And how many people with me? 'One'. It's all there, as clear as daylight, but still I'm not holding my breath that anything will be done. Open season on Tommy.

Another time I was walking round Luton with a Times journalist and got jumped by Muslim blokes – gang-handed, as usual. My skull and jaw were numb for a week.

When I got off licence we had a long overdue family holiday. We needed one. On landing back at Luton, after midnight, the police were waiting to arrest me over the incident in Peterborough nick with the Somalian.

They could have called my solicitor and made an appointment, but no. Far more fun to distress my kiddies, leave my wife to struggle late at night with four big suitcases. The following week when we went to a football match, my youngest saw some police officers and broke down crying, frightened they would take her daddy away.

I wasn't charged over Peterborough, I was bailed again and have since had a letter saying that they're dropping it. But the letter adds that it's only for now, and they might change their minds. They just never, ever let go, do they?

Oh, and the £125k so-called Proceeds of Crime claim that was dropped to £117k? It went back up again. I've paid it.

In the meantime I'll keep trying to do what I think's right, I'll try to stay out of jail, take care of my family – and above all else, I'll try to stay alive. Wish me luck.